Reference groups and the theory
of revolution

International Library of Sociology

Founded by Karl Mannheim

Editor: John Rex, University of Warwick

Arbor Scientiæ
Arbor Vitæ

A catalogue of the books available in the **International Library of Sociology** and other series of Social Science books published by Routledge & Kegan Paul will be found at the end of this volume.

Reference groups and the theory of revolution

John Urry

Department of Sociology
University of Lancaster

Routledge & Kegan Paul

London and Boston

HM281
U77

First published in 1973
by Routledge & Kegan Paul Ltd
Broadway House, 68–74 Carter Lane,
London EC4V 5EL and
9 Park Street,
Boston, Mass. 02108, U.S.A.
Printed in Great Britain by
Cox & Wyman Ltd
London, Fakenham and Reading
© John Urry 1973
No part of this book may be reproduced in
any form without permission from the
publisher, except for the quotation of brief
passages in criticism

ISBN 0 7100 7541 3

Library of Congress Catalog Card Number: 73-79116

Contents

Note on the text

Bibliography

I have divided the bibliography into three sections. The first details all the books and articles which make some contribution to the sociological analysis of reference group processes. I have not included every work in which the term is used since that would be time-wastingly irrelevant for the reader and for myself. It includes all the major contributions, any useful textbook discussions and other applications or statements which I thought were of interest or of importance. It is up to date to the end of 1971. All references in the text to this bibliography are preceded by a capital A; thus Hyman and Singer (A1968). That book, incidentally, contains until the present work the most exhaustive set of references; and it is still the most useful collection of articles in the field.

The second section is as extensive a bibliography as possible of books and articles (mainly in English) which relate to the history of Indonesia from 1870 to 1945, and especially to the 1920s and 1940s. Again it includes all the major works as well as a number of other more marginal contributions. And again, apart from Jaspan (B1961), such a bibliography does not exist at present. All references in the text to this bibliography are preceded by a capital B.

The third section is a list of other works to which reference is made in this book; references here are not preceded by any letter.

Note on the text

Introduction

This book is based on a dissertation that was awarded a Ph.D. by the University of Cambridge in 1972. In this introduction I think I should try to do two things. First, I shall indicate briefly why biographically I came to write a dissertation with the content that this one has and thus point out where my intellectual and personal debts lie. Second, I shall then try to show why such a dissertation should be published as a book, and especially as a book with such a contemporary title. Why another book on revolution and revolutionary change?

After taking an economics degree at Cambridge I began research in sociology under David Lockwood. After very brief prevarication, it was decided that I should explore some themes and problems in the study of the concept of the 'reference group'. In this endeavour I made two false starts: the first was in trying to tie in differing patterns of reference group selection with Parsonian pattern variables – the latter proving to be extravagantly elusive; the second was in trying to carry out a premature empirical study of the patterning of social comparisons and their relationship to different structures in which manual workers found themselves. Part way through this second false start, I was finding that the study of revolution in a seminar in King's College, Cambridge, on twentieth-century political revolutions was proving to be more enticing. Participation in this seminar both encouraged my general interest in the study of revolution as well as my specific interest in the Dutch East Indies. I should point out my gratitude to all members of that seminar and especially to Martin Bernal, John Dunn, Dick Geary, and Bob Jessop.[1]

John Goldthorpe became my supervisor for a brief period before he went to Oxford. From 1969 Philip Abrams supervised my dissertation. I would here like to express my great thanks for all the assistance that he, John Goldthorpe and David Lockwood have given me. It was in discussion with Philip Abrams that I conceived of the plan of working out a dissertation in which these various interests mentioned above were related both with each other and with certain aspects of so-called critical sociology. The latter enjoyed a great vogue in Cambridge as in many other places in the late 1960s and Schutz and Mead became the 'guru' figures in the history of sociology. I gained very greatly from protracted discussion with, especially, Mike Gurstein, Mike Pickering and John Skorupski.

In 1970 I moved to Lancaster and completed the dissertation the following year. Here I should like to thank Nick Abercrombie and Russell Keat with whom I have discussed some aspects of this book. Finally, I would like to thank my parents for their very great interest; also especially Pat, for her help and criticism throughout.

That is by way of personal history. I now want to justify the existence of yet another book on revolution. I think that this is to some extent justified by the first part of this book which is, as far as I know, the only extended discussion of the concept of the reference group which tries to work through some of the major problems in a reasonably systematic and historically-oriented way. Thus, to an important degree, that part of the book can be read on its own both as a contribution to the analysis of reference group processes and as a historical exegesis of the relations between Cooley and Mead on one hand, and the study of the reference group, especially in American sociology in the 1940s, 1950s and 1960s, on the other.

However, it is clear even from the chapter headings that my interest in reference groups is not confined merely to such a social-psychological discussion in itself. I try to develop my discussion and try to make the criticisms that I do so as to enable me to incorporate certain aspects of reference group analysis into an explanation of mass revolutionary consciousness and action. I ought to say here that since I see such explanation as singularly problematic, the formulation and application I present in parts 2 and 3 are clearly provisional and tentative.

Some of the issues with which I will be dealing result from the oddness of revolution as a phenomenon. It is on the one hand the result of a long, complicated and by no means inevitable, process occurring within the pre-revolutionary society, and on the other, it occurs, at least in some aspects, more or less instantaneously. Partly for these reasons, it is very difficult to identify just what are the features of revolutionary change which separate it from non-revolutionary change. All sorts of different aspects are involved, and because the concept of revolution is also irreducibly one employed by actors themselves, the satisfactory identification of what is a revolution, what are its *particular* features, and what would count as a satisfactory mode of explaining such features, are supremely problematic. But while revolution is unquestionably never inevitable and depends very importantly on exactly how people feel about their world and specifically, on what they intend to do about the fact that they are feeling revolutionary, revolution is also not accidental. Clearly we can say minimally that it results from the interplay between social structures and social actors, from the dialectic between object and subject.

Nevertheless, existing works on revolution, where they are concerned with explanation and not with description or discussion of the concept itself, concentrate on only one of the levels of analysis. They either imply a systemic or structural analysis where men are taken to be determined by external social forces; or they employ the model of a highly rationalistic man who self-consciously and intentionally acts so as to bring about the desired post-revolutionary outcome. The problem with the former is that whatever else revolutions are, they are indubitably carried out by actors – they are made and do not merely happen. And although, clearly, they cannot be made at any time, in any place, in any form, they will just not occur unless very many people come to interpret their experience as indicating that the world needs changing and can be changed. Revolutions are irreducibly projects worked out and carried through by men and women seeking to transform their world. The great problem with the latter focus is that it is hardly ever the case with the big revolutions in history that the actual outcome is intended at all. Indeed, it is clear that had the post-revolutionary regime been available for consideration prior to the period of revolutionary change, many people would have been far less enthusiastic in their militant support for such change. In other words, it is a very important fact about revolutions that they are not normally brought about by people who act with complete knowledge and foresight as to the ends which their actions will bring. Indeed, since this is itself clear to many revolutionaries, they tend to focus not on what will be produced in detail by revolutionary action but rather on how change is justified merely because of the very features of the pre-revolutionary society. Thus to set about explaining why revolutionary events take place we have to know why it is that so many people feel so strongly that the pre-revolutionary society is so unattractive and unfair to such an extent that they are willing to engage in activity certain to be excessively uncomfortable, unpleasant and personally-traumatizing. And for us to be able to provide that explanation implies that we look to the relationship between on one hand, the historical development of the elements comprising the structure of the society, and on the other, the changing meaning and interpretation that actors themselves place on their experience in that society. Why, in other words, is it that the structure of the society creates so many people who feel so strongly that that society is irredeemable and should be replaced, although it is not known at all what the new society will actually be like?

It is to enable me to account for this that I attempt to integrate aspects of the analysis of reference groups into my explanation of the genesis of dissent. Specifically, this book is focused on the contribution that the study of social comparisons can make to the analysis of why people are dissatisfied with *their* society and wish through militant dissent to replace it. It is secondarily concerned with considering how the other aspect of reference group analysis, the study of normative reference groups, can help to elucidate the way in which alternative sets of values and criteria of social justice are possible and are maintained within different social groupings within the pre-revolutionary society. It is the attempt to fit these considerations into the study of revolutionary consciousness that is the main argument for producing this particular book on revolution.

Finally, though, I might point to another justification, my explanation of Indonesian dissent, where I attempt to demonstrate that a number of interesting issues and themes in historical analysis can be treated and analysed sociologically. What I do in part 3 is to take the history of the Dutch East Indies over the last two hundred years up to the declaration of independence in 1945. Specifically, I consider the period of dissent in the 1920s and see how certain aspects of that can be explained in terms of particular features of colonial rule and of the response to that rule. I then consider what it was about the period of Japanese rule from 1942 to 1945 that resulted in what turned out to be successful dissent in the sense of establishing an independent Indonesian Republic. Now, clearly, there are many accounts already available of this period, but there are no explanations which specifically take as their explanandum the genesis of revolutionary consciousness in Indonesia in the twentieth century, and base the explanation of this partly on the symbolic interactionists and partly on a fairly ordered theory of dissent. Ultimately, what I wish to claim is that even the history of very specific events in the Indonesian archipelago, such as the geographical distribution of militant dissent in 1926–7, can be made more intelligible by considering the postulates of symbolic interactionism, the way in which notions of role and reference group have developed from this tradition, and the inadequate uses normally made of these concepts.

part one

Symbolic interactionism and the reference group concept

The significance of the dialectical relationship between man and society is rarely grasped within sociology which is a study conventionally premised upon the rigid conceptual dichotomies of individual and society and subject and object. The one tradition which places this dialectic at the centre of its sociological concern is one towards which Durkheim was moving (see Stone and Farberman, 1967) and is one implicit within Weber's focus upon action. The first chapter is, initially, an outline of the symbolic interactionist perspective; it is, second, an exposition of what I take to be certain critical lacunae of argument and an indication of the relationship of this perspective to other sociological traditions. I will argue that contemporary sociology should have followed the presuppositions inherent within this tradition. And although it has derived the concepts of role, self and reference group from symbolic interactionism, it has in their more precise specification, emasculated the originally dialectical presuppositions.

In chapters 2, 3 and 4 I try to show this with particular respect to the concept of the reference group. This discussion reveals both an unfortunate lack of specification in some places in the interactionist tradition, as well as the imperatives within American sociology to render the actor's dependence upon each group as precise, quantifiable and determinate. In parts 2 and 3 I attempt to elaborate and apply an explanation of mass revolutionary consciousness and action which focuses on how different actors come to develop differing conceptions of what sorts of social arrangements are and are not just. A more dialectical formulation of the reference group concept is, I argue, an essential element in such an explanation.

1 Of symbolic interactionism

An outline

The inadequacy of conventional dichotomies is pointed out by Baldwin[1] when he says of man that: 'He does not have two lives, two sets of interests, two selves; one personal and the other social. He has but one self, which is personal and social in one, by right of the essential and normal movement of his growth.' William James, even earlier, both distinguished between the self as known and the self as knower, and emphasized that they were not separate but simply aspects of the one person.[2] Although Mead claimed in 1930 (p. 700) that James's significant contribution was to show the nature of the self's spread *over* his social environment, his importance has, in fact, been largely in showing how the self as known, that is, the social 'me', grows out of the recognition that men receive from other men (James, 1892, p. 179). But since different men respond differently to the same person there must be as many social selves as there are distinct groups of men about whose opinion one cares. James importantly anticipates reference group analysis when he argues that it is a man's image in the eyes of his own 'set' which exalts or condemns him as he conforms or not to certain requirements that may not be made of him elsewhere.[3] Dewey (1925, ch. 5) indicates something of the process by which the actor comes to act in accordance with the expectations of his particular 'set', that is, how through language and communication the self and the meaning of actions arise. He maintains that because of language the individual is compelled to take the standpoint of other individuals and to live out his life from a standpoint common to them as co-operative participants in a joint enterprise. But like James, he indicates that because of multiple membership the individual may be divided within himself, have conflicting selves, or be relatively disintegrated.[4] Also like James, his writings have been largely used to show how meaning and

3

communication exercise control *over* the individual actor. There are two major attempts to depart from such mechanistic interpretations. They are both derived from these early writers and they have importantly influenced contemporary reference group formulations. I will consider first Charles Horton Cooley; and then George Herbert Mead.

Cooley criticizes the *merely* precise study of details, advocates the constant use of 'instructed imagination', and asserts that statistical uniformities 'do not show that it is possible to predict numerically the working of intelligence *in new situations*, and of course that it is the decisive test'.[5] In seeing society and self as dialectically related temporal processes, Cooley (1966, p. 396) argues against the Cartesian postulate of the primacy of self-consciousness. This is because the consciousness of 'I' is not part of all consciousness since it belongs to an advanced stage of development, and because of the individualistic assertion of the 'I' to the exclusion of the social or 'we' aspect (1956b, pp. 5–6). Rather, society and self are phases of the common and evolving totality which Cooley terms 'Human Life' (ibid., pp. 8–9; 1956a, pp. 35–7). 'Society' and the 'individual' are not separate phenomena but simply the collective and distributive aspects of the same ongoing reality. Society is both made up solely of individuals, and is more than their sum since there is an organization in the whole which cannot be found in the parts (ibid., pp. 48–50). Thus it is not an error to claim that the individual is the product of society, since everything human about him has a history in the social past and the individual can only in an external sense be separated from society. But at the same time the individual is free in an organic sense which is worked out co-operatively with others. There is no freedom in the sense of a complete absence of restraint (see ibid., pp. 422–3). Man has no existence apart from social life and thus the freedom of any single individual depends upon the nature of that life. The perception of this as 'a creative process' (ibid., p. 50) of which both men and society constitute an organic whole, emphasizes how man's freedom depends upon the existential possibilities available to him within that society.[6]

Thus Cooley says that the quality of human life in any society is dependent upon the relationship between its social and individual aspects. That in turn depends upon the processes of communication, processes which are not so much a consequence of thought as an inseparable part of it.[7] Thought and mind only develop through communication, since without it, a truly human nature cannot emerge (see 1956b, p. 62). And, importantly, this communication may realize itself not only on the level of society, but also within various groups of which the actor may or may not be a member, but within which the individual develops by means of its common thought (see ibid., ch. 3). Mead (1930, p. 699) summarizes Cooley's recognition:

> that the self is not an immediate character of the mind but arises through the imagination of the ideas which others entertain of the individual, which has its counterpart in the organisation of our ideas of others into their selves. It is out of this bi-polar process that social individuals appear. We do not discover others as individuals like ourselves. The mind is not first individual and then social. The mind itself in the individual arises through communication.

But over and beyond the argument for the social genesis of mind and self there is a further implication of Mead's statement; that is to say, for Cooley, the self arises out of the imagination of the ideas which others entertain of the given individual. Thus, through imagination one perceives in the mind of another or others, their thoughts as to the nature of one's appearance, manners, aims, deeds, character, friends and so on, and one is, to a varying extent, affected by it. As Cooley (1956a, p. 184) says:

> Each to each a looking-glass
> Reflects the other that doth pass.

Cooley (1956a, pp. 183–5) stresses three elements in this process: the imagination of an individual's appearance to the other person, the imagination of his evaluation of that appearance, and a consequential sense of self-feeling, such as pride or mortification. He concludes (ibid., p. 203) that the imagination of how one appears to others is a controlling force in all normal minds.

This derivation of an individual's self-conception from his imagination of how he appears to others is a crucial consideration: what is inadequate is the conclusion that Cooley draws from it (ibid., p. 119). He says: 'My association with you evidently consists in the relation between my idea of you and the rest of my mind. . . . *The immediate social reality is the personal idea* . . . Society, then . . . *is a relation among personal ideas.*' But although one might acknowledge that the personal idea is the immediate social reality, this idealism cannot accommodate an objective reality out there comprised not of these personal ideas held of each other, but of other social selves who are realizing themselves within concrete patterns of social interaction, albeit mediated by conceptions of the self mirrored in the minds of various others. Perhaps Mead (1930, p. 704) should be allowed the final word on Cooley:

> In the process of communication there appears a social world of selves standing on the same level of immediate reality as that

5

of the physical world that surrounds us. It is out of this social world that the inner experiences arise which we term psychical, and they serve largely in interpretation of this social world as psychical sensations and percepts serve to interpret the physical objects of our environment. If this is true, social groups are not psychical but are immediately given, though inner experiences are essential for their interpretation. The *locus* of society is not in the mind.[8]

Mead is thus important in maintaining that mind, consciousness and the self all result from the concrete patterns of interaction between these individuals. They are all premised upon human group life.[9] But to claim that is for Mead to reject psychological associationism (1934, pp. 18–19), the parellelist thesis (ibid., pp. 40–1) and individual behaviourism (ibid., *passim* and pp. 10–11, 104–5). He does call himself a social behaviourist, but maintains that this indicates that the study of social psychology must commence with observable activity, that it must not ignore the inner experience of the individual, that it must not fail to locate the individual's acts within implicating social processes, and that it must be dynamic (ibid., pp. 6–11 and 24).

Mead emphasizes the temporal and logical pre-existence of the social process to the self-conscious individual that arises within it (for example, see ibid., pp. 186 and 233). Thus, like Cooley, he objects to any social contract model since society exists prior to the individual. The self, as we shall see later, is not there at birth but arises in the process of social experience.[10] But this is a dialectical rather than a determinate relationship because 'the individual is no thrall of society. He constitutes society as genuinely as society constitutes the individual' (quoted in Morris, 1934, p. xxv). Action originates and is built up in coping with processes within the social and natural world. It is not released simply by the individual as a consequence of factors playing externally upon him (see Blumer, 1966, p. 537).

The construction of such conduct arises within and through communication with others. Thus, instead of commencing with individual minds and working outwards to society, Mead begins with the ongoing social processes and works inwards through the importation of processes of communication into the individual by means of the vocal gesture (see Morris, 1934, p. xxiii). Human society is thus dependent upon the development of language for its own distinctive form of organization. Human rather than animal beings do not only interact within a world of conditioning stimuli (non-symbolic interaction where there is direct response to another's gestures or actions); also they inhabit a world of objects meaningfully significant in terms of shared symbols (see Mead, 1934, pp.

43–9, 89 and 122; 1912). Language thus emerges out of particular social processes rather than being the result of simple inter-individual imitation (Mead, 1934, pp. 59–61). Two related criticisms of Mead should be noted: first, in his conflation of the notion of mind with language-symbols of a social-vocal origin, there is a failure to consider certain individual aspects of man resulting from non-linguistic and thus non-social signs and gestures (see Morris, 1934, pp. xiv–xv). And second, on occasions, Mead appears to suggest that language is important not only in conceptualizing order, but in determining the very nature of *that* order.[11] Both of these seem erroneous intrusions of an idealism reminiscent of Cooley where social reality for each actor *is* the set of socially acquired symbols.

The importance of communication follows from the fact that certain gestures arouse the same response in the individual as they do in the other to whom they are directed. In addressing himself in this way, the individual's self is developed – in his social conduct he becomes an object, or an other, to himself. Mead (1938, p. 428) says: 'it is primarily in social conduct that we stimulate ourselves to act toward ourselves as others act toward us and thus identify ourselves with others and become objects to ourselves'. It is the vocal gesture which enables this to occur. Internalization and a shared consciousness of the meanings of such gestures result from the fact that they arouse the same attitudes in the individuals making them that they arouse in the individuals responding to them (1934, pp. 47 and 109). But Mead points out that the social relationships upon which this process is based are directed to different individuals and groups with the result that different selves develop in relation to these varying social encounters (ibid., p. 142). But *the* self does not exist apart from such social experience.

The development of the self, in the sense of an agent being the object of his own activity, is a two-part process. First of all, there are the mechanisms through which the individual internalizes the attitudes of various others by placing himself in the role(s) that they are playing; second, through the capacity for role-taking, the individual comes to look at himself through the eyes of these various others and thus to be an object of his own consciousness. He stands outside himself and evaluates himself in various ways. Thus Mead points out that the development of the self is dependent upon the presence of other objects with which the individual can identify himself. During play, the child plays a succession of roles with various role-partners as significant others. There is no stable organization of the child; he is unpredictable, he has no definite character or personality. The individual's self at the play stage is constituted solely by an organization of the particular attitudes of

7

particular individuals in the specific social acts in which he partici-
pates with them. The game, on the other hand, is a social activity
based on the assumption that each individual takes the attitudes
of the social group of which he is a member towards the organized
co-operative social activity or set of such activities in which that
group as such is engaged (ibid., pp. 152–64). Thus the self as an
object becomes a part of the individual through its having assumed
the generalized attitude of the group to which that self belongs (see
Mead, 1938, p. 375). Mead argues that the self reaches full development by organizing the individual attitudes of others into the
organized social or group attitudes; he puts himself in the place of
the generalized other, which represents the organized responses of
all the members of the group. For Mead then, for the development
of the self, the individual needs to be a member of a group or community, since it is only in the acquisition of such generalized attitudes
that a definite character or personality develops.

This is a crucial and difficult argument. In the way in which *Mind,
Self and Society* is normally interpreted it leads to the thesis that the
beliefs and actions of individuals are determined by the organized
social group in which that individual is implicated. This, I think, is
too simple since in the same work (p. 210) Mead claims that 'Social
control is the expression of the "me" over against the expression of
the "I". It sets the limits, it gives the determination that enables the
"I", so to speak, to use the "me" as the means of carrying out what
is the undertaking that all are interested in.' In other words, although
the self arises out of the assumption of the attitudes of the generalized
other, in doing so it begins to be able to look at itself and to act in
specific ways. That the internalization of the other is simply one
moment in the dialectic can be seen from the following (Mead,
1936, p. 163):

> That reflexive experience in which the individual realizes
> himself in so far as, in some sense, he sees himself, hears
> himself. It is the sort of situation in which the individual is both
> subject and object. But in order to be both subject and object,
> he has to pass from one phase to another. The self involves a
> process that is going on, that takes on now one form and now
> another – a subject-object relationship which is dynamic, not static;
> a subject-object relationship which has a process behind it, one
> which can appear now in this phase, now in that.

Thus, in acting as a subject, he acts with reference to himself as an
object; he turns back and directs himself just as he influences others.
The human actor thus is put not merely within the world but is set
over and against it; he is required to meet and handle his world
through a defining process instead of merely responding to it, and

this forces him to construct his action rather than simply to release it. Thus, for Mead, there is made possible 'the purposive control and organization by the individual organism of its conduct, with reference to its social and physical environment, i.e., with reference to the various social and physical situations in which it becomes involved and to which it reacts' (1934, p. 91). Mead distinguishes the 'I' and the 'me'; it is the former that gives the sense of freedom, initiative and self-conscious action – it is the latter which is the organization of the generalized attitudes held by others and internalized by the individual. The dialectic between man and society finds its internal reflection within the self in each individual. By being both subject and object (ibid., p. 137), the self is neither a purely initiating 'I' nor a simply habitual 'me' (ibid., pp. 197–8, 202 and esp. 215–16).

However the precise nature of the actor's determination of his own conduct does vary. Mead in *The Philosophy of the Act* distinguishes between immediate experience, trial and error, and reflexion. The first of these occurs when the individual does not act as an object of his own consciousness since the introduction of one's self into the act would be hampering and embarrassing (1938, p. 368). In the second case, control is secured through discovering and emphasizing the appropriate stimuli in their relation to one another. Mead argues that this experimental, non-reflexive activity accounts for a significant proportion of men's conduct. Reflexion results from the occurrence of novelty and change in a world which was previously unproblematic. He gives the example of meeting someone new or meeting someone already known in a new context (ibid., p. 416). In chapter 5 I will discuss other situations likely to produce reflexion.

Finally, in this account of Mead's social theory, we must consider briefly the nature of the self that develops. I have already mentioned that a single individual may possess a number of different selves depending upon the various contexts within which he takes and plays roles. Mead also considers that the result of this may be to break up the unity of the self such that two (or presumably more) separate 'me's and 'I's develop so destroying the personality itself. Such self-disintegration is never elucidated or explained though; only two points emerge. First, deleterious consequences occur when the gesture does not arouse the same response within one's own self as it does in the other (1934, pp. 143–9). Second, Mead maintains the necessity for 'an expression of the individual himself if there is to be a satisfactorily developed society' (ibid., p. 221). Mead contrasts primitive with civilized human society, maintaining that in the former there is more complete determination of the actor's thought and action and less scope for individuality.[12] The development of the self is thus not fixed and immutable but is dependent upon the possibilities of symbolic social interaction available within that society.

Problems and remedies

No one would claim that the foregoing is a wholly adequate basis for contemporary sociology.[13] There are certain critical lacunae but I think that they can be filled without destroying the presuppositions inherent within the framework. To claim that is to claim the converse of most contemporary sociology.

The first and clearest inadequacy results from the failure of the interactive tradition to provide any satisfactory account of the social organization or social structure which results from the processes of symbolic social interaction and within which actors engage in symbolically mediated social interaction. This lacuna results from the derivation of this perspective from both social psychology and social philosophy and it leads Anselm Strauss to claim the necessity for fusing the orientations of symbolic interactionism and social organization.[14] Generally, the failure to allow for this means that there is no consideration of the fact that certain interpersonal relationships are predicated upon power, or that there may be contradictions between parts of any ongoing society. The latter is seen more or less as the generalized other.

But this term is itself confused; Natanson (1956, pp. 66–8) asks rhetorically whether there is *a* generalized other or others. Mead (1932, p. 192) varies his position, but he does maintain at one point that the effectiveness of social control depends upon the degree to which the individual assumes the attitudes of those 'in the group who are involved with him in his social activities'. The generalized other is here limited to those actual social groups in which that actor is directly implicated in one way or another. But even so, it is still very loosely specified there because of the unreflective use of the term 'group' and the failure to signify the various possible forms which this may take within any society.[15] Also, little or no attention is paid to which groups within such a society are actually involved for a given actor in a particular situation; Everett Hughes's question of 'what other?' remains unanswered (1962). It is, of course, this explanatory vacuum that reference group analysis was meant to fill; I will discuss later whether or not it has been successful.

The third issue raised by the discussion of symbolic interactionism both demands some solution within this book and relates to the failure up to the present time to solve the first two problems The interactive tradition is markedly ambivalent as to the possibilities of conflict within society. It is certainly admitted that the actor may be socialized into various subcultures and that over a period of time the nature of his subcultural orientations may change.[16] But Mead, for example, does not indicate whether conflict may materialize between two or more of these orientations. He says, on the one hand, that a self-possessing individual is always a member of a larger social community than that in which he immediately and directly belongs and thus the respective organized attitudes of the individuals involved always have a wider and more general reference; no indication is given here of conflict (see Rose, 1962, p. 16). Yet he does indicate the possibility of 'latent opposition' on the actor's part towards the organized society or social community of which he is a member, conflict between two aspects or phases of the same individual self, conflict between different individuals, and social situations in which individuals act as members of 'two or more different socially functional groups whose respective social purposes or interests are antagonistic or conflicting or widely separate'. Examples of the last type are the conflicts between labour and capital, producers and consumers, and buyers and sellers (Mead, 1934, pp. 272–3 and 306–7). It is also noteworthy that his prescribed mode of conflict resolution is 'an organization of common attitudes which shall be found in all individuals' (ibid., p. 323). Normally this is interpreted as the advocation of value consensus so as to produce social integration. It can also be seen as a plea for the radical re-establishment of man's relationship with his fellow men since for Mead man 'must be an organic part of the life of the community' (ibid., p. 324).

The final problem relates, not to the substantive content of argument, but to the pragmatic philosophy with which this sociological tradition is associated. Explicit attention will be paid to Mead, to the relationship between pragmatism and phenomenology and to the possibilities of selective synthesis.

Mead's philosophical pragmatism leads him to reject the 'vast amount of philosophic riffraff known as epistemology' (1938, p. 94).[17] The undisputed and undisputable framework upon which epistemology cannot encroach is the philosopher's experience within his taken-for-granted world. It is this assured reality within which all philosophical investigations occur and in terms of which all theories are validated. Without such a world, there could be no basis for the resolution of philosophical controversy. But this is, I think, profoundly confused. What Mead does is to conflate the completely desirable common-sense description of the nature of man's life within his everyday world with the wholly erroneous claim that the nature and the presuppositions of an investigating philosophy should commence and continue with and be validated by the philosopher's everyday world. But if we consider merely the former activity, the description of man's life within his everyday world, we still find problems. Let us consider Natanson (1956, esp. p. 81), who prescribes a

11

phenomenological suspension of the natural attitude so that the actor's day-to-day life may be described and understood. But although that is no doubt desirable, it is an extremely restricted vision of socio-logical and philosophical activity. We can see this by considering the case of Schutz who has most closely followed Natanson's directives.[18] Schutz's emphasis is upon the 'subjective *meaning*-context of action'; it is only half a description of men's actions within the world. Indeed, it is a world where practically nothing ever happens, where there is no change and nothing too much interferes with the actor living out his taken-for-granted life within his everyday world. It is a study of consciousness not of reality. It is the advocation of disdainful con-templation where only the phenomenologically trained philosopher can suspend the natural attitude and critically describe the structure underlying common-sense reality. That actors can themselves suspend the imperatives of everyday life, can reflect upon their situation, and can do something about it, is beyond the bounds of Schutzian contemplation. Thus although some use is made later of Schutz's description of the taken-for-granted world of the everyday actor, this world is considered to be one of at least potential action, change and conflict. It will therefore be argued that in Mead's notion of the self, namely that the actor can be an object of his own reflexive consciousness, there is the mechanism through which an actor can both transcend the epoch of the natural attitude and the epistemological nihilism of American pragmatism. The logic of the Meadian dialect, rejected by Natanson, is that the individual con-stitutes and is constituted by his experience.

Actors, groups and roles[19]

The previous section has set out some ways in which the interactive perspective needs amplification. I have so far not discussed the crucial presuppositions of any sociological enterprise, the taken-for-granted or domain assumptions as to the relationship between the actor, roles and norms. The two main ways in which this can be considered stem respectively from Mead and Freud. I will consider the latter first.

An initial point to note is that Freud, for all his apparent emphasis upon the individual's identification with his immediate family during childhood, does not ignore the importance of other relationships. He says (1960, p. 3) that 'only rarely and under exceptional condi-tions is individual psychology in a position to disregard the relations of this individual to others'. For Freud, the key process within all groups is that of identification, which is itself based upon *eros* 'which holds together everything in the world' (ibid., p. 31). Freud argues that an individual's commitment to a group is a return to the individual's dependence upon his parents. The group member, in other words, becomes a dependent child; through identification, based upon the emotional common quality of the leader, he adopts the values and standards of the group (ibid., p. 50). In this, identification with the strong leader is the key mechanism, but Freud's two examples in *Group Psychology and the Analysis of the Ego*, namely the church and army, are unjustifiably favourable to his case since the central figure in each is father-like and both flock and army are characterized by child-like dependency.[20] Since Freud himself sometimes admits that the leader may be an abstract ideal rather than a human being, the main point to note is that identification (not necessarily with a leader) is the process through which an individual acquires and internalizes the values and standards of the particular group. This model of the relationship between man and social life is the basis of contemporary sociology. A sociology which has acquired the notions of self, role and reference group from the interactionist tradition, but which has located them within a Freudian ontology – an ontology where there is an overdifferentiation between the isolated individual and the 'individual in the mass' to such an extent that the essential dependence of each upon the other is obscured.[21]

This is a very significant point. Campbell points out that in the literature there are two overarching traditions which account for the way in which an actor comes to exhibit behaviour congruent with the norms and values of a given group.[22] The Freudian picture, austerely summarized above, can be further generalized. Thus the internalization of norms and values is a process that follows from identification with a group. The symbolic interactionist view, on the other hand, is that through role-taking the actor internalizes certain norms and values and it is as a consequence that identification occurs. I think that the latter account is more attractive, first, because identification is what needs to be explained rather than what is initially assumed, second, because the notion of role-taking emphasizes the sort of *social* process which is unquestionably involved in any individual's identification with a group, and third, because the emphasis of the latter upon interpersonal reciprocity rather than normative commitment is a way of transcending the normally over-socialized conception of man presented in the literature.[23] Yet for all these points, Campbell plausibly maintains that it is the former perspective which is the central tendency within modern sociology. But in the conflation of internalization and learning, even the original conflict within Freudian man between the id and the super-ego has been systematically denied. The reason for this is clearly related to the growing indistinguishability of scientific truth and the acceptance of social determination (see Lynd, 1958, p. 212). Two concepts, the role and the reference group, have been

13

taken over from the interactionist tradition and have been made precise and quantifiable. It is the former which is of greater importance since the assumptions that are made regarding the actor's relationship to his role are of crucial significance to the sort of sociology one engages in elsewhere, such as in the analysis of reference group processes. This must be briefly discussed.

That role analysis is typically based upon the former model of the assumption of norms and values can be seen impressionistically from the following pair of quotations:

> The *emphasis* in role theory is on overt role playing and on the researchable relation between role expectations and role performances; the emphasis is either less, or altogether lacking, on role-taking, on the interior processes of the self, and what Shibutani calls the sentiments are often ignored (Kuhn, A1964a, p. 67).

> Role theory, originally depicting a tentative and creative interaction process, has come increasingly to be employed as a refinement of conformity theory (Turner, 1962, p. 37).

This point may also be indicated by very brief consideration of the nature of personality in the writings of Talcott Parsons.[24] It is noteworthy that for all his intention to provide an integrated general theory on all four systemic levels (organism, personality, society, culture) he operates with a conventionally inadequate postulate of the independent individual set apart from the environing society and a simultaneous claim that the structure of personality is a 'mirror-image' of the structure of the social system (1954, p. 84). These two arguments are reconciled by synthesizing a sort of Freudianism (action being the expenditure of energy by the organism to 'optimize' gratifications in accordance with learnt, segmental need-dispositions (see Scott, 1963)) with a one-dimensional role theory. The link between these two is provided by the concept of identification used more or less in the Freudian sense above. Thus Parsons (1955, p. 229) says:

> The end product of this phase of the socialization cycle seems to us to be the appropriate place to use the term *identification*. This essentially means that internalization of the new object system has been successfully completed ... that from now on ego's major 'predispositions' or 'orientations' are to act in terms of the newly internalized object system and the motives which are organized in it.

The individual is seen as separate from society while he is not playing a role; but once he identifies with an object system he plays a role in accordance with its prescriptions with the result that the personality system precisely mirrors the social system. The social conformity posited in Parsons is even greater than in Freud, first, because cognitive and expressive features as well as moral standards are internalized after identification; second, because learning rather than innateness is emphasized as critical; third, because the content of an actor's identification is given by his identification not with the alter as a totality, but with the reciprocal role relationship; and fourth, because no indication is given as to how conflicts may occur between different stages of the life-cycle (see Bronfenbrenner, 1963, pp. 199–202). Although it is fashionable to criticize certain aspects of the Parsonian system, I think it is interesting to note that his social psychology has emerged relatively unscathed. This suggests that to criticize Parsons's account of the relationship between the personality and society is to criticize a widely-held position. But various writers have at different times made this criticism explicit.

Turner (1962, p. 22) emphasizes the importance of the argument above; that there is not only role-playing, role-taking, but also what he terms role-making. Goffman (1961) distinguishes between the normative role, the typical role and the actual role-performance; role-distance being the clear and expressed separateness between the typical role and the actor. He argues as to the generality of this phenomenon: 'a role-performer in our society has a right to some learner's licence and a limit to formality of obligation – by sheer virtue of being a role-taker'.[25] Wrong (1966) points out that the emphasis on the maximization of favourable self-evaluations from others ignores the obvious significance of material interest, sexual desire and the demand for power. To maintain that man is social is not necessarily to maintain that man is fully socialized. Both Dahrendorf's criticism of *homo sociologicus* (A1968) and Goode's argument (1960) that a given actor playing a role may experience strain in fulfilling the demands of that role relate to this point.

There are various conclusions that follow from this discussion. First of all, the norm which is internalized through role-taking should not be seen as a set of detailed standards and rules providing a precise specification of the expectations associated with an actor's performance within a certain role. It should be viewed simply as a broad cultural definition of desirable behaviour (see Williams, 1968). Second, an actor's performance within a role, even where that role is normally non-deviant (teacher, for example) is not *simply* integrative because on the basis of common social participation, role-taking and role-making among similar role-occupants, there is an internalization of common attitudes and the genesis of subcultural definitions of social reality (see Shibutani, A1955; Yinger, 1960). Third, conventional accounts do not allow for the

15

actor reflexively taking the role of the other and evaluating his actions through the eyes of a significant or generalized other. And fourth, most important and most problematically, what is ultimately significant about the processes of role-taking and making is that they are the bases of constitution and reconstitution of the very social norms which are taken and internalized by the social actor. The organization of society and of its constituent parts is the framework, within which actors act in certain ways; but the very nature of their acting serves to reinforce or to change the nature of this organization. It was with this point that I began this chapter.

2   Of reference groups

One aspect of my discussion so far is the claim inherent in symbolic interactionism and expressed in Thoreau: 'If a man does not keep pace with his companions, perhaps it is because he hears a different drummer.' That is to say, it was increasingly observed that the explanation of men's actions needed to be situated not only within the groups of which he is a member but also within those to which he refers in some way or other. The concept of the reference group was developed to help to account for the observation that the range of social objects to which an actor may relate is not necessarily coincidental with the groups of which he is a member. The major contribution of reference group analysis is thus in indicating that the attitudes taken by an actor may derive from groups other than his own, and that his sense of self-esteem may originate from unusual points of social comparison. In itself, this is a highly significant perspective, quite congruent with the presuppositions of the inter-active framework and a conceptual development of major importance within the sociology of contemporary society. This development is clearly not simply fortuitous within such sociology, but is derived from certain structural factors. In a stable, integrated and less-differentiated society there is little necessity for the development of the concept of the reference group separate from the notion of the membership group. But as Mead points out, it is a feature of con-temporary man that he is faced by a large number of alternative objects to which he can refer. He is caught in the throes of vertical mobility, in the dilemmas and contradictions of different statuses, in the painful predicament of cross-pressurization or marginality, and in role-conflict and exposure to conflicting and diverse means and ends of social life.[1] But simultaneously, as Mead also maintains, the nature of modern life, with its possibilities of escaping the limitations of a single, possibly claustrophobic, social world, is immensely liberating. The notion of a reference group is a fundamental adjunct to the analysis of the degree to which actors realize such potentialities within their world. It is noteworthy, incidentally, that, as Merton fails to realize, Mead explicitly emphasizes the importance of non-membership groups, in, for example, the child's role-taking during the play stage (see Merton and Rossi, A1957, p. 239; Mead, 1934, p. 150; Stone, A1958; Sowa, A1962, pp. 42 and 46). A sociological condition for the development of this concept was the emergence of the interactive perspective and its emphasis upon symbols and language for the genesis of social interaction and role-taking. This is an important point because it implies that reference group analysis is only necessary when it comes to considering human (symbolic communication) as opposed to animal (communication through signs) behaviour.[2] It is because of man's ability through symbols, language and communication to take on the role of the other that he is able to orient himself to groups other than those with which he is directly and continuously implicated. It is these symbolic processes which allow man to escape from the confines of a narrow environment; he relates to other social objects not only in terms of past and present affiliations, but also in terms of aspirations and expectations, means and ends, status and prestige (see Halloran, A1967, p. 41). The subject matter of reference groups is centrally placed with respect to any analysis of man within society since it is both psychological (involving motivation, perception and judgment) and sociological. It relates to *the* problem of the relationship between self and society.[3]

In outlining Mead's account of this interrelationship, I distinguished between two processes: on the one hand, the self was seen as emergent out of role-taking and internalization of the norms and values of significant and generalized others; on the other, by being able to take the role of the other, the self could look at and evaluate himself. The reference group literature has followed this distinction. The originator of the term, Hyman, showed that actors often took individuals of high status as their reference group since this enhanced their subjective status. But because this is counter-intuitive Hyman had to distinguish between two different orientations that might be taken by these actors, the identificatory and the judgmental (see Hyman, A1942, pp. 85–6). The identificatory orientation relates to the process of role-taking (internalization) leading to identification with a particular generalized other; the judgmental orientation refers to the actor evaluating himself in comparison with others.

Relatively little emphasis was placed upon the concept during the decade following Hyman's original article. Newcomb, in his study of attitude change and non-change in Bennington College, and Sherif and the Hartleys in their social psychological texts, concentrated upon the identificatory orientation. Stouffer, through the use of the

18

related term relative deprivation, implicitly, and Merton and Rossi, explicitly, elaborated how an actor may assume a judgmental orientation to a particular reference group (see Newcomb, A1943; Sherif, A1948; E. and R. Hartley, A1952; Stouffer, A1965; Merton and Rossi, A1957). This distinction was, however, hopelessly opaque to those employing the concept, and although Kelly made it explicit in 1952, there are some writers who still do not distinguish between the two.[4] Kelly differentiates between the normative and comparative functions of the reference group (A1968, pp. 80 and 81); he says:

> The first of these is that of setting and enforcing standards for the person. Such standards are usually labelled *group norms* so we shall call this the *normative function* of reference groups. . . . The second of these functions is that of *serving as* or *being* a standard or comparison point against which the person can evaluate himself and others. We shall refer to this as the *comparison function* of reference groups.

Although Kelly points out how such functions may appertain to one or more than one such group, there is something inherently confusing about his terminology since it suggests that the phenomena are similar in all respects other than in their function (see ibid., *passim*; Shibutani, A1962, pp. 133–4). In fact, it is clear from the discussion which follows in Kelly's article that he is aware that there are two quite different processes that are involved, which he terms the motivational and the perceptual. The maintenance of the distinction between them is of major importance; their only common property being that for either the derivation of norms and values or for self-evaluation, the actor will refer to others.

Various writers have suggested more sophisticated classifications. Out of a brief discussion of some of these, I hope that more satisfactory distinctions will be developed. One of the most recent and complex classifications is that produced by Theodore Kemper (A1968, pp. 32–4) who distinguishes between normative groups (where normative conformity is expected), audience groups (where an actor may act in accordance with norms but there is no demand for conformity) and four types of comparison group (equity, legitimation, role-model and accommodation). Three observations are relevant: first, this is more a list of possible references rather than a classification; second, the equity comparison group may be distinguished from the other comparison groups; and third, since no indication is given of the importance of role-taking, each group is described in terms of its effect *upon* the actor. This last point can be interestingly seen by considering the notion of a comparative reference group as found in Turner's classification (A1966, p. 158) the

19

major formulation based upon an interactive perspective. He says that when levels of aspiration, degrees of determination and the like are being compared, the individual must necessarily take the role of the other in order to make a comparison. But Turner then fails to provide a detailed account of the process by which an actor comes to judge himself in relation to his comparative reference group. The significance of the reflexiveness of role-taking was. we saw, explicit in Mead (1932, p. 190):

> We can talk to ourselves, and this we do in the inner forum of what we call thought. We are in possession of ourselves just in so far as we can and do take the attitudes of others towards ourselves and respond to those attitudes. We approve of ourselves and condemn ourselves. We pat ourselves upon the back and in blind fury attack ourselves. We assume the generalized attitude of the group, in the censor that stands at the door of our imagery and inner conversations, and in the affirmation of the laws and axioms of the universe of discourse.

Although it is correct and congruent with Mead to say that the individual compares himself with others in accordance with the standpoint of the generalized other, one needs also to know why such comparisons are made at that moment, which generalized other is relevant for which comparisons and what interpretation is placed upon this by the actor concerned. All this will be examined later in greater detail.

The significance here of role-taking implies that it will also be relevant to the other groups in Kemper's classification. Thus, within his normative category, a distinction may be drawn between a group based on identification through role-taking and internalization, and a group where this does not occur but where the standpoint of the former group designates it as a point of reference. Turner (A1966, p. 158) distinguishes between these two, the former being an identification group, the latter a valuation group; Maureen Cain (A1968, pp. 195–6) provides the same term for the former but names the latter a normative reference group. Kemper's audience, legitimator and role-model groups all seem varieties of the latter, all dependent upon signification *by* an identification group. Kemper's accommodatory group seems cognate with what Turner and Cain term an interaction group. This exhausts the types considered by Kemper; also mentioned by Turner (A1966, p. 158) and Cain (A1968, p. 196) are audience groups, that is, the groups by whom the actor sees role-performances observed and evaluated by means of reflexive role-taking. Thus, cognate with Cain, five sorts of social objects can be identified within an actor's social environment. These are identification, normative reference, audience, interactive and comparative reference groups. Cain's contribution is interesting first, because she ignores role-taking processes although she claims to base her approach upon Turner, and second, because her theoretical discussion is based solely upon identification groups.[5] It is also significant that Turner's classification appears at the conclusion of his article and no systematic justification is provided of the distinctions made. Before I attempt to provide some justification there are three other points to be considered.

First, and briefly, the identification and normative reference groups concern what one might term the *saliency* of different social objects. They indicate how significant is a given social object with respect to a particular configuration of behaviour (for example, within work or the family). It does not indicate what is termed here the *range* of importance of any given social object. A second point is to indicate the problems raised by the term 'group'; two lines of criticism have emerged. On the one hand, many writers have emphasized the distinction between reference groups and reference individuals, the latter being objects of comparison, audiences and models for role-playing (see Hyman, A1942; Merton and Rossi, A1957; Newcomb, A1943, Hyman and Singer; A1968; Kaplan, A1955; Etzkorn, A1966). On the other hand, Merton, among others, has distinguished between a group, a collectivity and a category; a group exists when there is an enduring and a morally established form of social interaction, self-definition as a member and the same definition by others; a collectivity exists when there is a sense of solidarity by virtue of sharing a set of common values and an attendant sense of moral obligation; finally, a category is simply an aggregate of those with like social characteristics with no necessarily common normative structure (see Merton, A1957, pp. 284–6 and 299–300; Kaplan, A1955, pp. 7–8; Smith, 1967; Warriner, 1962). The combination of these two sets of distinctions yields four different *forms* of social object to which an actor may refer; to fail to make such distinctions is to heighten the probability of reification. The third point is that the normal distinction between membership and non-membership of a particular social object is singularly naïve. Jackson points out the distinction between formal and psychological membership,[6] Patchen (A1968a, p. 168) talks of how 'the lines between in-groups and out-groups blur', and Merton[7] states that 'there appear to be *degrees* of membership' and 'basic distinctions in kinds of non-membership'. These problems relate to the former point and imply that the meaning accorded to different forms of membership (that is, with different sorts of orientation to different sorts of social object) will vary enormously and systematically. The following appear to be the possible structural *relationships* between the individual actor and a given social object: formal membership, psychological membership, regular interaction, intermittent interaction and no contact. Each of these implies very significant differences for the process of changing normative orientations. Between what Linn terms segments of society, models and norms of behaviour are unlikely to be readily available. The consideration of the degree to which they are necessitates the analysis of the varying possible relationships between the actor and the particular social object (see Linn, A1966, pp. 496-7).

There are thus four different aspects of any actor's normative reference group. These are its degrees of *saliency* and *range*, the various *forms* it may take, and possible structural *relationships* between the actor and the social object in question. I now want to return to the other set of distinctions that I drew earlier between types of reference group. I shall not discuss the general division between normative types, interactive and comparative, since there seems to be little to object to in the latter pair. What does need justification though is the division between types of the normative groups, that is, the distinction between identification, normative and audience reference groups. If this division can be maintained, I think that it is of major importance in analysing the actor-group relationship within contemporary society.

First, we must consider what is meant by the notion of an identification group. It is noteworthy that all those who make some contribution here write in theoretical terms and from a broadly interactionist perspective.[8] Mead (1932, p. 165) provides the basic outline when he says: 'The principle is that the individual enters into the perspectives of others, in so far as he is able to take their attitudes, or occupy their point of view.' For Mead, as for all symbolic interactionists, the basic epistemological position is that there is a symbolic structure interposed between man and his world. This is very important since it means that there is no question that thought and knowledge is socially determined in some way or other.[9] Yet Berger and Luckmann (A1967, p. 23) point out the paradox that Merton fails to see the significance for the sociology of knowledge of the development of reference group analysis. Berger himself (A1966, p. 112) suggests how the actor may not only take the attitude and the role of the other but also his world.[10] It is not simply a question of being born into or professing loyalty to a social object – it is rather to see the world and certain phenomena in that world in a particular way. It is to 'be-with' the other members, it is to share certain assumptions, partly temporal, of the nature of the world and of their places within it.[11] If the sociology of knowledge gives a broad view of the social construction of reality, reference group analysis (identification group variety) shows one the smaller scale locations where different sets of actors work out their own particular models of the cosmos (Berger, ibid., pp. 137–9). There is in this sense nothing new in reference group analysis but there is an indication of the variety of perspectives available to the actor. A reference group then for Shibutani is 'that group whose outlook is used by the actor as the frame of reference in the organization of his perceptual field' (A1955, p. 565; see also, p. 563). The development of these separate perspectives, or identification groups, is based on language and communication. Each social world, for Shibutani, is a cultural area, the boundaries of which are set by the limits of effective communication.[12] He does, of course, mention the possibility of holding more than one perspective and of the potentiality of conflict between them, of alternative definitions of their situation.

Shibutani's discussion, although provocative, is not, I think, fully satisfactory. This is both because it takes for granted the undifferentiated nature of each of these social perspectives, and because it ignores the structural configuration within which an actor may assume one rather than another. This latter point is fundamental not only in this specific context, but also to the more general sociology of knowledge; I will discuss it later. The former point relates to the reference group distinctions drawn above.

The distinction between an identification and a normative reference group should be clear from this discussion. Kaplan points to the difference by indicating the way in which Sherif conflates the actor's orientation to a social object and the consequences of that object for the actor in question.[13] If there is role-taking then the actor acquires norms and attitudes which relate both to his role-performances as well as to other social objects which may be more directly responsible for providing role-expectations for the actor. It is these latter objects which I take to be not identification groups but simply objects of normative reference. There may still be role-taking, but following Turner (A1966, p. 158) the actor in question does not take the role as his own but views it from a third-party standpoint. One further point should be noted and that is the possibility of Newcomb's negative normative reference group (A1952), or Nettl and Robertson's negative value reference (A1968, p. 77). There is a great danger of tautology here, which is only avoided by seeing such negative references as resulting from the directives of a quite different social object which is the source of identification. As a consequence of role-taking and internalization with an object of identification, there is specification of another object with which role-taking from a third-party standpoint occurs but from which there is valuative and normative dissociation.[14]

The undifferentiated nature of the social perspective formulation provided by Shibutani can also be seen by considering the way in which he views it as not only a shared world view similar to Mead's generalized other, but also as an audience before whom one tries to maintain or enhance one's standing. Each actor for Shibutani tries to gain and regain recognition within his own particular world (see A1962, pp. 132 and 143; A1964, pp. 250–60). This is not an implausible account, but it does presume that one seeks recognition within precisely the same group as that which is the basis of role-taking and identification. At one point Shibutani (A1962, p. 132) seems to say that this identification group is *only* a shared perspective while clearly, in referring to the judgment of others, one is relating specifically to other social *actors* within one's world. What seems important, therefore, is to distinguish between one's identification group, from which are derived one's major norms and values, and one's audience group, by which one's performances are judged in relation to the internalized values. Although empirically these two objects of reference may coincide, the maintenance of the analytical distinction is of considerable importance. The studies which show this are based on participant observation.[15] W. A. Rushing in his analysis of the psychiatric professions distinguishes between a comparative reference group, a normative reference group (provides individual with assimilated social norms) and an evaluative reference group (from which are derived expressive rewards of appreciation, recognition and respect). The last type, what I call an audience group, functions as a source of evaluation and appraisal for the actor, as a means by which his status and overall self-conception is confirmed and reinforced (Rushing, A1964, pp. 20–1). Thus specifically Rushing (ibid., p. 164) argues that psychiatrists function as an evaluative reference group for social workers since it is from them that they wish to obtain professional recognition. This point is made even more explicit by Berreman (A1964). His argument is that in the Aleutian village that he studied, although the whites were a fundamental audience group for the Indians, it was the membership group of modern, white-oriented Aleuts who constituted the main object of identification. This splitting of reference orientations was the result of the social separation of white and Aleutian society and from the power relationship existent between them (ibid., p. 234). Two further points should be made with respect to such audience groups. First, the degree to which actors self-consciously adjust their actions in relation to what they believe is expected by their audience group(s) is a variable.[16] Second, although an actor's audience objects may refer not only to power, wealth and status, but also to honesty, beauty and intelligence (see Goffman, 1963, p. 12), there will be occasions when there are radical changes in the relative significance of different audience groups as well as in the replacement of certain dimensions by others as primary.

These points will recur below – for the moment it is necessary to consider generally the value of the contributions within the field of reference group analysis. Although it will be seen later that such accounts are unsatisfactory in certain ways, they are most inadequate in failing to provide a satisfactory explanation. There has been conceptual confusion, the addition of *ad hoc* variables and the inclusion of a heterogeneous bundle of empirical phenomena. Deutsch and Krauss question whether there is anything that might be termed reference group *theory* since there is neither central notion, nor the postulation of any fundamentally new social processes.[17] Brian Barry more strongly questions whether there *can* be any such thing as 'reference group theory' (see Barry, A1966, p. 35; Nelson, A1961). Although this argument needs to be taken seriously, Barry (A1966, p. 35) is paradoxically the victim of the very conceptual confusion that provides part of the justification for his claim. Thus specifically he asks:[18]

> Is behaviour involving reference groups a special *kind* of behaviour, about which generalizations can be made? Or is 'reference group behaviour' logically on a par with 'Tuesday afternoon behaviour' – a slice of behaviour but not a slice with special characteristics? To support my view that it is the second possibility that in fact holds, let me quote two of Runciman's examples of 'reference group behaviour'.

The first example that he quotes is the experiment conducted by Charters and Newcomb (A1968), where a number of Catholics are split up into three equal and randomly selected groups. It is found that the third group, who meet together and who are told that their help is needed to perfect an attitude scale designed to be relevant to Catholics, give answers to a set of questions which are far closer to orthodox Catholic norms than those of the other groups.[19] The second study is that conducted by Chapman and Volkmann (A1939) and illustrates how in a situation of framework indeterminacy the suggested achievements of others, in advance of actual performance, can change the level of aspirations of different groups. Barry (A1966, p. 35) concludes from comparing these two studies that there is no common psychological mechanism that is involved. Unfortunately, this conclusion is arrived at by failing to make the simple distinction between the normative and the comparative reference group. The first study shows the saliency of different *loci* of groups of normative reference; the second, the effect of the making of comparisons upon aspirations. It is not surprising that there is no common mechanism visible.[20] Barry (ibid.) continues his argument:

> In both of these experiments the victims' behaviour is in some ways affected by their beliefs about the characteristics of certain

OF REFERENCE GROUPS

groups; but the trouble is that this would be equally true of practically all behaviour, whether public or private. Collecting information about 'reference group behaviour' will no more generate a 'theory of reference group behaviour' than collecting information about cats will generate a 'theory of cats'.

The first point to note is that he is now arguing that 'reference group behaviour' is a feature of all behaviour. Second, as a consequence of this, if information is collected about both types of reference orientation this should provide the basis for theoretical development; just as it is possible that the collection of specific sorts of information about cats should render plausible a theory of cats. Thus it does not seem that a theory of reference groups is logically impossible. But to say that is not to maintain that within this field of inquiry there is not a chronic lack of satisfactory explanation.

Runciman (A1966, p. 16) points out that such explanation would consist of two parts; the explanation of the selection of reference group, and the explanation of the consequences of such selection (see also Nelson, A1961). Typically, the first point has been ignored and where explanation has occurred, it has been overwhelmingly devoted to the interpretation of the consequences of such reference group selection. They have thus been primarily used for 'post factum sociological interpretation' (see Merton, 1957, pp. 93–5 and 99–100), especially in accounting for apparent disjunctions between independent and dependent variables. This has sometimes been of some heuristic use but it has rarely provided adequate systematic explanation. The reason for this is the looseness of the theoretical structure employed. Thus, B. P. Cohen (A1962, p. 103) maintains that it is where non-membership groups are considered (which after all is the significant emphasis introduced by reference group analysis) that there is a crucial lack of constraint upon the use of the concept:[21] the Sherifs (A1953, p. 159) argue that there is a danger of it becoming a magic term to explain anything and everything concerning group relations; and Barry (A1966, p. 36) points out that explaining a lot of things with a lot of different variables does not exhibit a theoretical structure even if all the explanations have one variable in common. The way out of this theoretical impasse is clearly to develop satisfactory explanation at the prior level of the processes of selection; it is only when this is provided that the explanation of the consequences of such selection can be theoretically tightened (see Merton and Rossi, A1957, p. 250). All of this will be now shown specifically with respect to the processes of identification and normative reference group selection.

26

3 Of normative references

Conceptual matters

I want to begin by dealing with a number of relatively controversial issues arising here. First of all, Kaplan (A1955, p. 24) draws attention to the question of whether an actor has to be aware of a particular normative prescription before we can argue that the social object associated with that norm constitutes a normative reference for that actor. He concludes that awareness is a minimal condition for establishing the existence of a reference.[1] This is not a fully convincing argument, however, since it is based on an identificatory model of the actor-group relationship. It is derived from the idea that the actor identifies or relates himself in some similar abstract way to the social object in question and as a consequence gains a normative prescription as to how he should behave in a certain context. In Kaplan's example he acquires a particular voting norm. But that seems to be highly implausible since no account is attempted either of why such an orientation is made in the first place or of the salience of a given norm of a given actor. This sort of argument leads almost to the conclusion that an actor refers to one social object rather than to another simply because he wishes to assume the norm of that particular 'group' in relation to that particular behaviour (ibid., p. 23). In relation to the identificatory group, it is clearly incorrect to suppose that an actor has to be aware of the norm for him to orient himself towards it. One's family of origin, or one's immediate social environment are given and for periods, probably objects where role-taking leads to identification and hence to behaviour partly congruent with their norms and values. One does not refer to either simply so that one can act in accordance with a particular norm that it espouses; one is engaged in continuous role-taking interaction. Kaplan's argument would have more plausibility with respect to the normative reference group, but even here, what is crucial is the significance which one's identificatory group places upon some rather than other references, and that it may only be in the process of orientation that the norm becomes apparent. Kaplan's argument is interesting since the significance of this awareness-consideration is not at all clear, even in the case of the voting norm. One wonders how much more ambiguous it would be where the norm in question was a highly generalized aspect of the actor's being-in-the-world and where temporarily distant elections did not bring about some degree of reflection as to the nature of a very specific norm. There are many sorts of norms crucial to man's behaviour, which are not obvious in this way but which are acted upon in taken-for-granted unreflective fashion. A crucial dimension, therefore, is the *degree* to which an actor is aware of the particular norms and values that are associated with it. It cannot be claimed, as it is by Kaplan, that a necessary condition for the imputation of a normative reference group to a given actor is that he is aware of its norms. The only situation where this is the case is where his orientation is to a social object with which he does not interact at all (in the past, present or through indirect mediation) and in which his reference and his acting in accordance with its norms cannot but be based upon his awareness. The empirical importance of this seems limited. It certainly does not refer to the situation that Kaplan outlines since he lays particular emphasis upon the immediate social context of each actor as being normatively significant. It is because most references arise from past, present or indirect mediation that it seems plausible to maintain that the assumption of a normatively prescribed pattern of behaviour is not necessarily based upon perception of the norm, or being consciously aware of it, or favourably evaluating it.[2]

It is not difficult to see that this argument has important implications. That an actor is aware of a particular norm espoused by a particular social object is no indication either that the norm is in fact salient for him, or that an alternative actor unaware of that norm is not in fact more influenced by it. A related methodological point which may be mentioned here arises from the difference between an expressed and a held opinion (see Smith, Bruner and White, A1956; Festinger, 1953). In other words, it cannot be presumed necessarily that what people say they believe is what they do in fact believe. Thus in a membership group the actor may often express particular opinions, congruent with the group's perceived normative climate, although actually he holds quite different attitudes.

Before proceeding further in this discussion I want to consider the implications of one particular empirical finding that reference group analysis has sought to support. A paradoxical consequence of Hyman's original article was that it focused attention upon how distant social categories were salient for the actor.[3] Much recent research has, on the other hand, tried to show that it is the more immediate and pervasive concrete relationships and social groups which shape an actor's orientation to the world.[4] Thus, some of the arguments here show that the recipient of a mass-communicated message rarely receives it directly; rather, it is mediated through the close and informal reference groups in which he is implicated.[5] Actors, during periods of crisis, tend to rely upon informal satisfactory personal relationships (see Sowa, A1962, p. 52). Face-to-face contacts are crucial for maintaining and validating actions congruent with attitudes which have been acquired much earlier.[6] How people behave politically very much depends upon the way in which the normative reference group of a class is *experienced* by actors in the political process, that is, via close and informal social groupings.[7] Finally, the 'acceptance' of a normative reference group is thought to be based upon the ease with which it is possible to establish satisfactory interpersonal contacts (see Hartley, A1968b; Ehrlich, A1966). The importance of these findings, among others, leads Rose to advocate the use of the term 'reference relationship' and Kuhn to suggest the 'orientational other'.[8] The former exists only where role-taking is involved, the latter being the basis of the actor's basic emotional and psychological commitment, his essential vocabulary, his categories of self and other, and his significant roles and sources of validating self-conceptions. However, the latter formulation ignores the distinction drawn above between an actor's objects of audience and of identification, the potentially conflicting orientational others, and the possibility that a more abstract group, collectivity or category may, at times, be an important point of reference. Rose acknowledges the last point since he notes how the other may be either a single individual or a group in a general sense. This possibility is very important. A further point of significance is the emphasis Rose places upon the nature of the 'group' as a relationship between the actor and another, or others; as such it avoids the danger of reification (see Sowa, A1962, p. 47). This is something of an exception here since although reference group analysis grew out of the symbolic interactionist tradition, what is interesting and important is the way in which this tradition has been emasculated. This can be seen in a number of respects: through reification of the notion of the other, through positing a determinate one-way relationship between this group and men's actions, through a failure to acknowledge the tentative and precarious quality of social norms, through ignoring time, the self and the actor's construction of his actions within the world, and through neglecting what it is about the totality of society which presents different opportunities for reference group selection to different sets of actors.

29

Reification occurs in two ways: most commonly through the conceptualization of the 'group' – less commonly through the meaning given to the notion of a 'norm'. Examples of both of these will be given below. I want to emphasize that most of the studies in this field are based on one or other mode of reification. Both modes are derived from a conception of the relationship between roles and actions in which once the actor's orientation to the group or the norm is established, then his behaviour will follow automatically. No attempt is made to show either the process by which norms are internalized through role-taking with others (who may or may not form a group), or the manner in which these norms are validated through actors acting in accordance with them.

A clear example of the less common reification is provided by Eisenstadt (A1954c, p. 194) who, although sensibly pointing out that a specific norm is not necessarily attached to a particular *group*, proceeds to consider a reference group as the norm that serves as the frame of reference towards which an actor seeks to orient himself. His aim is to show that reference orientations to the wider norms of society serve as a mechanism of social control (ibid., p. 197). What is inadequate is not any failure to realize that invocation of such norms arises within particular structured situations, since this is very plausibly demonstrated (ibid., pp. 199–203), but that the concept of a norm is postulated as the fundamental ontological category. There is thus neglect of the fact that it is only by acting in relation to a norm that it is reconstituted and probably partially changed through the actor's projection of his other norms and values into the external situation (see Bott, A1957, p. 166). Eisenstadt minimizes the importance of this fact that norms and values are only defined and redefined in concrete relationships between actors, and particularly, within this context, through relationships of power. To say that a reference to a wider norm is a means of social control is critically to neglect the very relationships within which norms arise, develop and change (see Kemper, A1968, p. 32, n. 12).

The other and more common form of reification results either from the basic presupposition that groups are the original givens within social reality, or from the practical sociological assumption that the study of the actor and of the way in which he constructs his actions is properly the domain of psychology or social psychology and can thus be dismissed. Either way, this sort of presupposition is very common in the analysis of reference group processes. Although certain people have at times pointed this out, they have neither acted upon their own prescriptions nor had a general influence.[9] Merton, for example, explicitly distinguishes between types of reference groups but fails to use the distinctions systematically in his analysis of such processes (Merton and Rossi, A1957; see Merton, A1957).

The dangers of trying to quantify these phenomena can be seen from Fishbein's testing of certain aspects of Merton's analysis. The acknowledgement by the latter, that the relationships between in- and out-groups and membership and non-membership groups are extremely vague and imprecise, is overlooked in the former. Membership and non-membership groups are here the given reality (see Fishbein, A1963). There are two comments that follow.

First of all, the notion of the reified phenomenon, the 'group', concentrates attention upon 'common interests', 'group structure' and 'defined statuses'. This leads to the neglect of orientations *to* collectivities and categories, and to the fact that within all orientations there is a process of reference group construction in which certain norms are imputed to the object in question.[10] Second, it is only where the social object is a group in the specific sense that there are values, norms and roles which the actor can simply adopt. But even in this case there are three other points: first, the variation in the actor's orientation and in the processes of role-taking and internalization; second, the importance of the actor's acting within a role and as a consequence, reconstituting or changing the norms in question; and third, the particular actions may result much more either from particular relationships with significant others or from some broader collective act with a high degree of normative construction.

For these reasons it is difficult to devise a non-reified conception of the 'reference group'. But because this term is part of the taken-for-granted conceptual apparatus of the sociologist, I do not think that it will be useful simply to abandon it. Rather, I will keep it as a category serving to cut off a general section of sociological research. A further general term to be used is that of the 'social object', that is, any other individual, group, collectivity, or category of human beings towards which the actor may orient himself and which is a constituent of his objective social world. More specific terms to be used are 'objects of identification', 'objects of normative reference' and 'audience objects'. Where attention is being directed to either the first two of these or to all three in general, the term 'normative reference group processes' may be employed.

Thus normally the nature of the relationship between the objects of identification or of normative reference is conceived of in reified form; more specific examples will be presented later. For the moment it is important to consider the direction of causality implied within such analyses. Kuhn (A1964a; A1964b) points out that although the theoretical statements of reference group analysis are indeterminate (or at any rate those of Shibutani (A1962), Turner (A1966) and Kuhn are indeterminate), the actual applications of the analysis have been characterized by a social object to actor determination. This contradiction between the theoretical statements and the operational research within reference group analysis is for Kuhn one of the most unfortunate aspects of modern symbolic interactionism.[11] Although perhaps overdrawn, this is an important point which relates to the ever-developing tendency within Western thought to believe that the source of truth in the world derives from the increasing fragmentation of observed phenomena into smaller and smaller units such that each part can be more accurately measured. The problem within the sociology of the reference group is that it is customarily based upon the breaking up of the actor's essential being-in-the-world into a number of separate, distinguishable and quantifiable forms, structures and functions. Later, it will be seen that this leads to a very peculiar ontology of the agent in the social world conceptualized in reference group terms. For the moment it must be seen that this way of conceiving of man's experience of his social world is to result in a series of more or less testable relations between the social object and the actor of a determinate kind (see Lynd, 1958, p. 75f). That the relationship is conceived of in these terms reflects the predominance of a model of role-playing which neglects the significance of role-taking and derives internalized behaviour from the actor's identification with the social object in question. It is based on a model where the role-performance more or less reflects the expectations implied within the role itself, where this role is derivative from either a status or a position, and where this status or position is located within a hierarchy such that the actions of men within their role(s) are approximately integrated. The possibilities that the actor himself defines his performance in the act of role-playing, that this role is the potential source of sub- or contracultural definitions of social reality, and that there is a lack of integration of this hierarchy, are all ignored. But to ignore these possibilities is, in the analysis of self and reference groups, to posit self-control as a function of social control and to conceive of normative reference group orientations as simply a non-dialectical assumption of the norms and values of a generalized other. The model of man, therefore, is simply one who acts in accordance with the norms and values that *play* upon him. There is no notion of action that is built up by actors through their interpretation of objects, situations and the actions of others, of their experience of others, of their experience of their world. An actor simply refers to, relates to or identifies with a social object and his action is seen to flow simply from the norms and values of that object. That *we* know from our experience of the world that human society consists of acting (and not simply of reacting) agents is systematically denied.[12]

Nevertheless a few studies of reference group analysis have not totally ignored the orientation taken by the actor, not in the form outlined here but to help to explain the selection of reference orientations. Again, interestingly, it is Eisenstadt (A1954a; A1954b) who has discussed this most explicitly (see also E. and R. Hartley, A1952, pp. 591–3). The problem is that it is very difficult to see how one could provide an explanation of the selection of normative reference groups without the imputation of some general psychological motivation to the actor. Most writers ignore the problem by simply providing an account of the consequences of such selection. Eisenstadt, on the other hand, commences with the assumption that it is the individual's status-image and collectivity-orientation that largely determine the choice of normative reference groups. He argues that about 90 per cent of his respondents gave their reason for reference in terms of status conferral (A1954a, p. 177). This is tricky, however, because first, the reason that actors give now for their actions in the past is no *necessary* indication of the actual reasons for their action; second, only two examples of the responses are given and if one is looking for signs of status conferral then it is typically not difficult to find them; third, even in these two examples (which are presumably particularly clear to illustrate the point) there are evident signs of alternative bases of motivation;[13] and fourth, Eisenstadt himself acknowledges this by distinguishing between economic goals, social participation and solidarity, and aspects related to cultural evaluation. Thus, to say that the reason for an actor's orientation to a given social object is status conferral is to say nothing much more than that the actor appeared to have *some* reason for such a reference. Status is here being used in the wide and diffuse sense discussed above, which is the counterpart of role-playing within the over-socialized conception of man; Zetterburg (1962, p. 91) plausibly suggests that status seeking in general is 'a strong contender for the position of the Major Motivational Theorem in sociology'. However, once an attempt is made to make the notion of status just a little more specific, it can be seen that there are a whole family of motivations that are here involved which relate not only to the chances of positive or negative honour, but also to power, wealth and satisfying interpersonal relationships.

I do not, therefore, think that postulations of *universal* reference group motivation have been particularly fruitful. Thus no basis has been provided for overcoming the 'group'-actor determinate model outlined earlier. This model is a particularly interesting phenomenon within the sociology of sociological knowledge. It reflects two tendencies: first, the desire for determinate and quantifiable answers within an increasingly empirical social-scientific establishment; second, an emphasis upon the group or even small group basis for social action. In that the former reflects the quest for methodological rigour within American social science, and the latter reflects the salience of pluralist philosophy within the USA, it is not surprising that the whole thrust of reference group analysis has been predominantly American. No particular objection to methodological rigour *per se* is to be suggested except that to be precise about something that is necessarily imprecise almost inevitably leads to systematic error. This has produced a form of social scientific project which has been rooted within the quest to quantify man's dependence upon various social objects, or reference *groups*. The objection to be levelled here is not only to the unfree, unliberating nature of the resultant sociological conception of man, but to the manifestly unsatisfactory explanation of human action that is provided. Further the empirical connection within 'American' sociology of quantification and pluralism[14] has led to another critical failure, that is, to the ignoring of the problems and nature of the social structure and a concentration upon small-scale research and the psychology of adjustment (see Coser, 1955, p. 6). This is very important. It has meant that restriction of attention to certain levels of analysis, even to conflict between different normative reference orientations, has allowed the nature of the structure *within* which such second-order conflicts are played out and discussed to go unanalysed. The very term 'reference group' implies that one 'group' (for example, class) is very much like any other (for example, family), and that it is sensible to consider changes from one to another or possible conflicts between them within a single conceptual framework. Conflicts are thus all brought down to the common denominator of the 'group' and this reflects the pluralist postulate that conflict occurs only at this level. The conventional study of normative references is thus an attempt to obfuscate different orientations to different social objects with differing potentialities of conflict at different levels of analysis. That the study of normative references is dragged out of the social totality within which such orientation occurs is to neglect the structure of this totality, to neglect real power relationships between actors[15] and the mobilization of bias (see Bachrach and Baratz, 1962). That the study of the part without reference to the whole is a distorted abstraction is perhaps nowhere so clear as in the study of the processes of normative reference group orientation. That study must be placed back into the analysis of the social structure in which various possibilities, both contradictory and non-contradictory, are presented to the actor. The degree of realization of such possibilities specifies the distinction between the real and the ideal that was manifest in the original interactionist tradition.

Empirical matters

I will attempt to show in this section that the empirical analyses are inadequate and that this is partly because of the unsatisfactory cluster of presuppositions lying behind the normative reference group concept.

The first empirical use of the concept that I will consider is that which employs it as a means of redescribing a behavioural or orientational pattern that we already know about. Very common in this respect is the conceptualization of an occupational community as a normative reference group. Lipset[16] argues that such a community will occur when there is either a geographically isolated job or a deviant work schedule.[17] Salaman argues that if two out of involvement in work skills, marginality and inclusivity occur, then we will find an occupational community.[18] A number of points stand out here: first, to redescribe an occupational community as a reference group does not achieve any theoretical advance but *may* obscure understanding as a consequence of its reified conceptualization. Second, as normally used, an occupational community constitutes an identification object in the sense used above. Finally, the degree of significance of such communities varies, partly depending upon whether the objects of audience and identification are synonymous.[19] The importance of the last point may be illustrated by Salaman's interesting use of the local-cosmopolitan distinction to characterize different forms of occupational community. The literature itself had got rather bogged down,[20] but it may be argued that the application of the identification-audience distinction overcomes certain difficulties within both Salaman's analysis and the literature in general. His argument is that the occupational reference group of railwaymen working in Cambridge consists of other railwaymen in their particular department. On the other hand, the occupational reference group for London architects is comprised of all members of the profession and not just of immediate work mates (A1969, p. 241). Different conclusions follow, however, if we distinguish between the audience and identificatory orientations. Thus it is probable that for both 'local' railwaymen and 'cosmopolitan' architects the local work group is the *principal* audience orientation; while identification in each case may well be provided by the national association. The point to emphasize here is that a failure to consider the meanings of different social objects within the actor's social world may result from the use of the normative reference group as a means of collective redescription.

Discussion of those studies which set out to be explanatory falls into two parts. On the one hand, there are two studies which attempt to explain the selection of an actor's reference objects on a relatively social-psychological level. On the other hand, there are a large number of studies which analyse the consequences of such selection.

Within the first section I will devote most attention to Maureen Cain's attempt to systematize the explanation of the selection of

35

different role-sets or counter-positions (A1968). Her argument is that the reason for one rather than another counter-position being selected is mainly a function of the degree of perceived functional interdependence between ego and the group (ibid., pp. 200–4). The problem is that since in her actual exposition she only tries to explain the relative potency of identification groups, it is very difficult to see how perceived interdependence can be distinguished from identification. Thus, if ego perceives himself as interdependent with a group then he will also identify with it; and if he identifies with it he will also perceive that he is dependent upon it and it is dependent upon him. This point is enhanced because Cain claims that her notion of an identification group both follows Turner and is predicated upon internalization, that is, upon role-taking.[21] But, in a very important way, that implies ego's clear perception of the interdependence between himself and the object of role-taking. This lack of clear-cut differences between identification and interdependence can be seen in how Cain elaborates her explanation.

The first structural factor affecting the relative potency of different identification groups is ego's perception of the group's dependence upon him. This is simply asserted and there is no reason for not arguing the converse, that if ego identifies with a particular group he will perceive its dependence upon him. Not to do so would be psychologically dislocating and might lead to the attenuation of identification. The second structural factor is treated a little differently. At first she maintains that identification with a group will follow if ego is *actually* dependent upon it. This is clearly false. The family of origin is a group with which ego identifies and upon which he is dependent, yet the marriage of ego may be accompanied by both an increase in his functional dependence upon it and a decrease in his identification. Cain, in fact, predicts this possibility since she says 'where there is no identification, ego will come to resent, and ultimately to avoid if possible, the power of the group' (ibid., p. 201). In other words, she admits explicitly that identification may act as the independent rather than the dependent variable.[22]

One interesting reason for the inadequacy of Cain's analysis is that the social psychological literature from which she deduces her basic proposition is only concerned with one combination of reference group characteristics, that is, situations where the ego is a member of a face-to-face group which acts as a source of norms with a limited behavioural range.[23] But there is no reason for supposing that relationships found useful to this ego-group relationship will be similarly useful to the explanation of the actor's orientation to other social objects, particularly to explaining the relative potency of various objects of identification.

Jackson (A1959a) argues on the other hand that in any group a person's attraction to membership relates directly to the magnitude of his social worth. A number of points need to be briefly mentioned. First, he emphasizes that the sentiments of an actor's immediate work group rather than a wider and more diffuse organization are crucial to his self-esteem (ibid., p. 323). Second, he points out the nature and importance of the power relationship between the professionals and the non-professionals in the agency that he studied. The latter he shows do not work *with* the others in the organization but *for* them. Upward mobility is practically impossible and so the relation between attraction and social worth is not relevant to their experience (ibid., pp. 322–3). And third, Jackson gives some indication of the probable circularity of the process. Thus, the communication to members that they are valued increases their attraction to membership; and this in turn increases their probable conformity and thus their status within that hierarchy (ibid., pp. 321–2). The point here is that correlations can tell one little of this historical process. Unfortunately his analysis concludes at this point. If he had continued it would have indicated: the different structural forms of reference groups which may exist, the distinction between identificatory and normative references on one hand, and the audience object on the other, and the various meanings which can be placed by actors upon different social objects within their environment.

I now want to consider the adequacy of those studies which attempt to explain the *consequences* of reference group orientation, especially where there is conflict between them.[24] Most are based, more or less directly, upon Newcomb's classic account of reference group processes in Bennington College (see Newcomb, A1957; A1968a; A1968b; Newcomb, et al., A1967). He observed that during four successive years, juniors and seniors were markedly less conservative than freshmen in terms of a number of contemporary public issues. The study of a cohort of individuals over the period of college membership showed the same trend. Comparisons with other colleges indicated that there were no major differences in original freshmen attitudes and that in the older years, there was much less conservatism in Bennington. Further study showed the connection of non-conservatism with high participation, involvement and status within the college. Newcomb's follow-up study showed the general persistence of the attitudes that had been established and accounts for this both in terms of the selection of husbands, friends and activities more or less congruent with these attitudes, and in terms of these patterns of interaction supporting the already established attitudes. Newcomb (A1968b) suggests that Heider's notion of balance helps to account for these validating processes. Although this follow-up study appears to be a plausible account of the way in which attitudes once established can be maintained, I want to consider whether the original conceptualization of Bennington as an object of normative reference was satisfactory.

Newcomb correctly points out that an explanation of the attitudes simply in terms of 'assimilation to the community' would be inadequate since it is also necessary to consider the student's orientation to the normative reference group of home and school. He maintains that where an actor's attitudes do not change, this can be explained by the fact that the home and the school and not the college were the objects of normative reference.

I think that there are two problems with this account. The first is outlined by Kaplan (A1955, p. 31f) who suggests three criteria by which we can judge whether a particular social object is an actor's normative reference group. These are agreement with the norm, identification (we may generalize this as simply a normative orientation) and awareness of the norm. Newcomb, however, ignores the latter two and by concentrating upon the first bases his analysis simply upon whether the girls were or were not conservative. Thus in all cases where the girls were conservative, the family was assigned as a positive reference group; and in three of four non-conservative cases, the college was so designated. But this is an obviously circular argument since if one only establishes the operation of a reference through the attitude expressed, it is erroneous to use this attitude as any sort of indication that a reference group has influenced the attitude. One thus needs some independent evidence for the operation of a reference group. Of the two suggested by Kaplan, the awareness of the norm has been criticized above as being of only variable significance. The other point, however, that Newcomb does not consider is the orientation of the actor to the college; this is crucial. Newcomb's failure here means that he ignores the meaning that these different social objects have for the actor in question. Thus it is clear that the actor's orientation to the family is not of the same form as his orientation to a college community. In the first case, he is a long-term member of a face-to-face group premised upon identification and exercising a high range of significance. In the latter, he enjoys short-term membership of a moderately salient collectivity, with which he may identify or which may act as a basis for normative reference. This is extremely important since it suggests that the two cannot be lumped together as variants on a single theme. All that one can say is that there has been a change from one orientation to one social object to a different orientation to a different social object and that certain attitudinal changes followed, but this does not indicate what it was that brought about the change. The importance of this variability of potentially different social objects and orientations is, in fact, indicated by Newcomb when he talks of subgroups within the community which may serve as focal points of reference.[25] This is crucial of course; it may be that it is these social groups that are important bases of self-evaluation. If so, it would suggest that Newcomb's general explanation in terms of becoming liberal in order to acquire status would need radical transformation. Two possibilities are ignored: first, that the adoption of non-conservative attitudes is associated with the fact that such attitudes represent more plausible interpretations of the student's experience of the world; second, that these normative orientations are placed within a larger whole such that the potential reference conflicts are seen to involve the whole process of structural change and development.

These points relate to the more general consideration of the explanation typically provided by reference group analysis; that is, of certain attitudinal or behavioural outcomes in terms of conflict or cross-pressurization between two or more normative references. These two points relate both to the interpretation of the actor's experience and to the wider structural context. Much analysis that has developed out of reference group analysis has ignored both of these considerations. This can be seen in the application of reference group analysis to the notions of marginality and cross-pressurization. Marginality for Park (1928) and Stonequist (1937) represents the psychological uncertainty resulting from an actor being situated between two or more social worlds, typically those based upon race or nationality. This has been generalized to include wider categories and more varied outcomes.[26] Although this has some use, it is theoretically limited. First of all, it is unclear whether cross-pressurization results from merely referring to different social objects, or whether it depends upon the actor interpreting his situation as cross-pressurized or marginal. Both perspectives are found in the literature. If it is the former, then the explanation is simply that an actor refers to conflicting normative references and this leads to cross-pressurization or marginality, the existence of which one only knows because his orientations conflict. In the latter case, although it is possible to discover whether an actor is or is not cross-pressurized simply by asking him, there is an enormous explanatory looseness that is introduced into the account. The reason for this is that it is erroneous to maintain that orienting to two social objects will *necessarily* involve conflict. It will depend rather upon the actor's interpretation of the relationship between his differing orientations. Intra-individual conflict will only materialize out of the particular interpretation of the relationship between particular references. Many people have pointed out parts of this argument: thus, there is no obvious relationship between marginal status and personality (see Kerckhoff and McCormick, A1955); a marginal culture may develop (see Goldberg, 1941; Stonequist, 1937); there is the possibility of being marginal to a situation of marginality (Riesman, 1951, esp. p. 114); there are all sorts of different social objects that may be involved;[27] the social objects may simply be uncontradictory (see Simpson, A1962; Rosen, A1955; A1968; Emery and Katz, A1951; A1952; Taft, A1952; A1953); different objects are relevant at different times and places (see Pugh, 1966); the actor may be unaware of any conflict (see Kriesberg, 1949); different responses may occur as to whether the conflict is internal or external (see Segal, 1969); the importance of the normative level of each object may not necessarily coincide (see Festinger, 1953); the relationship between the social object and the actor may vary enormously (see Berreman, A1964); and marginality may be minimized by retirement into, or resignation of, one social object, or by its disappearance, or their resignation (see Hughes, 1949).

This is relatively unproblematic and probably uncontroversial. What is surprising though is that many of the reference group contributions have remained unaffected by these arguments. Thus it is believed that the explanation of particular social phenomena can be derived from the more general formulation that an orientation to two apparently conflicting 'groups' leads to greater psychological stress. Although I take this argument to be inadequate, it is nevertheless interesting since it indicates certain presuppositions: first, that there is an approximate equality of importance of these different social objects; second, that conflict is undesirable because of its internal, psychological consequences; third, that there is no really *implacable* conflict between different and opposed collectivities and categories in relation to which the individual is said to be cross-pressurized or marginal; and fourth (see Riesman, 1951), that it is desirable to minimize marginality and to reintegrate the actor. The perspective I am adopting here rejects all of these presuppositions as being *necessarily* useful. However, there are a small number of points that can be made.

Thus, Stonequist's excellent discussion of the marginal man (1937, pp. 51–3) is important, first, in outlining the notion of a 'marginal area'; second, in his enumeration of the conditions under which racial assimilation is enhanced; and third, in his argument that marginality does not simply follow from a structural location between two cultures but from a 'crisis experience' which necessitates a reconstruction of the actor's fundamental self-conceptions (ibid., pp. 120–58). These considerations will be taken up later. The distinction developed above between normative references in general, and audience objects, indicates that although an actor's general values may be derived through role-taking with wide-ranging collectivities and categories, it is probable that the specific expectations of significant others are immediately important for any potential development of conflict.[28] One situation of clear stress is where one is evaluated negatively by an audience object of which one is simultaneously a member. A third point to note is that an actor may exhibit dual consciousness; he may, in other words, possess two or more sets of attitudes which although in themselves are highly contradictory, do not always come into conflict since they are mobilized in quite different situations.[29] Furthermore, certain orientations to certain social objects are not simply non-contradictory but are conditions which reinforce each other. Thus membership of, and some sort of normative orientation to, a social object may be a necessary condition for the actor's movement into a new social object in a more or less integrated way,[30] although most life-cycles in contemporary society will, at times, involve a certain marginality.[31] A similar congruence may arise through the coincidence of different social objects, all of which espouse the same normative emphasis (see Kemper, A1968). The most stressful form of conflict is where the actor experiences a contradiction between a single salient membership object and single salient non-membership object of identification and where he is unable to become a member (in a fairly normal sense) of the latter.[32] This process of changing references between fairly significant social objects is problematic. There are I think two fallacies: first, that conversion is simply a matter of building loyalty towards something whereas it may also involve the loosening or the abandoning of former allegiances (see Strauss, A1959, p. 123); and second, after partial conversion which then ceases, the actor will return to the previous situation.[33] The first point indicates that it is necessary to specify the meaning of an orientation for the actor in question; the meaning, that is, for the way in which he appears to others, his perception of this and the way in which he wishes to appear. Changes in adult objects of identification are problematic for this reason; Brim (A1966, p. 37) suggests that such socialization requires a relationship rather like that of childhood to effect equivalent changes in basic values. The second point indicates the non-reversibility of time in social life. As Mead argues (1932, p. 19), time is not simply passage but a becoming which affects the inner nature of the event itself. To stop orienting to a social object is not to revert to the former situation. Both the actor and his world are no longer as they were.

Temporal matters

Both these last points are important and usually ignored within the literature. The failure to consider them in systematic fashion means two things: first, that actors in normative reference group analysis appear only as a bundle of reference group orientations; second, that there is neglect of the temporal relations between such orientations.[34] These points are interdependent. The notion of the self is almost wholly disregarded with the consequence that the former acting agent of symbolic interactionism is conceptualized in vacuous terms. He simply and a-historically plays roles and relates to various social objects. But what we should take as important is the way in which the passage of time maintains, shapes and transforms the actor's self and the way in which this self refers to and internalizes certain social objects within his environment. Thus, at any point in time, the selection for reference among social objects is dependent upon the temporal development of the self up to that point and on the resulting orientations, expectations and aspirations which are brought to each situation. The reason, therefore, for the importance of the orientation of the actor is that he will not refer to any social object unless the meaning which it has for him is one more or less congruent with the form, content and development of the self at that moment in time. Explanation of an actor's total cluster of normative references cannot be divorced from the temporal development of the self; and the explanation of why a single reference is made must be in terms of the meaning which it has for the actor at that point in time.[35]

Now it is thought clear that the notion of a non-reversible, quasi-consistent self has always been open to criticism,[36] since ultimately it cannot be disguised as a purely observable phenomenon. It can be criticized as a figment of the observer's imagination (see Lecky, 1951, p. 105f; Allport, 1955, *passim*). In two ways, however, its use here will partly (but only partly) counter such criticism; this is because the self will neither be held to be the doer of all things, nor simply the outcome, or dependent variable, of certain social processes (see ibid., pp. 84–5; McCall and Simmons, A1966, p. 8). The self is to be seen as neither dependent nor independent but as intermediate between the objective facticity of society and the subjectively meaningful actions of actors. The development of symbolic interactionism has, of course, paid much attention to the processes by which this self is both generated and generates itself. In this account, which is neither actor- nor group-oriented in its perspective, the actor's orientation to, and the meaning of, certain social objects should be of seminal importance. Reference group analysis has so far failed to provide a specification of this relationship between self and society mainly because the self, as anything but an a-temporal repository of group- and societally-determined values, norms and attitudes, has been consistently denied. It is a significant indictment of this analysis and of symbolic interactionism in general that they have not said anything about what the neo-Freudian Erikson terms 'the *mutual complementation* of ego synthesis and social organization'

(Erikson, 1968b, p. 53). Further, in his castigation of psychoanalysis for its neglect of the environment, he says ' "former" environments are forever in us; and since we live in a continuous process of making the present "former" we never . . . meet any environment as a person who never had an environment' (ibid., p. 24). This is a clear statement of the temporality of the self and of how an actor's orientations derive significantly from the past, his interpretation of that past, and its relationship with the present. The grounding of the historical society within the historical self, and the converse, is the essential premise.

This duality indicates, however, that the self is not a unitary phenomenon which would rest under a single conceptual umbrella. Most especially there are two important aspects: first, the self as subject or agent; second, the self as the actor somehow known to himself.[37] Since the latter usage is crucial in Mead it seems best to refer to that as the self; the former will be termed identity. They are two aspects of the single actor.

This argument is complicated by the multi-dimensionality of the notion of identity. It is necessary to distinguish personal identity that relates to the individual's uniqueness, and social identity that derives from the actor being experienced in terms of certain broad social categories (see McCall and Simmons, A1966, pp. 64–5; Strauss, A1959, ch. 1); actual, potential and ideal identity (see Miller, A1963, p. 679); the existence of identity and the actor's belief in its existence (see Erikson, 1968b, p. 50); and activities that are crucial to the establishment of an actor's identity and activities that are peripheral.[38] Such non-peripheral activities are those that result in the individual acquiring money, labour, goods, status and power (see Erikson, 1968b, p. 132; McCall and Simmons, A1966, p. 78). A related distinction is that between the actor's self-image, that is, his way of looking at himself in taking and playing a single role and thus in establishing a short-run social identity, and the actor's self-conception, that is, his long-run sense of himself in activities crucial to his identity (see Turner, 1968).

The self, on the other hand, is the individual as seen by himself through the eyes of certain others. It is unequivocally social since it is dependent upon his perception of how he appears to others, how he appears to his audience 'group' or 'groups'. He may refer to different audience-objects to derive different self-images depending upon his roles and the social identities that he is trying to establish (see Smith, A1968). These objects will typically act to maintain and reinforce the actor's overall self-conception. Discrepancies between an actor's expectations of himself as derived from his audience-objects and his performance will customarily only bring into question his transient and passing self-images. This is because although it is endemic in social life that new relevant audiences are continually being derived for physical-maturational and social-situational reasons, these objects essentially act as validations of the actor's already established conceptions of himself. Thus they are unlikely to conflict with each other, they are mostly concerned with the provision of approval or disapproval (status in the general sense used above), and as a result of the continuity of interaction within which actors are engaged the actor is likely to adjust his actions unreflexively in accordance with his perception of the expectations of the particular audience-object in question. Most analyses concern themselves with either the judgments of this audience-object (as in Goffman) or the societal judgments of wealth, power and status (as in the status consistency literature, for which see below). What both of these approaches ignore is the possibility of radical and acute transformations of the actor's social situation and the consequential replacement of one set of audience objects by another. What it is that might bring this about, what it is that might lead the actor to view himself as an object of his own reflexive consciousness, needs serious discussion.

There are two aspects of identity: consistency and development.[39] As Anselm Strauss (1962, p. 65) says 'the open-ended, tentative, exploratory, hypothetical, problematical, devious, changeable, and only partly unified character of human courses of action'.

Perhaps the most systematic attempt to elevate the quest for consistency of identity into a social psychological theory is that of Prescott Lecky (1951): he says that the goal for which the individual strives is that of the maintenance of a unified organization.[40] Pleasure, he argues, is associated with satisfying the primary goal of the maintenance of unity; pain with conflict and disorganization. He talks of 'The principle of unification', which is the constant compulsion to unify and harmonize the system of ideas by which one lives (ibid., pp. 222–3). Three criticisms of this are pertinent. First, consistency for Lecky is seen purely as the outcome of the relationship between the ideas by which one lives and is not seen as dependent upon ongoing social processes. Second, he treats consistency as though it were an end in itself, and he thus ignores the ends that motivate actors, in relation to which a consistent self is the framework and part of the means used (see Kelly, 1963, p. 59; Gergen, 1968, p. 300). Finally, he does not consider whether the individual *is* unified or whether there is simply striving *for* unification. The former argument would, as Strauss suggests above, be simply untrue; the latter argument, if combined with both a specification of the nature of development and of the ends that motivate men, would seem correct. Gergen's criticism of all notions of consistency is inadequate; first, because he discusses only the individual as known to himself, and second, because he does not distinguish between self-images and self-conceptions (see ibid., Erikson, 1968b, p. 73; 1968a, p. 61). Most writers assume some such process of striving for a consistency of identity,[41] although it is clear that actors vary greatly in their striving for, and in their notions of, consistency, as well as the importance of apparently discrepant expectations (see Miller, A1963, pp. 696–8).

Some evidence can be adduced in favour of this argument: that is to say, it is observed that there is some behavioural consistency across various situations. Brim (1960) makes four points in opposition to this argument: first, that such consistency is only weak; second, it occurs most noticeably in functionally unimportant aspects such as sociability; third, to the extent that it does occur, it may result from response generalization from one role to another; and fourth, it may be most marked among inadequately socialized actors as a consequence of an inability to discriminate between roles (see also Miller, A1963, pp. 657–8). The third point, which is clearly correct, can, however, be used against Brim since it would certainly not be argued that a strain towards consistency could not be derived from the existence of a master-role vital to the actor's identity. What Brim ignores is that it is the actor's performance *within* this role that is generalized elsewhere; it is not the role itself. Thus Brim's further argument that the learned repertoire of roles *is* the personality is questionable (see also ibid., p. 657). His image of man, his *homo sociologicus*, is the rationally understandable and readily observable player of roles; it is not the image of man found here.

There are, on the contrary, three features of this image. The first is that it is not a partial image in the sense of being economic man or psychological man or sociological man, but is simply man living within his social and cultural world.[42] Second, I presume that there is some transformation of the actor's previous and present role-*performances* into a sort of subjectively meaningful whole. This is what Weber (1964, p. 101) means when he talks of 'the behaviour of one or more individual human beings' or of 'the subjective meaning-complex of action'. Third, the actor is seen developmentally, unlike Weber's conception of man which ignored the processes by which the actor was transformed and transforms himself over time. This last point is crucial since it means that the actor brings to any interaction situation a history of social experience; but because of the second point, it is important to note how such experiences are not just added together but exhibit organization. It is this feature which accounts for the emergent properties of both society and the actor since organization imparts to the aggregate characteristics (of either individuals or role-performances) not found in the components alone (see Buckley, 1967; Erikson, 1968a, p. 233). Actors thus exist in time and realize some degree of consistency among their organized

45

role-performances. It is important though not to posit the development of the actor as something preordained and quasi-inevitable; if it was, the explanation of various normative references would never be problematic. But that it is reflects the fact that the actor's identity develops out of the processes of symbolic social interaction, although there are constraints imposed by the physical maturation of the actor (see Sarbin, 1954, esp. p. 238f). Incidentally, any account of man's genesis based *solely* on physical maturation reduces man's development to inevitable and hidden presuppositions about the 'healthy' individual and to culture-bound values as to the nature of his functioning (see Strauss, A1959, p. 140). The identity of man is neither a simple development nor a consistent subject, but an organization, a totality of his past and present experiences, of his performances within particular roles (see Moustakas, 1956). Identity is based upon non-reversible time; it is not something that one has, but it is won and re-won through validation within one's experience within the world. The claim to a particular identity is not just, therefore, a statement of being, but rather one of becoming. An identity is not simply something that one is or has, but is a whole set of structures and processes, behaviours and attitudes specifying how one is, will be and could be.

A necessary adjunct to this notion is that of career since this relates one's image, conceptions and identities to one's official positions and life-styles within collectivities.[43] Unlike the concept of role, that of career emphasizes both the critical nature of certain of man's activities and indicates their temporality. Men and subcultures are not simply deviant or non-deviant, but have careers.

This notion of a career developed out of Van Gennep's formulation of *les rites de passage*, the effect being to reduce the harmful consequences involved in passing from one group or status to another.[44] Two features of contemporary society are significant in generalizing this notion: one is the high degree of role-differentiation and segregation (see Banton, A1965); the other is the possibility that the actor may engage in a project to bring about a progressive transformation of his situation over the life-cycle (see Touraine and Ragazzi, 1961). Both these points relate to the abundance of reference orientations available in the world of the contemporary actor. They also indicate two features of the notion of the actor's career. The former is the degree to which the stages of a single career are integrated with each other, such that when one has been completed the actor both aspires to the next and can reasonably obtain it. The latter is the meaning which is placed upon his life experience – that is to say, the degree to which the actor conceives of his life as consisting of a series of reasonably well-established stages and of a fundamental *raison d'être* for being-in-the-world. There is no necessary relationship between these two aspects. Thus a well-regulated status-passage may be antithetical to the actor's fulfilment of a project of successive transformations of his life-situation. It is important, however, not to overemphasize either of these two aspects, or to ignore other properties of status-passage.[45] Nevertheless to view the actor's experience in this way (as opposed to a role analysis) is very important, since it indicates the problems of pacing and timing, and of the temporality of expectations and aspirations. Reference orientations are not only multiple; they may also be sequential, timed and historically dependent upon each other. Most societies develop cooling-out or marking-out mechanisms by which some identity support is given to those who for personal or structural reasons do not fully realize their expectations regarding their development (see Goffman, 1962). There are two important considerations. The first is the degree of effectiveness of such cooling-out mechanisms which depend upon the lack of agreement or differences of status between demoters and demoted, or the long-range or collective nature of the demotion (see Glaser and Strauss, 1968, p. 89). Second, it is important to specify the structure of opportunities available at each stage; this varies not only between different stages of a single career but also between different actors depending upon their particular structural location. This, in turn, is important since such a location implies a career of some sort. And even where this career is well-regulated and conventional there is a necessary contradiction since, on the one hand, it implies estrangement from society, and on the other hand, it implies integration with it. Even the career of childhood within the family is partly the implication of the actor within a tiny subculture of its own, within which the structure of society is selected and interpreted (see McCall and Simmons, A1966, p. 32). A simple dichotomization of such opportunity structures into legitimate and illegitimate is thus problematic since it is based on a unitary conceptualization of the normative framework (see Cloward and Ohlin, A1960). All careers, roles and opportunity structures are partly conflictful and partly offer contradictory interpretations of social reality for their adherents.

The importance of the temporal nature of man's experience has another important consequence. This is that different categories of actors experience social reality differently from each other on account of their varying experiences not at the same point, but at different points. Thus, within the same society, different generations exhibit dissimilar orientations to the world. Heidegger says: 'The inescapable fate of living in and with one's generation completes the full drama of individual human existence' (quoted in Mannheim, 1952). Such generational differences do not result automatically from some age-graded status differentiation; rather, they result both from the overall structure, especially of occupations, and from specific events which create sudden discontinuities between the age-groups in question. The second point is made more specific by Mannheim's emphasis on how distinctive experiences during youth can create the basis of a common frame of reference (normative reference collectivity), or what Hyman terms a reference period (Hyman and Singer, A1968, p. 17; Zeitlin, A1967, pp. 212–13). The former point above is elaborated by Eisenstadt's work on youth movements (1956); these are more likely to develop, he claims, where the kinship unit does not provide the context for the division of labour. Contemporary youth within Western society is placed within what Erikson terms a psycho-social moratorium which although not allowing free role experimentation as he suggests, does enable a considerable degree of identity testing (1968b, p. 156). There is, of course, a fashionable tendency to explain a great many social phenomena in terms of generational differences. Again, if this were correct it would make the explanation of normative references relatively unproblematic. Unfortunately, it is not an adequate account since it fails to distinguish between the age-span, as given through culturally specified social roles, the consciousness of an age-group as indicated through fashion, the generation, as developed through the convergence of personal and social time, and the generation-unit, the historically-specific vanguard of transformation.[46] Thus, changes or stability within society are not explained *by* the relationships between age-groups. Rather, it is changes within society which explain the possible nature of the age-relationships, as well as a lot more besides (see Allen, 1968, p. 321 and *passim*; Cain, 1964).

Theoretical matters

This discussion of the relationship between the self, identity and processes of normative reference reveals two crucial points. First, the actor's orientation to certain forms of distant non-membership social objects is based upon the development of the self, that is, upon some degree of integration of the separate unorganized role-performances such that he can view himself as an object of his own consciousness (see Winnicott, 1965, esp. pp. 146–9). Second, the actor's objects of identification provide social identities which serve to direct and channel his role-playing within the social world (see Foote, 1951). Both these points raise potential difficulties for the actor; the first because the capacity for role-taking is a variable, depending both upon the actor concerned and the availability and clarity of the perhaps temporally and spatially distant social object; the second because the establishment of identity, both in general and within a specific social situation, is never totally unproblematic. Yet at the same time it is 'the binding thread of identity' (ibid., p.

20), which enables one to orient to various sorts of social object and to play roles. Without the concepts of self and identity, role and normative reference group analysis would be impossible.

That this is so can be seen from one particularly interesting use of the notion of an object of identification, namely Bettleheim's account of the Nazi concentration camp and the hyper-identification of its inmates with the SS guards (see Bettleheim, 1958). The paradoxical quality of this phenomenon arises because we would normally expect that the greater the coercive oppression, the less the probability of normative identification. That this does not always occur is a result of the peculiar nature of the concentration camp. Such a phenomenon is most nearly isomorphic with Goffman's ideal typical presentation of the total institution (1968). Stated a little more formally than in Goffman, the following dimensions of such an institution may be identified (see also Wakeford, A1969): multifunctionality, the degree to which the individual sleeps, plays and works in the same place; homogeneity, the degree to which the individual carries on his daily activities in the company of a large number of similar others; isolation, the degree to which the institution is separated from the society outside; temporality, the length of time expected or demanded of an inmate; and administration, the degree to which the institution's activities are formally prearranged, imposed and synthesized. The explanation of the inmate's identification with the SS guards lies both in the degree to which all of these features were found in the concentration camp, and from the lack of cathectic identification with the inmate's family and friends outside. In other words, the less persuasive were the latter as an object of normative identification, the more easily did the individual come to believe that the rest of his life would have to be spent in the camp. Once that was believed, once, in other terms, role-taking, internalization and identification with social objects outside the camp were precluded, then the only objects with which role-taking could occur were the other inmates or the guards. The former, because of the systematic disintegration of inmate behaviour until it most clearly resembled that of a child, was highly implausible. Rather, the high official valuation placed upon the guards, the explicitness of their role-model, the childlike inmate orientation, and the closing of all outside identifications, served to heighten the probability of the SS being the objects of identification for the prisoners after a certain period of time.

This account highlights a number of points related to the analysis of identificatory processes. These can best be summarized by saying that identification with a given social object is more probable, the more explicit the nature of the role-model, and the more attractive is the object in question. The first of these is enhanced by an interpersonal relationship between the object in question and the role-taker; it anyway demands some degree of visibility. The second depends on the lack of explicit and attractive alternatives. Thus, the greater the degree to which the object is a total institution, the more readily it can exclude other possible identification objects over time. Where it is not in this favoured situation, it is more likely to be an object of identification where either the object is not inconsistent with the individual's present social identities, or where a single identification in the past is both being superseded and suggests or predisposes the individual to orient to the new object in question.

This last point can be amplified by considering the distinction between an actor's identity comprised of a single social identity resulting from identification with a single social object, and an identity comprised of a number of social identities derived from various identifications. The latter arises because certain social identities are exhaustive and exclusive (that is, they are *the* actor's identity and do not countenance any competitors); others are not. This obviously relates importantly to the process of new identifications with different social objects. The relevance of that to the sociology of revolution will be seen in parts 2 and 3.

4 Of social comparisons

I tried to show in the previous chapter that the attempt to systematize the study of normative reference groups emasculated the interactionist tradition, although it had made a limited contribution to sociological knowledge. In the present chapter I want to develop a similar critique of the sociology of social comparisons. But I also want to show that such a sociology has not significantly added to the more attractively expressed social and moral philosophy from which it partly developed. Thus, the first section of this chapter will consist of a selective account of this philosophy which will highlight the degree to which significant issues, themes and problems had already been confronted and discussed. The later parts will concentrate upon showing both the limitations of the contemporary study of social comparisons and the possible lines of development which will serve to connect parts 1 and 2 of this book. The following passage from Herzberg (1968, p. 49) summarizes the concern both of this chapter and of the book in general:

> Man's ability to compare his situation with that of another, and
> to score himself as 'less than' his fellow worker because he
> makes less money, has a smaller car and has less status, causes
> him to suffer greatly. Thus it is apparent that the human
> capacity to be unhappy is inexhaustible, because the range of
> stimuli that can cause pain to mankind is so vast and the
> number of situations in which man can make comparisons is
> equally inexhaustible.

The past study of social comparisons

In the latter part of Plato's discussion of Imperfect Societies in the *Republic* he analyses certain processes of social comparison and of the individual's sense of justice.

First of all, he pinpoints the importance of perception in accounting for differing patterns of resentment (1955, pp. 328–9). He says:

Such being the state of rulers and ruled, what will happen when they come up against each other in the streets or in the course of business, at a festival or on a campaign, serving in the navy or army? When they see each other in moments of danger, the rich man will no longer be able to despise the poor man; the poor man will be lean and sunburnt, and find himself fighting next to some rich man whose sheltered life and superfluous flesh make him puff and blow and quite unable to cope. Won't he conclude that people like this are rich because their subjects are cowards, and won't he say to his fellows, when he meets them in private, 'This lot are no good; they've had it'?

Similarly, although more obscurely, the invisibility of real pleasure to those with none induces further perceptual distortion. This is because these people 'will be convinced that the transition from pain to the neutral state brings satisfaction and pleasure, whereas in fact their ignorance of true pleasure leads them to make a false contrast between pain and the absence of pain, just as someone who had never seen white might similarly contrast grey with black' (ibid., p. 360). This implies that in a trichotomous system of stratification, will not the individual in the middle 'think he has risen towards the top? As he stands in the middle and looks down to where he came from, won't he think he's at the top, never having seen the real top?' Plato's explanation of this is not that there are certain structural conditions which serve to ensure the invisibility of those at the top; rather, it results from the psychological state of the individuals concerned. Thus (ibid., p. 362):

Those, therefore, who have no experience of wisdom and goodness, and do nothing but have a good time, spend their life straying between the bottom and middle in our illustration, and never rise higher to see or reach the true top, nor achieve any real satisfaction or sure and unadulterated pleasure. They bend over their tables, like sheep with heads bent over their pasture and eyes on the ground, they stuff themselves and copulate, and in their greed for more they kick and butt each other with hooves and horns of steel, and kill each other because they are not satisfied, as they cannot be while they feed on unreality a part of themselves which is itself unreal and insatiable.

I think that Plato's general discussion, although interesting, is inadequate. This is because it is almost entirely psychologistic, because his psychology is one in which reason is only a restraint upon an uncontrollable passion such that there cannot be both rational and irrational desires, and because it presumes that unfulfilled desires necessarily produce dissatisfaction. There is a considerable similarity with the Nietzschean tradition which will be discussed below. The last quotation in particular contains an argument for the greater happiness of the just rather than the unjust life. This is an argument premised upon the image of man torn between the control of reason and the insatiability of passion. It is the unjust man who lets his desires run ahead of him, who seeks pleasure, and finds dissatisfaction and discontent (see Crombie, 1962; MacIntyre, 1967, esp. pp. 46–8).

Apart from a brief account in the *Ethics* (1963), Aristotle discusses these issues in the *Rhetorica* and the *Politics*. In the former (1942, 1386ᵇ, 20–5) he tries to distinguish between indignation, envy and emulation, the first two being sentiments excited by that which has happened or is happening to other individuals. Emulation, on the other hand, is felt not because other individuals have highly valued goods but because the specific individual does not have them. Indignation will tend to result from where those who are deserving because of their goodness, birth or beauty do not receive commensurate rewards of wealth and power (see ibid., 1386ᵇ, 13–17 and 1387ᵃ, 6–16). It will be felt more where there is a lack of a 'certain correspondence and appropriateness in such things' (ibid., 1387 , 28 and 30 f). Indignation is thus, for Aristotle, a morally justifiable feeling aroused when one does not get that which is appropriate; it is felt both by the deserving and the successful, who are indignant at the success of the undeserving, and by the deserving and unsuccessful. Clearly, the criteria of 'deservingness' will vary and there will be counter-definitions of who deserves what (ibid., 1387ᵇ, 4–13). Finally, it should be noted that indignation is far less likely to occur where tradition has endowed man-made differences with the appearance that they are endowed by nature. Aristotle (ibid., 1387ᵃ, 16–19 and 26–7) says that:

> What is long established seems akin to what exists by nature;
> and therefore we feel more indignation at those possessing a
> given good if they have as a matter of fact only just got it and
> the prosperity it brings with it. The newly rich give more
> offence than those whose wealth is of long standing and inherited
> ... what appears to have been always what it is regarded as
> real, and so the possessions of the newly rich do not seem to
> be really their own.

Envy, on the other hand, is pain at the good fortune of those close to or similar to the individual and is felt not because of an intrinsic desire for the good in question but merely because others possess it (see ibid., 1386ᵇ, 18–20). Thus Aristotle quotes both Aeschylus and Hesiod respectively: 'Ay, kin can even be jealous of their kin. Potter against potter' (ibid., 1388ᵃ, 7 and 16). More systematically he says that (ibid., 1388ᵃ, 8–15):

> We do not compete with men who lived a hundred centuries ago, or those not yet born, or the dead, or those who dwell near the Pillar of Hercules, or those whom, in our opinion or that of others, we take to be far below us or far above us. So too we compete with those who follow the same ends as ourselves. We compete with our rivals in sport or in love, and generally with those who are after the same things; and it is therefore these whom we are bound to envy beyond all others.

There are two further points. First, and importantly, envy results when the possession of a good by another is a direct reproach to the individual in question. Aristotle maintains that if it is clearly the individual's fault that he does not possess the good, then this is particularly annoying and likely to produce envy (ibid., 1388ᵃ, 16–20). Second, he mentions two processes by which a similarity between the envier and the potentially envied may be realized. These are when the envier is morally encouraged to possess that which he did once possess, or that which those close to him have obtained noticeably more quickly than he (ibid., 1388ᵃ, 20–7). Both of these points raise problems; the first because the invocation of self-blame may serve to limit rather than to exacerbate envy; the second because it makes the grounds for distinguishing between envy and indignation seem somewhat nebulous. There is, of course, a difference between comparing one's position with those close to one and those distant – but it is unclear that this should imply any difference or moral approbation. I have a similar doubt about the distinction between envy and emulation.

Aristotle certainly sees emulation as a good feeling felt by good people – unlike envy which is a morally bad sentiment (ibid., 1388ᵃ, 27 to 1388ᵇ, 17). The problem, it seems to me, is that these two phenomena are opposite sides of the same coin. Thus, to know that others have a particular good (envy) is to know that one does not have it oneself (emulation), and the desire to have the good oneself depends, at least in part, on the knowledge that it is possessed by others. Thus I think that there are serious problems in trying to use Aristotle's tripartite division, certainly as a basis of explanation of given social phenomena, probably as regards a moral philosophy. In Book 5 of the *Republic* Aristotle provides more systematic social theory without making any use of the distinctions between indignation, envy and emulation.

Aristotle (1962, pp. 189–92) starts by arguing that any particular society is premised upon some notion of justice and thus a revolution may result when its members cease to agree upon the application of the principles to the existing pattern of inequality. Thus (ibid., p. 192):

> For those who are bent on equality start a revolution if they believe that they, having less, are yet equals of those who have more. And so too do those who aim at inequality and superiority, if they think that they, being unequal, are not getting more, but equal or less. The lesser rebel in order to be equal, the equal in order to be greater.

Further, he maintains that such revolutionaries are motivated by profit and dignity, or conversely, by avoiding the loss of profit and dignity (ibid., pp. 192–3). Aristotle argues that there are seven causes of disorder, the first two of which are again profit and dignity; they are important here 'because men see others getting a larger share of these, some rightly some wrongly' (ibid., p. 193). Thus with respect to dignity, 'those who see others honoured and themselves degraded soon become revolution-minded' (ibid.). Aristotle adds to these cruelty, fear, excessive power, contemptuous attitudes and disproportionate aggrandisement as further causes of those with profit and dignity being both visible to and open to condemnation from those less favoured (ibid., pp. 193–5 and 199).

Although this work is a rich source of information, I want to make just two more points here. The first is to note that Aristotle (ibid., pp. 211–12) advocates the development of a middle class so as to avoid revolution:[1]

> Exceptional prosperity in one section of the community is to be guarded against. The danger can be met by not entrusting assignments and responsibilities to one section alone but to different and opposing sections. . . . An endeavour should be made either to merge the poorer with the richer or to augment the number of those of medium wealth; this dissolves the unrest that is due to the inequality.

The second point is his emphasis upon the various sorts of opposition that can occur within any society. Thus, in talking of oligarchies, he points out two sorts of changes (ibid., p. 202); the first results from opposition *to* the oligarchy; the second from internal dissension, that is conflict *between* the members of the oligarchy.

Apart from the famous condemnation, the 'evil eye' in St Matthew's Gospel (20 : 14–16), the next significant discussion of these issues was in Francis Bacon's essay *On Envy*. The following quotation from Bacon (1911, pp. 37–8), indicates a marked difference from Aristotle: 'Men of noble birth are noted to be envious towards new

men when they rise; for the distance is altered; and it is like a deceit
of the eye, that when others come on they think themselves go back.'
In other words, envy is taken to be possible between individuals of
some geographical and social distance, although it is more probable
(or only possible?) where there are *some* bases of similarity. Thus
(ibid., p. 38):

> near kinsfolk, and fellows in office, and those that have been
> bred together, are more apt to envy their equals when they are
> raised; for it doth upbraid unto them their own fortunes, and
> pointeth at them, and cometh oftener into their remembrance,
> and incurreth likewise more into the note of others; and envy
> ever redoubleth from speech and fame.

Like Aristotle, Bacon (ibid., pp. 38–9) emphasizes how 'persons of
eminent virtue when they are advanced are less envied. For their
fortune seemeth but due to them.' But unlike Aristotle, Bacon maintains that 'persons of worth and merit are most envied when their
fortune continueth long; for by that time, though their virtue be the
same, yet it hath not the same lustre; for fresh men grow up that
darken it' (ibid., p. 39). Three further points are emphasized. The
first is that envy is dependent upon processes of social comparison.
Thus 'envy is ever joined with the comparing of a man's self; and
where there is no comparison, no envy; and therefore kings are
not envied but by kings' (ibid.). A second point is that for envy to
occur, the envier must clearly perceive the envied. Bacon (ibid.)
says that:

> Envy is as the sunbeams, that beat hotter upon a bank or steep
> rising ground than upon a flat; and, for the same reason, those
> that are advanced by degrees are less envied than those that are
> advanced suddenly and *per saltum* . . . and nothing doth extin-
> guish envy more than for a great person to preserve all other
> inferior officers in their full rights and pre-eminences of their
> places; for by that means there be so many screens between him
> and envy.

Finally, Bacon emphasizes that envy is less probable where the rich
and successful can justify themselves by virtue of the work, effort
or danger involved in their acquisition of such wealth and fame
(ibid.).

I think that the arguments of Aristotle and Bacon are the most
systematic statements on this subject up to the present day. Nevertheless, other writers have made less impressive contributions which
I will now summarize. It should be reiterated that the intention here
is not only to summarize a particular theme in social philosophy, but
also to indicate how much had been discussed before the contempor-

ary social sciences made their contribution. Also, it should be noted that apart from brief discussions of Scheler on resentment and Schoeck on envy, no more attention will be paid to these terms *per se*. This is because although there are a whole family of phenomena occurring within and relating to different social situations, the classical notions of envy, jealousy, indignation, resentment, and emulation do not seem to represent useful distinctions. This is because they were developed as concepts of explicit moral approbation or reprobation. In leaving this tradition behind, one could perhaps conclude by quoting Kant (1922, p. 316) and noting his explicit recognition of the importance of social comparison. Envy, he says, is 'a disinclination to see our own good overshadowed by the good of others, because we take its measure not from its intrinsic worth, but by comparison with the good of others and then go on to symbolize that evaluation' (see also Mandeville, 1970, p. 158 f).

The importance of this can be seen in the second volume of de Tocqueville's *Democracy in America*. First, he argues that in aristocratically dominated societies, revolution is less likely because individuals get used to their poverty and most especially, they are not concerned with physical comfort since 'they despair of getting it and because they do not know enough about it to want it' (1966, p. 685). The upsetting of this world 'when distinctions of rank are blurred and privileges abolished' leads 'the poor [to] conceive an eager desire to acquire comfort, and the rich think of the danger of losing it' (ibid.). The establishment of a 'lot of middling fortunes' means that their owners 'have enough physical enjoyments to get a taste for them, but not enough to content them' (ibid.); there is continual striving for further physical comfort. Some pages later, however, the development of such a middle class is unquestionably seen as counter-revolutionary. These two arguments can be reconciled, since the growth of the middle class and of middle-class aspirations for physical comfort is revolutionary in the sense of producing bourgeois-capitalism; but that middle class is then counter-revolutionary in any other sense. Thus, de Tocqueville's prescriptions are hedged; ideally, there should be a dominant aristocracy, but where this is precluded, then a strong middle class is to be preferred. The argument for the latter commences with the observation that revolution has something to do with equality and inequality. Further, although he argues that extreme wealth and extreme poverty will never be totally abolished, contemporary society has both eliminated a great deal of poverty and its law 'has not drawn them [the poor] together by the link of an irremediable and hereditary state of wretchedness' (ibid., p. 824). At the same time, the clarity of a simply dichotomized society of rich and poor is destroyed. De Tocqueville (ibid., my emphasis) says of the rich that:

They have no conspicuous privileges, and even their wealth,
being no longer incorporated and bound up with the soil, is
impalpable and, as it were, *invisible* . . . the rich daily rise out
of the crowd and constantly return thither. Hence they do not
form a distinct class, easily *identified* and plundered; moreover,
there are a thousand hidden threads connecting them with the
mass of citizens, so that the people would hardly know how to
attack them without harming itself.

Thus the first reason for the non-revolutionary character of the
middle class is that although 'their eagerness to get rich is unparal-
leled . . . their trouble is to know whom to despoil' (ibid., p. 825).
The second reason is that such a middle class 'have enough property
to want order and not enough to excite envy' (ibid., p. 824). It is their
very closeness to poverty that prevents them from conceiving of
action that would upset their tenuous situation.

De Tocqueville's explanation of what it is that changes is outlined
in his famous interpretation of the French Revolution (1933, p. 186).
Thus he says: 'A people, which has supported without complaint, as
if they were not felt, the most oppressive laws, violently throws them
off as soon as their weight is lifted.' The reason for this in eighteenth-
century France was that the growth of prosperity led to an unsettling
of men's minds, to the increasing bitterness of public discontent and
the ever-developing hatred of ancient institutions. In other words,
the belief in the inevitability of progress led to heightened expectations of the future since: 'Imagination therefore made men insensible
to the blessings they already enjoyed and hurried them forward to
novelties of every kind' (ibid., p. 1817).[2]

Walter Bagehot (1963, p. 249) provides at least part of the explanation why this did not occur in Britain. He argues that although there
are many very poor people 'the most miserable of these classes do
not impute their misery to politics'. And part of the reason for this
is that they would say that (ibid., pp. 249–50):

for all they have heard, the Queen is very good; and rebelling
against the structure of society is to their mind rebelling
against the Queen, who rules that society, in whom all its most
impressive part – the part that they know – culminates. The
mass of the English people are politically contented as well as
politically deferential.

Veblen's approach (1899) differs partly from both de Tocqueville
and Bagehot. He starts by noting that in the primitive stage of social
development, there is a weak incentive to emulate; but as development occurs, so the opportunity and incentive to emulate increases
greatly in scope and intensity. Invidious comparison between men

becomes ubiquitous (ibid., pp. 16–17). Emulation contributes to the accumulation, ownership and the development of private property (ibid., pp. 24-6), and this reacts back upon the form of comparative reference. In primitive communal society, the object of comparison is the enemy, the other group, from whom plunder has been acquired. In modern society based on individual ownership, invidious comparison is made with members of one's *own* group. The dimension of such intra-group comparisons is that of individual ownership (as well as physical prowess); those who are so deprived suffer from a lack of esteem from others and thus from themselves (ibid., 27–30). The incentive to emulate is never assuaged, first, because if the comparison reveals that the individual is deprived then until he reaches 'the normal pecuniary standard of the community' (ibid., p. 31) he will remain chronically dissatisfied; while second, once he reaches this normal standard, he will experience a restless striving to heighten the distance between himself and the average. Veblen's argument is well indicated by the following (ibid., pp. 31-2): 'The invidious comparison can never become so favourable to the individual making it that he would not gladly rate himself still higher relatively to his competitors in his struggle for pecuniary reputability.' Relative success, the outcome of invidious interpersonal comparison, becomes the end of action (ibid., p. 33).

This process of emulation reflects itself in the conspicuousness of leisure and consumption. It is as an outcome of the melting-pot effect of contemporary industrial society that people find themselves close to each other where they live, shop and play. The only way by which one can show what is one's worth is to engage in an unremitting demonstration of the ability to pay (ibid., pp. 86-7). Veblen emphasizes the visible component of these processes; thus, leisure pursuits are only justifiable if they leave a tangible, perceptible outcome amenable to measurement and comparison (ibid., p. 49). The nature of this expenditure should furthermore be seen to be wasteful since no merit is acquired through consuming the necessities of life (ibid., pp. 96-7). The end result, therefore, of invidious comparison and emulation is the wastefulness of conspicuous consumption (ibid., p. 100 and ch. 5 onwards).

Two further brief points should be made. First, in chapter 12, Veblen outlines 'Survivals of the non-Invidious Interest'. Second, even within a historical epoch characterized by ubiquitous emulation, each class tends only to emulate the class just above it in the system of stratification (ibid., pp. 102–5). This in turn has two implications: that standing at the apex of this emulative process is 'the highest social and pecuniary class – the wealthy leisure class' (ibid., p. 104); and that a class 'rarely compares itself with those below or with those who are considerably in advance' (ibid.).

I think that there are four further traditions, besides that of symbolic interactionism, which have contributed to this discussion. They are Marxism, classical sociology, psychoanalysis, and late nineteenth-century German philosophy. I will discuss them in that order.

There is no doubt that there is some ambiguity in Marx's writings as to the precise nature of the process of immiseration. The conventional discussion (see, for example, Bober, 1948, pp. 218–21) maintains that Marx argued that increasing misery meant not heightened psychological dissatisfaction but increased physical impoverishment. Marx's most explicit statement supporting this interpretation is 'that in proportion as capital accumulates, the lot of the labourer, be his payment high or low, must grow worse' (1954, vol. 1, p. 645). But what it is that grows worse is not, in fact, the absolute standard of living but rather the rate of exploitation. Yet once a certain surplus has been established, it does not imply that an increase in exploitation necessitates any reduction in the actual wage level. What happens is that the worker 'is forced to become impoverished . . . since the creative power of his work establishes itself against him as an alien force, the power of capital' (see McLellan, 1971, p. 81). Thus, what is important is the relationship *between* the power of capital and that of labour (see Marx, 1919, vol. 2, esp. p. 141). It is this relationship which is taken by Marx to worsen increasingly as capitalism develops. There are two premises of his theory here. First, an actor's satisfaction or dissatisfaction depends upon how much he has in comparison with others. Marx's characterization of his simple psychological model is as follows (1933, p. 33):

A house may be large or small; as long as the neighbouring houses are likewise small, it satisfies all the social requirements for a residence. But let there arise next to the little house a palace, and the little house shrinks into a hut.

The second premise is that as capital is accumulated and productivity enhanced, there is realized an increased disjunction between the power of labour and of capital (and specifically of relative factor shares in national income) (ibid., p. 39). Thus:

If, therefore, the income of the worker increases with the rapid growth of capital, there is at the same time a widening of the social chasm that divides the worker from the capitalist, an increase in the power of capital over labour, a greater dependence of labour over capital.

And (ibid., p. 33):

Rapid growth of productive capital calls forth just as rapid a growth of wealth, of luxury, of social needs and social pleasures. Therefore, although the pleasures of the labourer have increased, the social gratification which they afford has fallen in comparison with the increased pleasures of the capitalist, which are inaccessible to the worker, in comparison with the stage of development of society in general. Our wants and pleasures have their origin in society; we therefore measure them in relation to the society; we do not measure them in relation to the objects which serve for their gratification. Since they are of a social nature, they are of a relative nature.

The problem with this is that it is hardly a theory of revolutionary social change. All it suggests is that, over time, the consciousness of workers in general, or some workers in particular, will become a little more revolutionary. But we also have to know, whether there are not other features attendant on the accumulation of capital that might not lessen such relative deprivation; or whether such sentiments only occur in certain situations as a consequence of *particular* experiences; or whether there is variation in the non-bourgeois class or classes as to the degree to which there is perception of the alien power of capital; or whether the objects of comparison will be capitalists as bearers of capital or perhaps as specific personalities, or with managers or sectors of the middle class; or whether even if the alien power of capital is perceived this is not interpreted as an unchangeable, and thus partly justifiable, state of affairs (see Marx, 1922, pp. 24–5; 1909, pp. 715–16).

So Marx's relative deprivation argument, although quite clear, is full of problems. Kautsky's argument is similar and also problematic. He argued that the proletariat was relatively worse off than other sections of the population, that it was receiving a smaller percentage of the gross national product, that bourgeois prosperity was increasing at a faster rate than that of the working class, and that crucial to dissent is the *perception* of deprivation.[3]

I now want to consider the contributions of Weber and Durkheim. The latter can be dealt with quickly since I shall not be making explicit use of the concept of anomie, although it is clearly implicit in a great deal of discussion. Nevertheless, a couple of points within Durkheim's *Suicide* should be emphasized. Durkheim indicates the importance (for suicide rather than relative dissatisfaction) of crises which upset the taken-for-granted world of the actor. He says (1952, pp. 246, 252, 253):

> If therefore industrial or financial crises increase suicides, this is . . . because they are crises, that is, disturbances of the collective order. . . . In the case of economic disasters . . . something like a declassification occurs. . . . So they are not adjusted to the condition forced on them, and its very prospect

61

is intolerable. . . . . It is the same if the source of the crisis is an abrupt growth of power and wealth . . . there is no restraint upon aspirations. . . . Nothing gives satisfaction and all this agitation is uninterruptedly maintained without appeasement. . . . All classes contend among themselves because no established classification any longer exists.

The reason for the significance of such crises is that regular and consistent poverty is according to Durkheim the best protection against suicide. It is in itself a restraint. The less that one has, the less one aspires to, while the less limited one feels, the more intolerable any and all limitation appears (ibid., p. 254). Thus specifically and importantly for later argument (ibid., p. 257): 'At least the horizon of the lower classes is limited by those above them, and for this same reason their desires are more modest. Those who have only empty space above them are almost inevitably lost in it, if no force restrains them.'

Weber's contribution is more varied. First of all, there is a sense in which the notion of comparative reference is recognized in his argument that the degree to which 'communal action' and 'societal action' emerge from the 'mass actions' of class members depends on 'the extent of the *contrasts* that have already evolved' (1948, p. 184, my emphasis). He also outlines the conditions in terms of which a perceived deprivation is judged to be unjust. He argues that this is linked both to 'general cultural conditions, especially to those of an intellectual sort' (ibid.) and to 'the transparency of the connections between the causes and the consequences of the "class situation" ' (ibid.). Further, he pinpoints the importance of the development of the feeling among the fortunate that they have a *right* to their good fortune. Weber (ibid., p. 271) says: 'He wants to be convinced that he "deserves" it, and above all, that he deserves it in comparison with others. He wishes to be allowed the belief that the less fortunate also merely experience his due. Good fortune thus wants to be "legitimate" fortune.'

Finally, Weber turns his attention to the notion of resentment. He is very clear that this is not a general basis of motivation for the development of 'the religiously determined rationalism of socially disadvantaged strata' (ibid., p. 276; see also, Weber, 1965, p. 115); rather, it is sometimes part of the basis. Resentment 'teaches that the unequal distribution of mundane goods is caused by the sinfulness and the illegality of the privileged, and that sooner or later God's wrath will overtake them' (1965, p. 110). Weber argues that this has been most influential in the development of the Jewish religion. Thus he maintains that the Psalms are full of the need for vengeance in order that the pariah status of the Jews can be overcome. It is a religion of retribution in which there is an expectation of the day of restoration. Because of the lack of a theodicy of rebirth it is quite different from Hinduism or Buddhism. There the caste system is seen as eternal and absolutely just. There is no conflict between the social claims based upon the promises of God and a dishonourable social reality.

There is, I think, a certain affinity between Durkheim's image of man and that of Alfred Adler. This can be seen in two ways. The first and less important point, is indicated by the following argument of Adler (1938, p. 30) which is an adumbration of the internal consequences of a Durkheimian crisis:

> It is obvious that these myriad interpretations may and do come into contact with the world of reality and its social demands. An individual's wrong idea of himself and of the demands of life sooner or later clashes with harsh reality. . . . The result of this clash may be compared to an electric shock.

The second point is Adler's postulation of an innate striving for superiority within man (1965, p. 39); thus: 'Individual Psychology has shown that the striving for superiority and perfection is . . . given to *every* person and must be understood as *innate*, as a *necessary and general foundation of the development of every person.*' All human life is based upon such striving for perfection, upon overcoming innate feelings of inferiority (ibid., p. 31; see also, Adler, 1938, p. 96). Yet although Adler's individual psychology unquestionably presumes the individual innateness of such sentiments, I think it is clear that these do arise within social contexts, or rather importance should be attached to the individual's social interest.

Elsewhere in this thesis I criticize the presupposition that these processes are innate and universal. Sullivan similarly argues from an interactionist-psychoanalytic viewpoint in a way that can be used to criticize Adler's formulation located within the psychoanalytic tradition. Thus, central to Sullivan's argument is both that there is a self-system, similar to the self of Mead and Cooley (1955b, p. 17), and that it is constituted by the reflected appraisals of significant others with whom the individual is interpersonally implicated (1955a, pp. 22 and 46). The self comes into existence in order to preserve the individual's feelings of security. Without this, the occurrence of particular unfortunate experiences can realize 'feelings of inferiority' within the interpersonal situation (1955b, p. 350). Such low self-esteem arises by virtue of the fact that 'the person's personification of himself is not very estimable by comparison with his personifications of significant other people' (ibid.); although within that situation anxiety may be minimized 'by concealments and social isolation', or individuals 'may channel their anxiety and

63

disjunctive motivations in interpersonal relations by exploitative attitudes and substitutive processes, or may manifest them in dissociative processes' (ibid., p. 351; all emphasized in original).

The final tradition to be considered is the one mainly represented in the writings of Nietzsche and Scheler (see Ranulf, 1938). This involves a temporary return to the concepts of envy, indignation, resentment and the like, but this return has two advantages. The first is to strengthen the argument that such concepts do not represent useful distinctions. The second is to prepare the ground for the next section, Helmut Schoeck's account of envy.

The first point to recognize in Nietzsche is his account of the smouldering, developing quality of resentful sentiments. He distinguishes between ordinary envy, which may be simply dissipated, and silent envy, which grows more and more angry (1911b, p. 37). The sentiment of envy is one which would be inconceivable in a state of nature. The envious are aware of every sign of individual superiority and wish to depress everyone once more to the common level, or to raise themselves to the superior plane (ibid., p. 209; see also p. 172). The envy which Nietzsche particularly abhors is the envy of the gods, that is, when the despised person puts himself on an inappropriate equality with his superior. In the 'social class system': 'no one shall have merits above his station . . . his prosperity shall be on a level with his position, and . . . his self-consciousness shall not outgrow the limits of his rank' (ibid., p. 210). But regrettably for Nietzsche (1911a, p. 266), there are individuals who do not accept such ranking. They argue when they have been unsuccessful: '"May the whole world perish!" This odious feeling is the height of envy which reasons thus: because I cannot have one thing the whole world in general must have nothing! The whole world shall not exist!'

The result of the existence of such enviers is that 'they insinuate their evil natures into the consciences of the ruling classes' (1910, p. 210). Thus (ibid., pp. 210–11):

> The great desideratum is to find guilty people in it. The botched and the bungled, the decadents of all kinds, are revolted at themselves . . . they at least require a semblance of justification, *i.e.* a theory according to which the fact of their existence, and of their character, may be expiated by a scapegoat. . . . In short, resentful pessimism discovers responsible parties in order to create a pleasurable sensation for itself – revenge . . . 'Sweeter than honey' – thus does even old Homer speak of revenge.

The explanation of the unrelenting concern of the modern world for equality (see Nietzsche, 1909, p. 117) lies at least in part in Christianity, with its emphasis on the world as the outcome of souls and not of individual action, on inducing the individual to be the judge of all things, on the equality of all souls before God, and on the instinct of revenge (1910, pp. 211–14). But the modern world, with the development of psychology, has also contributed. Thus Nietzsche says that 'out of the spirit of rancour has this new nuance of scientific "equity" sprung to the service of hatred, envy, malevolence, and distrust' (1956, p. 206). The consequence of this is the development of 'bad conscience' as 'man began rending, persecuting, terrifying himself, like a wild beast hurling itself against the bars of its cage' (ibid., p. 218). Especially the man strong, happy and successful became increasingly doubtful of the right to such strength, happiness and success. Of those who develop the sense of guilt in others Nietzsche (ibid., pp. 260–1) says:

> Nothing less than to succeed in implanting their own misery, and all misery, in the consciences of the happy, so as to make the happy one day say to one another, 'it is a disgrace to be happy! *There is too much misery in the world!*' But no greater and more disastrous misunderstanding could be imagined than for the strong and happy to begin doubting their right to happiness.

Such prescriptions will recur within Helmut Schoeck's sociology of envy. For the moment I shall elaborate Max Scheler's extension of Nietzsche and especially his concept of *ressentiment*.

Ressentiment for Scheler results from the cumulative repression of feelings of hatred, revenge and envy. Where such feelings can be acted out no such *ressentiment* arises. But where the individual is unable to release these feelings against the persons or groups evoking them then there is developed a sense of impotence, and if this is continuously re-experienced, the sentiment of *ressentiment* develops. Such feelings can only arise where there is some similarity between the aggrieved person and the object of *ressentiment*. Thus Scheler (1961, p. 177, n. 4) quotes the best known example of *ressentiment*, the French Revolution; he says:

> The enormous explosion of *ressentiment* in the French Revolution against the nobility and everything connected with its way of living, and indeed the very emergence of this *ressentiment*, would have been entirely inconceivable if . . . more than 80% of the nobility itself had not been intermingled with bourgeois elements, who acquired names and titles by buying aristocratic estates. Besides the nobility was racially weakened by money marriages. The *ressentiment* of the insurgents was sharpened by the feeling that they were equal to the ruling class.

Similarly, he points out that a slave who accepts his status and has a slavish nature will not desire revenge against his master who has injured him. What is crucial to the genesis of *ressentiment* is a discrepancy between the political, constitutional or traditional power of a group and its factual power. Thus *ressentiment* is low in a society where there is both social and political equality, or in a society based on castes or sharply divided classes where there is a congruence of inequality. *Ressentiment*, Scheler suggests, is heightened in modern society where formal social equality is accompanied by wide differences of actual power (ibid., pp. 49–50). Four other points, I think, need to be made here. First, revenge is likely to be transformed into *ressentiment* where it is directed against lasting situations which are felt to be injurious and outside one's control, being the outcome of fate or destiny (ibid., pp. 51–2). Second, *ressentiment* only follows where the object of *ressentiment* can be identified and thought to be responsible for the inequality of the relationship (ibid., pp. 52–3). Third, Scheler locates the genesis of *ressentiment* within the tendency to make comparisons between oneself and others. He thus disagrees with Simmel's claim that the 'noble man' does not compare his own values with those of others. The explanation of *ressentiment* in Scheler is, therefore, heavily dependent upon the explanation of the patterning of social comparisons. Thus (ibid., p. 56):

> The medieval peasant prior to the 13th century does not compare himself to the feudal lord, nor does the artisan compare himself to the knight. The peasant may make comparisons with respect to the richer or more respected peasant. . . . Thus every comparison took place within a strictly circumscribed frame of reference. . . . Therefore such periods are dominated by the idea that everyone has his 'place' which has been assigned to him by God and nature and in which he has his personal duty to fulfill. His value consciousness and his aspirations never go beyond this sphere. . . . In the 'system of free competition', on the other hand, the notions on life's tasks and their value are not fundamental, they are but secondary derivations of the desire of all to surpass all the others. No 'place' is more than a transitory point in this universal class. The aspirations are intrinsically *boundless*, for they are no longer tied to any particular object or quality.

Social identity is thus realized through competing with others and is not given by the individual's placement within an accepted hierarchy. Further, there are in modern societies certain social situations which are more likely to induce sentiments of *ressentiment*.[4] Finally, it was mentioned above that such sentiments arise from a position of impotence. In relation to the social situation of a whole class this means that it develops where that class is unable to develop a set of alternative values to those of the society which are being devalued. Thus *ressentiment* is more probable in the *petit bourgeoisie* than in the industrial proletariat (ibid., p. 66).

It seems to me that Scheler's potential contribution to the sociology of social comparisons is considerable. The following points found in his work should be emphasized: his emphasis upon the repetition of experiences for producing *ressentiment*, his discussion of the nature of the similarity between the resentful and the resented person, his recognition of the possibility that situations may be thought to be beyond one's control, and the importance he attributes to certain situational determinants of the patterning of comparisons.

The sociology of social comparisons

Before showing the contribution of modern sociology to this subject I want to consider three emphases which are not part of the conventional literature on the sociology of social comparisons. They provide a means of linking the two main sections of this chapter.

Helmut Schoeck's sociology of envy

Envy for Schoeck refers to the state of mind of a person who is unable to bear someone else being something, having a skill, possessing something or enjoying a reputation which he lacks, and who in consequence will be pleased should the other lose the asset, although that loss will not mean his gain.[5] Schoeck (A1969, pp. 1–3 and 105) maintains that envy is a universal of human existence, and that it is universally proscribed. The claim for the former is a hotch-potch of three arguments: that many writers have in many societies described envious behaviour; that envy is a basic, primary core-like drive; and that envy is anthropologically necessary to human existence. Thus, on the one hand, he claims that the social control exercised by men over each other is based upon the latent envy inherent within each man; it is as a consequence that societies are established and persist (ibid., pp. 10, 87 and 356). And, on the other hand, envy is said to result from the exceptionally lengthy period of childhood socialization, and especially from the pervasiveness of sibling rivalry (ibid., pp. 7, 67–8, and 76).

There are two aspects of the patterning of the sentiments of envy: first, as a consequence of sibling rivalry, the object of envy is normally proximate (ibid., pp. 17, 40, 77–9 and 94); second, the degree and intensity of envy bears no relationship to the actual differences between the envier and the envied. By positing something innate about the envy-drive, Schoeck is able to maintain that it is doubtful whether the responsibility for envy can ever be placed upon the object of envy itself. He consequently claims that such sentiments can result from 'quite imaginary inequalities' and that 'the envious man so distorts the reality he experiences' (ibid., pp. 197 and 103).

Thus, Schoeck maintains that beyond a point envy is a bad thing, both because it induces people to commit crimes or to attempt to bring about revolutionary redemptions of the envious society, and because as a result of the fear of being envied, other people will not engage in creative and purposive action. Consequently, his objection to socialist millennia is that they will not abolish envy, although it is unclear whether he thinks that this follows empirically or logically. The good society for Schoeck is contemporary society except that individuals within it are less preoccupied with their own envy-feelings and with the envious feelings of others. This last Nietzschean point is crucial. Schoeck's message to the happy and successful is not to doubt their right to such happiness and success but rather to be even more happy and successful, to forget that others may envy them, to act as though envy did not exist and to act without any sense of guilt. To bring all this about he advocates the direct encourage-ment of the mechanisms of fortune, fate and religion, all of which encourage the under-privileged to realize how their life-chances are determined by external and uncontrollable forces (ibid., ch. 9 and *passim*).

This extraordinarily explicit work of conservative political phil-osophy is difficult to evaluate. On the one hand, as a piece of erudite literary accumulation it has an important value, although there are some omissions. On the other hand, as a work of sociological explanation it is extremely diffuse and confused. Initially this is because it is unclear whether the function of the notion of envy is simply to show that all men at all times are envious, or whether it is to argue that a widely divergent range of social phenomena can be explained in terms of the universal envy-drive. But this leads to confusion since in terms of the first objective, Schoeck admits enormous variation in the extent of envy-behaviour; indeed, he quotes John Gay to the effect that it is possible for some individuals to be completely devoid of it (ibid., p. 16). But if this is so, then first, it does not follow that socialist societies will necessarily be envy-prone, and second, the envy-drive cannot be used as the universal basis of explanation when it is not universal. This is the first contra-diction in Schoeck.

The second is whether envy is or is not desirable, since he claims both that it is necessary for human existence and that one should act as though there were no envy. By the last chapter he realizes the contradiction and claims that there should be a minimum of envy in society, anything in excess of which being indigestible by the social system – but that is problematic since the only way by which one knows that such a societal envy-ration is indigestible is because various social phenomena have materialized which Schoeck would judge to be undesirable (ibid., p. 348).

The third contradiction is whether the objects of envy are or are not proximate. If they are, then it is difficult to explain socialist movements where some notion of class-envy is clearly relevant – if they are not, then it follows that at least this form of class-envy can be eliminated. Schoeck maintains both at different stages of his argument; this is achieved by being unbelievably confused about the meaning of the term envy. The work commences by drawing precise distinctions between envy, jealousy, resentment, and so on; but in his desire to describe or explain an increasingly wide range of phenomena he places more and more sentiments under the single conceptual umbrella of envy. As a consequence he can castigate policies unrelated to envy, can invent irrelevant evidence, can suggest insupportable interpretations (ibid., pp. 112, 346 and 355), and can criticize utopian visions of the future. On the last point Schoeck argues that socialist societies will not eliminate envy since 'there will inevitably be some individuals who believe they have been hard done by' (ibid., p. 29). But, of course, no one would claim that socialism would eliminate all forms of dissatisfaction, but if that is all that will result then there are *no* grounds for supposing that the smaller the inequalities the greater the dissatisfaction.

Finally, it is necessary to consider Schoeck's view of the guilt-ridden modern man who dedicates himself to transforming the world by which he has already been blessed, who eschews prizes and distinctions, and who is so riddled with self-doubt that he cannot act forcefully and take pride in his achievements (ibid., *passim* and esp. pp. 224–5, 280 and 351). There are three objections to this view. The first is its limited empirical significance in Protestant acquisitive societies where most men most of the time are very willing to be rewarded, to accept prizes and to feel distinguished.[6] The second objection is that if Schoeck's argument that the smaller the differentials the greater the envy is true, then there would be much encouragement for the happy and successful to become even more happy and successful and to put a greater distance between themselves and the potentially envious, unhappy and unsuccessful. The third objection stems from a further inconsistency. On the one hand, Schoeck argues that there is no greater stimulus to envy than inequalities of food distribution *and* that within a stratified society the quest for equal opportunity is an empty chimera (ibid., pp. 121 and 240–1). But on the other hand, he generally fails to place such sentiments of envy within the structure of inequality, fails to allow for the justifiability of certain feelings of envy, and fails to see that not all such sentiments should be proscribed. Furthermore, paradoxically to preach the opposite is not to advocate a life of perfect

69

moral rectitude. The castigation of envy and the sanctification of guiltlessness at one's superiority is to argue for pride in one's success and happiness. Pride rather than envy is the moral imperative of Professor Schoeck's sociology of envy.[7]

The study of consumption

A second unconnected area of analysis which has been affected by this social philosophical theme is the theory of consumer behaviour in economics – most especially in the very Veblenesque version of the theory found in Duesenberry's relative income hypothesis.[8] While Keynes (1961, p. 97) had argued that the proportion of income consumed was a declining function of increasing income, Duesenberry (1967, esp. pp. 37–9) claimed that the income proportions consumed and saved were independent of the absolute income level but were dependent upon the individual's position within the income distribution. Duesenberry criticized two assumptions of traditional consumer theory; the independence of consumer behaviour and the reversibility of consumption relationships. The former point is most germane here. The implication of this criticism is that the preferences of each individual consumer cannot be taken to be independent of the purchases of others. This point permits solution of the statistical paradox that while budget study data indicate that a declining proportion of income is consumed as income increases (that is, average propensity to consume exceeds marginal propensity), time series data indicate a constant consumption proportion (that is, average and marginal propensities are equal). The solution can be seen if one considers the situation of a single individual faced by a rising income for both himself and for everyone else, and thus of a movement away from a previous equilibrium position. Both consumption and saving increase and in terms of the absolute income hypothesis and perhaps in terms of common sense, one would expect the latter to rise faster than the former. However, if that does occur the individual in question will find that the quasi-established relationship between his consumption and that of relevant others has not increased as he had expected. The reason for that being, of course, that everybody else's income and consumption has risen. The given individual is thus surrounded by superior goods and a general increase in consumer spending. To maintain his relative position (from the previous equilibrium) his consumption will increase such that his savings:income ratio remains constant.

This is not the place to provide an extensive criticism of this account. I would merely like to mention two points. First of all, Duesenberry argues that American society is classless and that, as a consequence, one can take the whole income distribution as the frame of reference relevant for each person. We would, however, want to argue that there are both classes and status groups such that the patterning of reference orientations will be variable as between different sectors of that society. Second, Duesenberry assumes a very simple model of reference processes and specifically fails to consider the normative-comparative-audience reference group distinction discussed earlier. Further, he assumes that such orientations will be necessarily upward such that the revealed deprivation automatically gives rise to an increase of consumption. There are two other points related more generally to this thesis.

The first is its interesting application intersocietally. Nurkse (1953) points out the fallacy of the development strategy that presumes that increased foreign investment will lead to a rise in savings consequent upon increased productivity and income. The fallacy arises from two features of the modern world. The first is the relative decline in the income position of the developing countries, which, combined with a perception of such growing relative deprivation, enhances consumption. The second point is that the increasingly interconnected nature of this world means that those in the developing countries are increasingly aware of new consumption patterns rendered available by modern technology. Thus the irony that increased income may (through improved communications of all sorts) heighten the sense of relative deprivation and the attractiveness of western consumer goods. That is a specific manifestation of the second point raised by Duesenberry's thesis. The whole thrust of contemporary western capitalist societies is upon industrial growth; and this has two implications. The first is that in some sense or other, economic expansion provides an increasing supply of goods and services to most individuals so that their welfare is enhanced. The second is that to bring about such expansion it is necessary for individuals to widen their aspirations and to seek to acquire greater and greater supplies of such goods and services. Thus the contradiction that the latter is necessary to bring about the former which is only necessary because of the latter.

Comparisons, expectations and revolution

There are certain sociologies of revolution which incorporate an explicit or an implicit comparative approach. Examples of the former are Sorokin, Gurr and Ruttenberg; of the latter, Brinton and Davies. I will deal with each briefly.

Sorokin (1925, pp. 367 and 369) says:

The immediate cause of a revolution is always the growth of 'repression' of the main instincts of the majority of society. . . .

> The growth of repression is, as everything else in the world, a relative conception. The poverty or the wealth of a man is measured, not by what he has at present, but by what he used to have before, or what others have.

In his model of revolution, 'this relativity of "repression"' is 'the primary and universal cause of revolutions' (ibid., p. 370); and when combined with the inability of the groups supporting the *status quo* to suppress subversion, it makes revolution inevitable. A more systematic exploration of a similar theme is Gurr and Ruttenberg's attempt to quantify the determinants of 'internal war'.[9] They maintain that most human aggression occurs in response to frustration. Relative deprivation is the actor's perception of a discrepancy between his value expectations (goods and conditions of life which are believed to be justifiable) and value capabilities (the determinants of the chances of getting or keeping the values they expect to attain). Relative deprivation is the perception of frustrating experiences, the emotional response to which is anger and aggression. Thus the occurrence of civil violence presupposes the existence of relative deprivation among significant numbers of actors. But because Gurr and Ruttenberg are only attempting to explain civil violence, they neglect the structural sources of both the 'frustrating situation' and of its perception by actors, the connection between the nature of the frustration and of the resultant aggression, and the particular direction of aggression.

Crane Brinton emphasizes that in the four revolutions he studied there was an improvement rather than a decline in the economic situation in the years prior to the outbreak.[10] He places two related riders on this however. First, in such pre-revolutionary periods certain groups were in very considerable poverty; for example, as a result of the bad harvest in France in 1788 and of the following cold winter (see Brinton, 1953, pp. 32–3; Rudé, 1959). Second, he points out that what is critically important is the *feeling* within certain groups that the prevailing conditions act to limit or hinder them economically (ibid., pp. 34–6). I do not want to pay any further attention to Brinton since he does not provide a systematic explanation of revolution but only an inventory of its more pronounced features. Nevertheless his formulation has not been without its effects, most noticeably upon James Davies's influential theory (1962, p. 6) that:

> Revolutions are most likely to occur when a prolonged period of objective economic and social development is followed by a short period of reversal. The all-important effect on the minds of people in a particular society is to produce, during the former period, an expectation of continued ability to satisfy needs –

which continue to rise – and, during the latter, a mental state of anxiety and frustration when manifest reality breaks away from anticipated reality. The actual state of socio-economic development is less significant than the expectation that past progress, now blocked, can and must continue in the future.

Certain criticisms are relevant. First, there are certain cases which are not congruent with this simple economistic thesis, but if the theory is extended into a broader formulation related to non-economic development as well, the problems of operationalization become extremely significant (see Stone, A1966, p. 172). Further, this state of mind may be the outcome of alternative patterns, such as constant expectations and declining rewards, or even falling expectations and even faster falling rewards (see Geschwender, A1968, pp. 128–9). Davies also does not specify the extent of the gap between expectations and satisfactions which is critical, or of the rate at which it may develop and not be critical (see Willer and Zollschan, 1964, p. 128). Essentially his account is one of precipitation which neglects both the actual makers of any particular revolution, and the structural conditions which lie behind it. This last point is crucial. On the one hand, Glock (1964) points out that the significant deprivations experienced by the different elements within a movement of dissent may vary, and thus Davies's exposition may only be relevant to explaining why certain structurally located actors express dissent. And on the other hand, Davies critically fails to place the outcome of revolution within the environing structure which produced his required configurations of economic development followed by regression, and the resulting interpretations.

I shall now consider the contemporary sociology of social comparisons beginning with one of the earliest and more interesting applications.

The American soldier 'promotion finding'

In a survey given in the American army in the Second World War, the pattern of responses to the question:

Do you think a soldier with ability has a good chance for promotion in the army?

was:[11]

Air Corps men tended to take a dimmer view of promotion opportunities for men of ability than did the Military Police ... [although] chances of promotion ... were about the worst in any branch of the Army – among this sample of men in the

Army one to two years, only 24% of M.P's were noncoms as compared with 47% of the Air Corps.

This was a general relationship found throughout the American army, and one that could not be explained in terms of the cultural differences between high and low promotion rate units.[12] The Research Board's explanation is simply that 'such opinions ... [with respect to promotion] represent a relationship between their expectations and their achievements relative to others *in the same boat with them*' (see Stouffer, *et al.* A1965, p. 251); Merton argues that a 'high rate of mobility induces excessive hopes and expectations among members of the group so that each is more likely to experience a sense of frustration in his present position and disaffection with the chances for promotion' (see Merton and Rossi, A1957, p. 237); and Runciman (A1966, p. 18), who claims to generalize Merton, maintains that:

Those who were not promoted in the Military Police tended to compare themselves with the large number of their fellows who were also not promoted, while those few who had been promoted were likely to appear to themselves to have done relatively better. In the Air Corps, by contrast, the man who was not promoted would be likely to compare himself with the large number of his fellows who *had* been promoted, while these, though successful, would appear to themselves to have done relatively less well.

The Research Board's interpretation is not amplified further; Merton fails to explain why group members are here relevant to the formation of hopes and expectations, why higher mobility leads to *proportionately* greater expectations (an implication necessary for his explanation), or why a sense of frustration should necessarily bring about disaffection with the actual promotion chances within the army; and Runciman's account boils down to the claim that the promoted always compare themselves with the promoted, while the non-promoted compare themselves with the other non-promoted when few are promoted, but with the promoted when many are promoted. The account Runciman gave has been analysed elsewhere. Briefly, the main objections to it are, first, there does not seem to be any justification for arguing that the comparisons would have taken this form, and second, too much is required from the comparative reference group concept which seems to be used to explain all stages in the genesis of relative deprivation.

All three accounts suffer from the *ad hoc* use of variables not subject to the constraints of use which would result if they were derived from a more general explanation. The one exception to this is James Davis's account, but since this is extrapolated directly from the Research Board's study it would be surprising if it radically contradicted the promotion finding.[13] From inference five of his theory he deduces that the amount of felt unfairness should equal $2PQ$, where P and Q are the probabilities of deprivation and non-deprivation respectively among two groups. In terms of the promotion example of high school graduates or college men with army service of one to two years, this means that in the MP 0·45 should experience feelings of unfairness as compared with 0·49 in the AC. Davis does not compare these with the original where the corresponding figures are 0·26 and 0·47 respectively. No indication is provided by Davis of whether this is a refutation or a confirmation of his theory; but one result deducible from his explanation is clearly false. Thus he maintains that the distribution of $2PQ$ is curvilinear such that there would be a decline in dissatisfaction after 0·5. However, in the case above, more than one half of the AC had been promoted (0·56) and yet there was still an increase in promotional dissatisfaction.

One reason for his difficulties lies in his assumptions. The first, that the non-deprived state is universally preferred, is not necessarily correct in the American army while the second, that comparisons are random, is sociologically nonsensical. The remaining assumptions, that comparisons with another automatically produce relative deprivation or subordination, simply ignore the fact that such sentiments depend upon the deprived actually *evaluating* the deprivation as unjust.

It is Brian Barry's intention to dispense altogether with assuming that it is necessary for actors to compare with others in order to derive self-evaluation (A1966). He attempts to explain the promotion finding in terms of an analogy with the heights of Oxford undergraduates – the latter roughly corresponding to a normal distribution. He considers the giving of a prize to, first, the tallest undergraduate, second, the tallest hundred, third, the tallest thousand, and fourth, the tallest four thousand (where there are eight thousand in total), and the consequential sense of grievance that would result in each case. The degree of relative deprivation would depend upon the number of undergraduates clustered around the four cut-off points. Given the approximately normal distribution the amount of dissatisfaction would rise reaching a maximum when half the undergraduates were being rewarded 'since the cut-off point would be in the most densely-populated sector of all' (ibid., p. 45). Although Barry admits the a-typicality of height because of its objective character, he maintains that dissatisfaction with ability would follow the same pattern (given a normal distribution) although at each point the amount of dissatisfaction would be greater. This then

75

explains why there would be more personal dissatisfaction with the promotion rate in the A C than in the M P.

Now that, Barry admits, is not the same thing at all as the American soldier promotion finding. I have discussed elsewhere my objections to his attempt to show that the differential rates of dissatisfaction about promotion opportunities for a 'soldier with ability' can be related to the rates of personal dissatisfaction. My conclusion was that at least one way of accounting for this promotion finding would be partly based on a comparative analysis; a point made also by exchange theorists, Blau and Homans, and by Runciman in the postscript to his *Relative Deprivation and Social Justice*.[14] It is to Runciman's book in general that I now turn.

Relative Deprivation and Social Justice

In the remainder of his work Runciman[15] makes some use of the generalization, derived from his discussion of the promotion finding, that the higher the actor's social ranking the more, rather than the less, relative deprivation that results. Specifically he argues that manual workers have extremely restricted comparative reference groups; indeed, although their relative deprivation with respect to status is increasing, their class deprivation is argued to be on the wane. Certain non-manual workers make wider and more class-conscious comparisons. Before discussing the survey from which this conclusion is derived it is necessary to consider his account of recent British social history.

This is so not simply because of its undoubted intrinsic interest but also because of Runciman's explicit methodological pronouncement that by itself the sample survey is no more than a snap-shot of social reality at one time and place, and thus that it is only the historical account which can provide an explanation of the findings revealed in the sample survey. The latter, he claims, is merely descriptive; it is only the historical survey which is explanatory.

My objection to this argument is not that such historical accounts are necessarily inadequate, but only that Runciman does not provide the sort of account that his work requires. Most of his attempted explanation rests on the idea that an increased standard of living leads to wider comparative references, to enhanced relative deprivation and to a growth of dissent. There are two objections to this. First of all, Runciman only provides evidence for and only tries to explain the first and the fourth stages; that an increased standard of living leads to a growth of dissent (rather like de Tocqueville and Brinton). The second point is that the relationship between these stages is taken to be necessary and not what it surely is, contingent. It follows from this that we have to know much more about how each of these stages come to be realized and how each of them needs to be explained. In general, Runciman fails to consider what it is to be an actor within an environing structure. Thus, first, the response to a rising standard of living is not simply an expansion of the range of comparative reference groups *pari passu*, since between such changes and the selection of comparative reference groups lies an actor's structure of meaning; and second, various changes may occur within the structure of society which will differentially affect the process by which 'rising optimism' is transformed into relative deprivation.

As a result, the sample survey is located within a historical vacuum such that Runciman is unable to explain the restricted patterning of comparisons that he finds.[16] Strangely, though, he commences the survey section of his book by introducing two variables, high/medium/low income and self-rated class, which he suggests are independent and might be explanatory. However, not only does this contradict the methodological pronouncement above, but the income variable suffers from the disadvantages already mentioned with respect to the standard of living, while Runciman (A1966, pp. 164–5) himself says that self-rating may be a symptom of the response to inequality rather than a variable explaining such a response.[17] He further suggests (ibid., p. 165) that 'the occupational composition of the immediate neighbourhood' may be a determinant of self-assessment; but then fails to consider it in his survey research. I will now consider the descriptive value of this research.

The first dimension of relative deprivation considered by Runciman is that of the actor's class-situation: 'his approximate shared location in the economic hierarchy' (ibid., p. 38). Some conceptual difficulty is raised by the fact that the three dimensions of class deprivation that he considers are income, consumer goods and state provision, that is to say, they are all dimensions of economic rewards and the consequences *of* class and class relationships. But even allowing for this, there are aspects of the content of his survey questions which have important implications. Thus all the questions he asked emphasized comparisons with other social categories (rather than with individuals, or groups, or collectivities) brought about by *recent* changes in the 'economic hierarchy'. Attention, therefore, is directed away from respondents identifying significant long-run collective classes and groupings as possible objects of comparative reference.

Runciman's account of relative deprivation with respect to status is also problematic. He points out himself that it is impossible to question individuals directly as to how much status is enjoyed and ought to be enjoyed by themselves and others, and that as a consequence, indirect measures of status deprivation must be used. But, as he further admits, to take one example, the fact that parents

77

express high educational aspirations for their children does not necessarily indicate high status aspirations, neither does it indicate the possibility that the frustration of such aspirations will necessarily provoke intense status deprivation (see Urry, A1972; Runciman, A1966, pp. 228–31; Goldthorpe, A1969a, pp. 132–4 and 144, n. 1). In general, he does not support his argument that there is a large and growing degree of status aspiration and deprivation.

I want, in conclusion, to consider three other points raised by the sociological sections of this extremely provocative and interesting book. First of all, Runciman identifies three dimensions of social inequality, class, status and power. Now although I will discuss this division more in the next chapter it can be said here that the use of these distinctions leads to a neglect of the interrelationships between these dimensions. This means that he does not consider in his detailed analysis either that an actor's rankings on one dimension may determine his rankings on another, or that his feelings of relative satisfaction or deprivation in relation to one form of social inequality will depend upon his rankings elsewhere. Second, he gives no indication of the possible political responses that may follow from a situation of relative deprivation. Thus, what is the significance for political action of the fact that the comparative reference groups of manual workers are extremely restricted?[18] Third, is it possible to extrapolate from this population to another in a different time and place, given Runciman's claim (A1966, p. 195) that 'reference groups tend to be closely circumscribed at all levels of society except under some abnormal stimulus'? What is the general importance of such stimuli; do they render a sample survey necessarily or sometimes ineffective?

Relationships between social inequalities

This is a theme which is, in general, neglected in Runciman's *Relative Deprivation and Social Justice*.[19] First, I will consider an analysis of wage comparisons made by workers within a single workplace.

These were first pointed out systematically by Roethlisberger and Dickson (A1964, esp. pp. 250 and 576) who observed that many workers who expressed a wage grievance maintained that this was not because of any dissatisfaction with their own wages but because the wage differentials were not congruent with the differences in social significance between the various jobs. W. H. Scott, *et al.* (A1956, pp. 245 and 254–7) add a temporal dimension to the argument. They maintain that where there is no *radical* transformation of the occupational structure, workers will evaluate any change in terms of the goals and experience of their own category of worker. To the extent that comparisons occur, they are made with other workers of the same sort. Inter-group comparisons only result where there are very significant changes which dramatically affect a particular sort of worker. Thus, for instance, the expansion and enhanced status of craft-workers led to their claiming that their wages were unsatisfactory relative to those of process workers, although there is no evidence that their wages had actually fallen.

Martin Patchen (A1961; A1968a) tries to make this speculative argument explicit. He points out that comparisons along one dimension cannot be made in a cognitive vacuum – in other words, the meaning an actor gives to his 'primary' comparison depends upon his ranking on relevant secondary dimensions. Thus it is wrong to presume that once one identifies the object of comparison, then one knows whether the comparison is favourable to the comparer. Patchen postulates that the actor undergoes a cognitive interpretation of comparing the ratio of his pay (given this as primary dimension) to the pay of the other(s), with a ratio of his position along dimensions relevant to pay to the other(s)'s position on such dimensions. Although there are some damaging criticisms,[20] there are two points which should be noted. The first is that Patchen maintains that it is not simply the probability of mobility which leads to dissonant comparisons; but rather such comparisons occur where mobility is possible but not assured (A1961, p. 86). Second, in his interpretation of the consequences of social comparisons, he emphasizes the degree to which the actor accepts personal responsibility for his life-situation (A1968a, p. 183). But, unfortunately, because his study focuses upon a single industrial workplace, he is unable to detail the significant structural factors that would explain the variations in the degree to which men do accept such personal responsibility. I now want to consider some further studies, similar in their concentration upon the dimensions of social inequality, but different in that they focus upon the wider society.

The theory of status congruence maintains that certain consequences follow where actors are ranked discrepantly along particular dimensions of status. In Lenski's classic formulation, he found that men in incongruent statuses along the dimensions of occupation, income, education and ethnicity, exhibited higher scores to certain indicators of 'welfare liberalism' than did those with better crystallized statuses.[21] Since then, however, many people have shown that all sorts of other outcomes follow from such discrepant status ranking. As a consequence, the first reason for concluding that the theory of status congruence is essentially unsatisfactory is that, as Blalock (1966) has shown, it reduces to a series of equations containing more unknowns than equations and is thus indeterminate. Mitchell (1964) also points out that the single variable of ethnicity may account for the response variation. More generally, the theory fails to provide any account of the mechanism by which the various outcomes follow from the relations between the dimensions; this reflects itself in two ways. The first is that there is no analysis provided of how a situation of status inconsistency arises, develops and effects the various outcomes. I will discuss this failure to analyse time later. The second consideration is that it is simply assumed that the particular actor will be involved in his ranking along all the dimensions all of the time. No attention is thus paid to the audience object or objects in terms of which the actor performs various roles in particular ways. There are the possibilities of compensatory statuses, of concealing certain statuses and thus, identities, through audience segregation and playing-at-a-role, of deviant ranking within particular dimensions, of the importance of alternative ranking dimensions, and of the irrelevance of some dimensions within certain social contexts (see Box and Ford, 1969; Homans, A1961). Two further points should be emphasized. First, there is implicit in all such theories some assumptions relating to the psychological organization of the individual actor of a cognitive dissonant variety.[22] To say that particular outcomes follow from the contradictory social ranking accorded by society is to say that the actor cannot accommodate such strains within his day-to-day life. The second point is that an inconsistent situation only leads to the outcome of political liberalism where particular grievances are felt against particular 'other-categories'. This argument can be made most clear by quoting Homans's status inconsistency thesis (Homans, A1961, p. 243, my emphasis):[23]

> The address girls made no such complaints about the relative position of their job against cash posting, the next job above it on the ladder of advancement. . . . They did not complain of being deprived *in comparison with others*, and it is always relative deprivation that raises the question of distributive justice.

The study of status congruence highlights a number of concerns. First, it directs attention to the processes of identity formation and the relationship between the actor and his audience object or objects. Further, it shows the wide variety of responses that may follow from a psychologically stressful situation. Specifically, in relationship to the processes of social comparison, it has indicated, first of all, that some comparisons with those more highly ranked do not produce a feeling of injustice since the 'investments' of the other are held to be greater (see Adams Stacy, A1965, p. 273). Second, as Runciman (A1966, p. 36) says in what will be seen to be a statement of some importance that returns the discussion to the point made earlier: 'such conflicting criteria of status and the "incongruences" to which they give rise create the possibilities of sudden changes in reference groups or a sudden intensification of relative deprivation from which revolutionary situations in the fullest sense are born' (see also A1967, p. 127).

There have been two main attempts to integrate these considerations relating to the theory of status congruence with the study of social comparison processes.[24] Johan Galtung (A1964) distinguishes between a TU position ('topdog' – 'underdog' along different dimensions) and a UU position ('underdog' along both dimensions) and maintains that aggression is more probable in the former. This follows, first, because the latter has less resources for aggression and less potential for developing self-righteous claims for equality with TT ('topdog' along both dimensions), second, because the disequilibriated is never left in peace with his disequilibrium unless he cuts out certain interaction channels, and third, because the TU will use TT as his reference group even if he is a member of UU. The TU thus has relative deprivation built into his situation. The other contribution here is that of Anderson and Zelditch who make two points ignored by Galtung. First, they point out that no effects are going to result from a situation of status incongruence unless some actual comparison process does occur. The second point is to emphasize that the patterning of relative deprivation does not necessarily follow from the overall structure; thus, even if an actor compares himself with another, he may say, either, 'I'm doing quite well since I make as much money as B although he has more prestige', or 'Although I make as much money as B, he still does not accept me' (see Anderson and Zelditch, A1964, pp. 115–16; Urry, A1972). Furthermore, even in the second case, relative deprivation and dissent need not follow, since the actor's attempt to change his situation may be mitigated either by insulation, that is, in-group interaction and comparison, or by mobility.

Thus, although such comparison processes are of importance they do not provide a full explanation of relative deprivation. Furthermore, the selection of such comparisons is problematic; in Galtung it is based upon similarity between the object of comparison and the actor – in Anderson and Zelditch it is based on actual interaction between the two. This point will now be discussed.

The choice of comparisons

Hyman and Singer (A1968, pp. 13–14) quote the example of the Amba of East Africa who were willing to work for Europeans at a much lower price than for employers from another tribe. This was because 'a European is on a much higher social plane, and therefore comparisons are out of the question' (see also, Winter, A1955, p. 40).

81

In other words, an actor will not compare himself with another unless there is some similarity between the two. Although this is emphasized by Merton and Rossi (A1957), Hyman and the whole of the social comparison literature,[25] which of the potential bases of similarity are actually pertinent is somewhat unclear. There are two possible dimensions, similarity and propinquity; this can be seen in Helen Strauss's study of social comparison processes among the blind.

I should point out first of all that this work is in the Festinger, cognitive, social comparison tradition. In general, there are three reasons why I do not think that this perspective is useful here. First, the dimensions considered are normally abilities and opinions rather than power and rewards; second, most of the literature stems from artificial experimental situations (groups of American psychology students) and no guarantee is provided that such findings are relevant to the behaviour of actors in real groups; and third, it focuses upon the small-scale social psychology of adjustment and ignores the structural context within which comparisons occur. Thus, although we will not pay systematic attention to this tradition, Helen Strauss's study (A1968, pp. 230 and 237) is exceptional in that it is neither a-structural nor artificial, although the dimensions she considers are those of personal appearance, learning and character. She notes first, that one-fifth of her respondents do not compare themselves with anyone and this may strengthen their self-regard. This mirrors an original claim of Hyman's (A1942) that not all actors make comparisons all of the time. A second point made by Strauss is that 63 per cent of her respondents choose the sighted rather than the blind as their comparison object, but within the sighted they choose those within their immediate social environment. Propinquity rather than similarity is the basis of selection. The final point here is that the consequence of such comparisons is not upsetting since, although the blind know they are inferior, they also know that it is not their fault. This point serves to emphasize the claim that the fact of comparison does not necessarily entail the sentiment of relative deprivation.

Other writers support this second point. Thus, Form and Geschwender (A1968) argue generally that an actor cannot evaluate his occupational position by comparing himself with others unless such others are in an occupation in some sense comparable to his own. Specifically they maintain that in the USA those born in the south, the country, abroad and as Negroes, all use standards prevailing in their families and subcommunities as a basis for evaluating their present occupation; and that working-class males judge their occupational success by comparison with their early life peer group. Reissman (A1953, esp. pp. 241–2) similarly attempts to explain the low aspiration of both policemen and junior businessmen, the former on account of the high mobility compared with their brothers who are salient objects of comparison, the latter because of the existence of friends, family and local community as their source of both normative and comparative reference. This is even more systematically shown by Stern and Keller's analysis of two hundred responses to an open-ended question on the standard of living (A1968). They find a low degree of class resentment, a high emphasis upon family and friends as comparison objects and a low tendency to cite non-membership objects. Two points derive from this. First, that it is 'upper class people' who explain differences of social class in terms of the 'system', while 'lower class people' tend to make personal interpretations such as: 'Well, when one works hard, or is good, or has the ability, one can rise in the world.' Stern and Keller account for this by the fact that this survey was conducted in 'low-mobility' France and they expect that the opposite would be found in 'high-mobility' USA. The second important point is that they argue that the aim of such comparisons is to arrive at a harmonious continuance of social relations with people close to one. There is, according to Stern and Keller, a desire to keep relationships functioning smoothly, and not to excite jealousy, envy and status-striving. Perhaps the best way to conclude this section is by returning to the original Hyman article (A1942; p. 24) and quoting his claim that:[26]

> The rare occurrence of the total population as a reference group and the great frequency of more intimate reference groups are characteristic of the process of judging status. Individuals operate for the most part in small groups within the total society, and the total population may have little relevance for them. Far more important are their friends, people they work with.

The methodology of comparative reference

Ideally, as Merton and Rossi (A1957, p. 249) argue, an effort should be made to discover 'which reference groups are spontaneously and explicitly brought into play'. The apparent impossibility of achieving this leads them to posit the second-best 'the study of responses to reference group contexts provided by the experimenter or suggested by the interviewer' (ibid.).[27] However, this seems to be a policy beset by difficulties.

I want to argue here that given certain reasons as to why it is not possible to describe directly an actor's comparisons, it is appropriate to use the concept of social comparisons as a non-observable term. It is, in other words, one term in my theory, but a term which is not

83

to be translated observationally. There are, of course, significant reasons why non-observable terms are important in sociology; one can point to their importance in natural science, one can point out that the tremendous emphasis within science to operationalize theoretical terms reveals a great faith in the importance of such non-observables, and one can see that the very process of operationalization is problematic. So what I am arguing is this; the social comparisons made by an actor are of great importance in leading actors to engage in various sorts of activity. However, there are tremendous difficulties in observing and describing such comparisons. But this does not mean that we should therefore dismiss such processes as not being our concern. Rather, they are real and substantive phenomena, crucial to explaining various courses of action in which people engage, but that they become part of our theory which we set out in the next chapter. Now in my basic non-positivist view of theories and theory construction I clearly do not see the objections to operationalizing theoretical terms as merely pragmatic. But in the case of social comparisons I do think that there are certain features which make their observation singularly difficult.

The first point is that there are few possibilities of satisfactory replication of social comparison studies. The best 'goodness of fit' between a research and its replication occurs to the extent that there are the same observers, researching at the same place at the same time.[28] The significance of the fact that replication is not perfect depends upon the nature of the object being studied. It is very important in the study of comparative reference, where it is thought that such patterning varies significantly with time (with the occurrence of normal and abnormal stimuli), probably varies with place, and certainly varies with the observer. The two empirical techniques by which an actor's comparisons have been observed and systematized are the experiment and the survey interview. The argument that follows is that both are inadequate.

Neil Friedman's brilliant discussion of the psychological experiment (1967) shows that the results customarily obtained indicate far more about the nature of the experimenter/experimentee relationship than they do about the intrinsic details of the experiment.[29] He points out that there is a peculiarly individualistic ontology attributed to the actor within the psychological experiment. This is because a congruence is presumed between experiments in the natural sciences and in psychology. The object-matter in each is treated in the same way. The experimentees are taken to be objects in no way entering into a structured and meaningful social relationship with the person conducting the experiment. It is important to note that while psychological and social psychological information is normally gained within the experiment (the Festinger social comparison literature for example), the data of sociology are mainly acquired within the interview. But the problem is that this is again premised upon the same individualistic assumptions. That is to say, the interview is not viewed as a particular sort of social relationship, the form and content of which is the main determinant of the responses to the questions asked. Again, this is a generally valid point but in the case of the study of comparative reference this objection has even more force. This is because there are no very good grounds for presuming that an actor's comparisons are consistently conscious. Merton and Rossi (A1957, pp. 249–50) argue that individuals unwittingly respond to varying frames of reference and thus that non-sample survey techniques are implied (see also, Anderson and Zelditch, A1968, p. 124; Urry, A1972). But that they have not been used means that in judging any particular revealed comparison pattern it is not obvious that there are not other comparisons more salient for the actor concerned than those observed and described.[30] But even if this is correct, one still does not know the precise nature of the relationship between an actor's attitudes and his actions. Of course, to the extent that the conventional techniques simply elicit the attitudes *expressed*, the relationship between them and men's actions is even more unclear.

C. Wright Mills (1963, p. 467) claims that the 'disparities between talk and action' are 'the central methodological problem of the social sciences'. In other words, to take the case of Runciman's work, what is the importance for working-class dissent of the fact that he found a highly restricted pattern of comparison among the working class? All it in fact shows is the response of one set of respondents within a particular interview situation to a small number of questions at a particular point in time. The difficulty arises, first, because most individuals do not by any means have stable and consistent attitudes, and second, because they cannot know in advance the concrete decisions that they will have to take, what possible alternatives there will be, or what influences may then be pervasive. LaPiere, in fact, once suggested that there may be a high inverse relationship between what people say and do.[31] The conventional inquiry based upon the single individual at a point in time ignores both that times change and that individuals interact. Most sociology ignores or evades these possibilities.[32] That the study of comparative reference cannot, means that it only effectively operates as a concept where some specification is provided of the relationship between men's attitudes and actions. This, combined with the former justification of non-observational concepts, suggests the importance of using the notion of social comparison to explain actual phenomena within history. It is in the latter that one both knows that various attitudes have been acted out in various patterns of action and that certain events are of importance and some are unimportant. As LaPiere wrote, shockingly perhaps, many years ago (1934, p. 237): 'it would seem far more worthwhile to make a shrewd guess regarding that which is essential than accurately to measure that which is likely to prove irrelevant'.

Conclusion

L. Stone (A1966, p. 173):

> Human satisfaction is related not to existing conditions but to the condition of a social group against which the individual measures his situation.

It is as a consequence of the lack of direct physical standards that actors have a need to compare their situation with that of others whenever they wish to evaluate themselves. This seems to be an anthropological necessity without which human life would not be possible, although critically, its empirical form is enormously variable. In view of the apparently universal nature of this phenomenon it is surprising that it has been relatively unstudied. Of Festinger's theory of social comparisons, Latane pointed out twelve years after its original formulation (A1966, p. 1) that it had been virtually untested; while Hyman and Singer in 1968 (A1968, p. 18) talk of the state of neglect into which the comparative reference group concept has fallen. However, since this notion of comparative reference is one potentially capable of explaining why actors within a given society are dissatisfied with some or all aspects of it, it may not be purely accidental that it has been so neglected. That actors can be an object of their own consciousness presupposes a relationship between man and society of some uniqueness within the sociological perspective. It is consequently not surprising that where the implicit notions of moral philosophy have been made explicit within the sociology of comparative reference, this has typically exhibited a form serving to neutralize, or perhaps dehumanize, the processes of interpersonal comparison. Indeed, the argument of this chapter is that practically all of the substantive conclusions that contemporary sociology has reached within this field were to be found, explicitly or implicitly, within the philosophical writings austerely summarized in the first section. Such sociology has, moreover, through an excessively over-enthusiastic systematization, neglected certain concerns that were very importantly part of especially the interactionist emphasis within this tradition.

All that is to be said here is that the study of social comparisons is customarily a-historical, both in the sense that it neglects the historical self who is the outcome of reflected self-appraisals and who acts as a limiting constraint upon the choice of comparisons, and the historical society, which produces continual transformations of the possibilities of comparative selection; it is reified since while phenomenologically such comparisons are intermittent, inconsistent and segmental, they are conventionally given a precise, fixed and unambiguous value; and it is a-sociological in the sense that such work has been abstracted out of specific sociological formulations and thus out of explanation in terms of changing historical structures. The combined consequence of these three points is that the sociology of comparative reference cannot specify why particular actors at particular times seek to transcend the constraints of their historical situation; but to the extent that that is not possible is to indicate the inadequacy of the explanation. Instead of being used to explain actual historical movements of dissent, the concept has been used to plot a-historically and a-structurally certain reified configurations of comparative reference.

part two

Reference groups in the study of dissent

The second part of this book is intended to show the way in which reference group analysis can help to explain the genesis and nature of mass revolutionary consciousness. I attempt to explain why actors are dissatisfied with their world, why they dissent individually and collectively, and why they may organize to transform that world. I am not asserting that such an analysis is a theory of revolution in the sense of explaining every aspect of revolutionary social change. Rather, I think that certain aspects of reference group analysis elucidate some of the processes which on occasions lead large numbers of people to become revolutionary.

In this chapter I shall make some use of the themes developed in chapter 3, but the bulk of my argument will be derived from chapters 1 and 4. Thus, one of the criticisms made of the conventional uses of the comparative reference group concept was that it is a-sociological. This present chapter consequently starts with a brief analysis of a framework by which social structural considerations are part of the explanation of the varying patterns of social comparison.

5 Of a theory of dissent

Structure

The common argument that 'functionalism' is a-historical and conservative does not do justice to the multiplicity of forms of functionalist analysis. In particular, it is possible to distinguish between structuralism, a concentration upon the parts of society using the whole as a kind of base off which to bounce effects and consequences, and functionalism, a model where the various parts are constituent elements and only significant in their contribution to the whole.[1] It is in the second sense that functional analysis is a-historical, conservative and concerned with functional unity rather than with change and conflict. Structuralism as used here does not exhibit these inadequacies, although in the hands of its most famous sociological advocate, Robert K. Merton (1957, esp. pp. 60–84), it has been used unsatisfactorily in a restless search for the latent functions of various phenomena.

I do not think that structural analysis needs to be inadequate. Admittedly, *in itself*, it excludes consideration of the actor, precludes explanation except through changes in exogenous variables, and, because of the physical and biological heritage, normally analyses time-free relationships of form. However, the last point is neither inevitable nor, given the historical character of the social world, is it desirable. In consequence, I will use the term social structure to refer to the dynamic relationships between the parts of the social system. Two further points need making. First of all, to maintain that the social world is historical is not to argue that there are no significant discontinuities within that history. Later I shall attempt to show how one may begin to conceptualize these disjunctions of history. Second, it is customary for structural (and functional) analysis to rest upon the assumption that value consensus is necessary to realize social integration. There are many objections: it is

91

empirically common for there to be conflicting value systems; the existence of shared values does not preclude a great deal of conflict depending upon their content (individualism, for example); conflict may occur between two or more shared values (for example, liberty versus equality); and the sharing of a value does not preclude antagonistic interpretations (see for example Gouldner, 1967, p. 168; Mann, 1970; van den Berghe, 1967, pp. 295–6; and Williams, 1963).

Van den Berghe suggests as an alternative the postulate of a dynamic equilibrium. But this too is, as he shows, not fully adequate since it fails to allow for the fact that 'reaction to extra-systematic change is not always adjustive', that 'social systems can, for long periods, go through a vicious circle of ever deepening malintegration,' that 'change can be revolutionary,' and that 'the social structure itself generates change through internal conflicts and contradictions' (1967, pp. 296–7). As a result of these points, van den Berghe argues for a *rapprochement* between dynamic equilibrium theory and the Hegelian-Marxian dialectic. Regrettably, he does not detail how this would actually be brought about and so we must direct our attention elsewhere.[2] But his analysis is important in indicating the sorts of social phenomena that must be explained by any satisfactory theory.

Lockwood (1964) provides a similar critique of the normative functionalist position, most particularly by distinguishing between social integration, the relationships between actors, and system integration, the relationships between parts of a society.[3] Normative functionalism neatly makes the connection between the two by maintaining that since the only differentiated parts of a society are its institutional patterns, the only source of social disorder arising from system disorder is that which takes the form of role conflict resulting from incompatible institutional patterns (ibid., p. 245). However, as Lockwood argues, if it is the case that such institutional patterns do not exhaust the generally relevant parts of a society, then this particular articulation of social and system integration is only one way in which conflict is related to the operation of the society as a whole (ibid., pp. 245–6). Lockwood continues by showing how the so-called conflict theorists (Rex and Dahrendorf) have failed in their critique of normative functionalism actually to specify the other *parts* of a society which may be in conflict. Instead, they have limited their attention to showing how the postulate of social (and not system) integration is inadequately treated by normative functionalism. Rex and Dahrendorf construct alternative models of society which systematically neglect norms and values and emphasize coercion and conflict.[4] But this is an unacceptable procedure since what is crucial is not a normative functionalist model to explain some sociological phenomena and a conflict-coercion model to account for other phenomena, but rather, a theory which incorporates both. In actuality, what is significant is the incessant interplay between norms and power within all major institutions.[5] That this is so can be seen paradoxically, from the following quotation from Parsons (1960, p. 173): 'Beliefs and values are actualized, partially and imperfectly in realistic situations of social interaction and the outcomes are always co-determined by the values and the realistic exigencies.' Further, if one turns instead to Merton (1957, p. 122), we find that in a study of such processes: 'The key concept bridging the gap between statics and dynamics in functional theory is that of strain, tension, contradiction, or discrepancy between the component elements of social and cultural structure.'[6]

Lockwood (1964, p. 249) points out the paradox that Rex and Dahrendorf claim to be generalizing Marx yet they do not use the distinction between social and system integration and this resulting notion of contradiction. Thus in Marxian theory what is decisive for change is not only the power conflict arising from relationships within the productive system, but also the system conflict arising from contradictions between the institutions of private property and the forces of production.[7] Therefore for Lockwood, contradiction is not primarily a relationship between actors or of conflict within the value system, but is a specification of the nature of the relationship between different parts of the society in question. There are though a number of important points raised by this highly interesting and well-nigh unique discussion within academic sociology. The first is the admirable way in which Lockwood places emphasis upon the responses that are made by those with vested interests when they are faced by this particular contradictory relationship (ibid., pp. 251–2). Thus, how can the capitalist resolve the functional incompatibility between the material means of production and the property framework? There are three limitations of his analysis. First of all, although following Weber, he mentions the material means of organization and violence, he does not indicate how these might be introduced systematically into his account (ibid., p. 251). Second, he does not analyse the contradictions implied above which occur within the value system.[8] Finally, Lockwood does not show the possible relationships between his structural contradiction and conflicts of power between actors. It is interesting incidentally that Blackburn who makes this last point (1969, p. 184), similarly fails to specify the various contradictions that may materialize except to make Althusser's point that there is over-determination. This is because a non-Hegelian formulation of the dialectic based not upon an indivisible genetic totality experiencing self-division, opposition and ultimate reintegration, does more than simply invert the circularity of a Hegelian contradiction (see Althusser, 1969, pp. 192–215; Hyppolite, 1969). But that in turn very pervasively demands the specification of all the contradictions existent within a society and of their possible accumulation and exacerbation that may fuse into a 'ruptural unity' (see Althusser, 1969, pp. 20 and 22).

Three different contradictions have already been identified: the contradiction within the value system, the contradiction within the actual organization of society (within capitalist society between workers and capitalists, or more generally, between those with and those without power), and the contradiction between various parts of society. To these may be added a fourth, the contradiction between different entire structures such as capitalism and small peasant property, or between capitalism and socialism. The most complex contradiction is that between the parts of the structure; before I elaborate this further it is necessary to identify the particular parts in question. Two have already been noted: values and social organization. It might appear that these are directly equivalent to Merton's culture structure and social structure (1957). This is incorrect, however, since in Merton the distinction is intended as real and not as analytic. Why I want to maintain that the distinction is only analytic is that, as the ongoing critique of normative functionalism and the quotation from Parsons above serve to emphasize, there is co-determination of actions by the values and by the realistic exigencies of the situation. The intention here is to take this argument very seriously. But if one does, then one realizes that there is another component within the notion of 'realistic exigencies' besides that of social organization: this is what Lockwood calls 'the material conditions' of acting. Thus with respect to any course of action in the social world there are three components: values, patterns of social organization and material conditions. This set is, moreover, not incongruent with Marxian discussion and bears a strong relationship to the hierarchy of action components as found in Parsons and Smelser.[9] The latter suggest one terminological change, that is, the replacement of material conditions by what they call situational facilities, or facilities for short. Thus the three components of action are values (general statements of desirable end-states); social organization (actual regularized patterns of interaction in the social world); and facilities (material conditions of production, organization and violence). Although this account approximates to that of Smelser there are two important differences. The first is that this set is not seen as a hierarchy with values at the top and facilities at the bottom. The second is that Smelser's component of norms is discarded as a component of action. Incidentally, the formulation here seems superior to Merton not only because it does not destroy the unity of the act of the actor, but also in enabling an explanation of individual behaviour in terms of the emergent properties of the society and in permitting a greater specification of possible relationships between the parts (that is, values, organization *and* facilities) of that society.

There are thus a variety of forms of contradiction. Godelier's analysis of the contradictions of capitalist society (1967) suggests three types. I think though that it can be shown that these are specific varieties of more general contradictions already identified. His first one is that between workers and capitalists, or put more generally, it is the contradiction found within any epoch where there is an inequality of power built into the structure of society. A second contradiction he specifies is that between feudalism and capitalism, that is, conflict occurring at all three component levels. But again there is nothing unique about the capitalist epoch in realizing such a contradiction. Finally, Godelier discusses the contradiction between 'property institutions' and the 'forces of production', or more generally, between social organization based upon private property and the increasingly social nature of the economic facilities (see Mandel, 1962; Marx, 1956, p. 244). There are two points to note about this capitalist contradiction. First, it is specific to only a part of the capitalist epoch, is born during its development and is not present from the beginning (see Godelier, 1967, p. 105). Second, this sort of structural contradiction is qualitatively more significant than what may be termed the simple contradictions that occur within a single action component. As Godelier says of the simple contradiction between worker and capitalist (ibid., p. 107) '[it] does not contain within itself the set of conditions for its solution' (see also Marx, 1954, p. 20) (all emphasized in original). But although we must attach particular importance to the structural contradiction of capitalist society it is clear both that there are other structural contradictions within capitalism (for instance, between the value of becoming bourgeois and the social organization which precludes the realization of this universal), and that other societies exhibit such contradictions, as will be seen in the study of bureaucracies in chapter 6.

What is the implication of the contradictory character of the objective facticity of society for the argument that 'in the last instance' the economy is determinant (see Engels, 1962, p. 488)? In other words, I want to consider the claim that ultimately all accounts of human action can be reduced to statements about the economic facilities. However, because of the non-monist assumptions upon which my argument is based, the process is dialectical rather than mechanistic. There are three critical moments: the developing self-generative quality of the economic facilities, the consequences of this for the values and social organization, and their feedback upon

95

the economic facilities. The dialectical quality of this process results in significant discontinuities, that is, in different epochs of history as given by the nature of the economic facilities. However, the consequence of this is that the values and social organization need not, at any moment of time, be the mirror-image of the economic facilities. Rather, it is only where they take on a specific form that such isomorphism is found. Elsewhere their importance is mediated by various institutions, in post-capitalist society still based on scarcity by the political system, in feudal society by religion, and in primitive society by kinship (see Godelier, 1967, p. 112). It is only in an extreme form of capitalism that the determinant economic facilities result in their domination so that the values and organization of society perfectly mirror the economy. All actual societies are departures from this type to varying degrees. This is relevant here not only in terms of the general meaning that can be attributed to the economy-society relationship but specifically in terms of one's analysis of class and status, of one's analysis of social organization.

We will commence discussion here by considering Marx's statement (1954, p. 625) that: 'Accumulation ... presents itself ... as increasing concentration of the means of production, and of the command over labour.' In other words, there is a duality in the capitalist-worker relationship. It is similar to the distinction drawn by Lockwood (1958) between an actor's work – and market-situations. Since though the importance of class for varieties of political action lies in the fact that it is a relationship and not a thing (see Thompson, 1968, p. 11), it is the former, the actor's work experience, which is immediately and importantly implicatory for the actor. The actor's market-situation, on the contrary, is something set apart from the actor's everyday experience. Since I am not interested here in explaining the class consciousness of a particular category of workers ('blackcoated' workers) but in providing the general basis for the explanation of class and status structures, groupings and degrees of consciousness, it is necessary to distinguish a number of dimensions by which the work structure is differentiated. The three most significant are the idle and the working, the employers and the employees, and the situationally favoured in their work-situation and the situationally unfavoured.[10] The first dimension is definitionally dichotomous, the second is either dichotomous or trichotomous (may be the category of self-employed) and the third is variable.

The argument here is that it is the relationship between the market structure and the various dimensions of the work structure which determine the form of the class and status structures and groupings.[11] Initially, the ideal typical two-class structure will be considered. This occurs in the situation where both the work and market structures are dichotomized and overlapping. The first point means that in the market structure there is private ownership of the economic facilities by less than the whole population. In the work structure it means that there is no category of the self-employed and the work-situation is such that there are two polarized categories within each workplace.[12] The notion that these structures are overlapping means that there is a one-to-one congruence between the 'top' and 'bottom' categories within each structure. Thus any actor will belong to either the top work and market category or the bottom work and market category.

The degree to which any society does not approximate to this is of course variable. Much Marxist analysis is incorrect because it presumes that a dichotomized market structure must realize a dichotomized and overlapping work structure. Thus, although this is one consideration, the nature of the work structure also depends upon the stage of the society's economic development, its previous economic history and the societal values relating to economic activity. This is very important. It means that the degree to which classes in the 'in-themselves' sense exist depends on the general character of economic development, upon the economic nature of that particular epoch. There are three ways in which a dichotomized market structure does not necessarily imply a whole society torn by the polarization of two antagonistic classes, one of which is structurally dependent upon the other.

The first point arises simply because this particularly dichotomized class structure may only exist within part of the ongoing society, and there will be other stratification structures elsewhere. The second consideration is that although all such structures may be dichotomized they may not be overlapping, and as a consequence there will be certain structurally ambivalent groupings and categories. Thus to take a well-known example, the blackcoated worker, is in three senses in an inferior situation – he does not own the economic facilities, he works, and he is employed. But in one sense he is in a superior situation – that is, he has a favoured work situation. It is then possible to apply this sort of analysis in various other situations. The third point occurs where there is such differentiation of the work structure that each formally specified class (that is, all actors in common relationship to economic facilities) is completely split up into multiple and possibly conflicting status-groups. Further, as a consequence of the nature of this economic structure, there is the probability that dimensions other than economic will be dominant. I now want to consider what these might be.

An adequate account would entail a long and detailed discussion of the nature of power. I do not have time to do this here.[13] Rather, I want to consider briefly Runciman's article on 'Class, Status and Power?' (1968; see also Ingham, 1969). In this he maintains that it is always possible to rank individuals with respect to class, status and

97

power in such a way that the position of each can be designated as a vector in a three-dimensional space. One objection to this claim is to question whether the establishment of such distinctions between the dimensions has any significance for the actual study of the ongoing processes of class and status grouping development, conflict and change. A further objection is terminological. Runciman considers 'power' to be a category at least logically distinct from 'class' and 'status'. This is derived from Weber (1948), but he is himself confused on this point since he says *both*: 'Now: "classes", "status groups", and "parties" are phenomena of the distribution of power within a community' (ibid., p. 181); but 'parties' live in a house of power (ibid., p. 194). I think that the former more adequately reflects Weber's general orientation because he also talks explicitly about economic power and implicitly about the power basis of status (ibid., pp. 180–1). The ambiguity in Runciman can be seen from an earlier work of his where, within the space of four pages, he maintains that there are '"classes", "status-groups" and "parties" (or "power-strata")' and that 'all societies are somehow stratified in terms of class, status and power' (1965, pp. 137 and 141). I think that the way out of this confusion is to maintain that, on the one hand, there are classes and status groupings which exist as structural manifestations within society, and on the other, there are the bases of power of such groupings, and these are economic, political and cultural.[14]

These three bases vary as to the means that are used to make the other in the relationship comply with the wishes of the subject.[15] One actor gets another to do something because he is able to threaten or to enforce compliance, that is, he can use one or more of the power bases. These are distinguished in terms of the means of control that are used. Political power is based upon the applicability or threat of applicability of the facilities of physical coercion; it corresponds to what Etzioni calls coercive power.[16] Economic power is based upon control of the economic facilities; it roughly corresponds to Etzioni's remunerative power. Cultural power is based upon the control of the means of value creation, maintenance and interpretation, or following Etzioni, it is based upon the manipulation of 'symbolic rewards'. Etzioni claims that this typology is exhaustive although he also points out that this can only be shown by indicating how every type of power can be reduced to one or more of these categories.[17] There are two further points that need making here: they are both illustrated in Diagram 1.

First, then, coercive facilities produce coercion, value facilities produce inequalities with respect to cultural power; but economic facilities produce not only differentials of economic power but also, through the processes of capital accumulation, differentials of goods and services and thus of incomes. The relationship between economic power or control and the economic production of goods and services is not one-to-one. Thus, an actor can acquire more goods and services but in no way increase his degree of economic control. One does not necessarily imply the other. But if this is so, in what sense is it still legitimate to talk of the three dimensions of power? It is obviously convenient to do so, but if we are interested in changes within them then we must indicate whether it is the economic control or production aspect of this dimension which is relevant in any particular instance. Typically, most actors most of the time are more involved with the latter than with the former. Thus when we draw attention in the future to the three power dimensions, it is economic rewards rather than economic control which is being considered along the economic dimension.

DIAGRAM 1: *The sources of power*

Control source	Non-zero sum rewards	Zero-sum power distribution	
Economic facilities	goods and services	economic	⎫
Political facilities		political	status
Cultural facilities		cultural	⎭

The second point indicated by Diagram 1 is that it is impossible to identify any independent sources of the status-situation of an actor other than his power held with respect to the three power bases.[18] This is contrary to most Weberian stratification analysis where status enjoys the position of something of an independent variable. Thus one sees *Class, Status and Power* (for example, Bendix and Lipset, eds, 1966; Runciman, 1968), and *Class, Status and Party* (for example, Weber, 1948; 1964), and Runciman (1968, p. 33) says: 'The millionaire, the celebrity and the ruler enjoy a high social position'. The problem with this last argument is that who is and who is not a celebrity within a particular society depends upon the particular values predominant within that society. Thus an actor without significant political or economic power may only acquire status through the possession of cultural power, through the maintenance, interpretation or creation of societal values. But similarly it is not possible to maintain that status is simply cultural power since it can accrue to actors by virtue merely of their economic or political power. The exact way, therefore, that status is a derivative varies. For some actors, their status may be an aggregation of their three power rankings, while for others, there may be a master-status dimension,[19] or simply different dimensions with no tendency to aggregation.

Thus in consequence of its derivative character status will not be a major component of the explanation of dissent. The importance of power for the genesis of dissent will now be shown.

The world upset

Alfred Schutz (1962; 1964; 1966; 1967) provides the most plausible account of the way in which men live out their lives with their fellow men (see also, Garfinkel, 1960). Fundamental to his account is the way in which the world out there becomes transposed for each actor into his world in the here and now, in accordance with the relevant elements of his biographical situation. Each actor considers himself the centre of his world which he groups around him according to his specific interests. The crucial feature is that at any moment in life this individual actor has a stock of knowledge at hand; a stockpile of typifications which is endemic to common-sense life. It is this stock of knowledge which provides the structuring of his perception and of the initial formulation of the thousands of concrete problematic situations that arise in each actor's daily life. And this world-as-taken-for-granted is intersubjective – it is their world which is the underlying common-sensical typification. The elements within this world are taken-for-granted; they are socially acceptable as the good and right ways for coming to terms with both things and men. They are taken-for-granted because they have so far proved satisfactory and are thus held to require neither an explanation nor a justification. Man, within the world of common-sensical typifications, puts in brackets the doubt that the world and its objects might be otherwise than it appears to him; it is the epoché of the natural attitude (Schutz, 1962, p. 229). The world-as-taken-for-granted is thus a world of common situations within which common problems emerge within a common horizon, problems requiring typical solutions by typical means for bringing about typical ends.

Schutz's description of the world of common-sense reality (1944) approaches closest to conflict and change in his essay on the stranger. He outlines the assumptions upon which 'thinking-as-usual' continues: these are that social life will remain as it has been, that the same problems requiring the same solutions will recur so that one's former experiences will suffice for the mastering of future situations; one may rely on handed down knowledge even if one does not fully understand its origin and intrinsic meaning; one has some knowledge about the general type of events that may be encountered in one's life-world; and the assumptions are validated intersubjectively (ibid., pp. 500–2). But if one or more of these cease to operate then thinking-as-usual becomes unworkable. There is a crisis which, as W. I. Thomas puts it: 'interrupts the flow of habit and gives rise to

100

changed conditions of consciousness and practice' (quoted in ibid., p. 502). Schutz applies this notion of the breakdown of the system of tested recipes at hand to the problem of a social group encountering a stranger. But I think that it has a wider applicability. Schutz himself argues that life is highly uncertain, that there is a possibility of a cataclysm which will destroy one's experience and will mean that one will act once more as a subject, as a centre of spontaneous activity (1964, p. 82). What it is that brings this about is a fundamental disturbance of the customary preoccupation with the next step, when there is the intrusion of an experience which cannot be subsumed beneath the stock-of-knowledge-at-hand such that solutions are no longer typical and unproblematic? (See Bergson, 1913, p. 170.) The world-as-taken-for-granted is, at least partially and temporarily, transformed into the world-that-may-be-made-by-men; this transformation is, I am arguing, the consequence of a significant dislocative experience. I am now going to summarize a number of differing writers who emphasize the importance of such experiences in leading actors to attempt to remake their social worlds.

First, it will be remembered that Runciman mentioned the effects of an 'abnormal stimulus' in widening the selection of comparisons and thus in heightening the sense of deprivation and the degree of dissent (see chapter 4). Specifically in the literature on millenarianism, Norman Cohn (1957, pp. 310–11) claims:

Whether in the Middle Ages or in the twentieth century, revolutionary chiliasm has flourished only where the normal, familiar pattern of life has undergone a disruption so severe as to seem irremediable. When a way of living which has long been taken for granted is called into question, invalidated or simply rendered impracticable, a situation of peculiar strain is created.

Aberle (A1962, p. 210) connects this explicitly with the notion of relative deprivation since probable dissenters will experience 'not only relative deprivation, but a deprivation which stems from change' (see also, Worsley, 1968; Key, 1956). Engels's emphasis upon how workers in the early period of industrialization will exhibit greater revolutionary consciousness as a result of rapid and discontinuous changes, which occur to an inexperienced working class with primarily agricultural origins, is confirmed both in much contemporary literature[20] and by Trotsky (1965, p. 33):

The proletariat did not arise gradually through the ages, carrying with itself the burden of the past as in England, but in leaps involving sharp changes of environment, ties, relations, and a sharp break with the past. . . . The Russian proletariat was forever repeating the short history of its origins.

101

Similarly, in *The Hidden God*, Goldmann adumbrates the transforming consequences of the onset of industrialization (p. 48):

On a social as well as an individual plane, it is the sick organ which creates awareness, and it is in periods of social and political crisis that men are most aware of the enigma of their presence in the world.

The degree to which such crises occur is highly variable. One point to note is that during the course of the life-cycle there are certain critical periods where there is a much reduced possibility of preventing 'those radical crises during which options multiply and group rationales become inadequate for handling personal dilemmas' (see Strauss, A1959, p. 142; Brim, A1966, p. 22). Erikson has devoted himself most consistently to describing the nature of such transformations of the individual's biography.He discusses necessary turning points, how certain crises induce radical selections, the possible simultaneity of socio-economic and psycho-sexual crises, and the importance of significant historical transformations, especially in their capacity to disintegrate the inner consistency of a child's hierarchy of expectations (1968b, pp. 16, 53–5, 74 and 159). Most contemporary sociology, in stressing role-incompatibility and the failure to meet role-expectations, ignores the importance of such temporal change. Nevertheless, of the five explanations of dissent set out by Geschwender, four (Davies's, rising expectations, relative deprivation and downward mobility) do involve some notion of historical discontinuity (see Geshwender, A1968, p. 131; Strauss, A1959, p. 144; Bagley, A1970a; Gouldner, 1955). Geschwender suggests that the a-temporality of the fifth, status inconsistency, can be overcome through synthesizing it with the work of Homans and Festinger. Thus his own explanation of dissent is in terms of the dissonance that arises between an actor's various cognitions as a result of changes in his circumstances (ibid., pp. 132–3 and ch. 4). In itself, this is excessively imprecise but is nevertheless significant in emphasizing, first, the importance for dissent of changes within an actor's experience and their connection with the notion of status consistency; and second, the emphasis upon the psychological consequences of dissonant cognitions which result from these changes. These two points are another way of expressing the fact of the fundamental dislocation of the actor's world as taken-for-granted which results from changes in his status dimensions. There are two implications of this discussion: first, that change is a crucial social variable; and second, that it is something to do with change which through reflection enables the actor to dispense with taken-for-granted, limited and partial assumptions about the world. Thus, on the second point, Mannheim (1936, p. 95) says that the actor is enslaved by a particularistic and partial point of view until he reached the crisis which brought disillusionment. Not until the moment, when he for the first time conceived of himself as being a part of a larger concrete situation, would the impulse awaken in him to see his own activities in the context of the whole.

It is as a consequence that Eric Hoffer points out the paradox of revolution, the paradox of the apocalyptic intention to transform, to remake the world in one's image. Revolutions are normally thought of as intended to bring about radical change. Whether they do or do not there is no doubt that it is radical change which presages revolution. Where life has not changed, where the social world continues in its Schutzian bliss, there will be no attempt to change it.[21]

I now want to provide some greater specification of what it is that has changed, rather than simply to indulge in the monotonous incantation of the homily that it is change that produces change. Earlier we discussed the way in which there are three bases of power, and how each actor can be located along dimensions related to each of them. If then we ask what it is that changes, could we not argue that it is the actor's rankings along these dimensions of power? Thus, the initial and a necessary condition for the expression of dissent is the radical dislocation of an actor's power rankings. It is not simply that there is incongruence (as is detailed in the status inconsistency literature), since that can normally be accommodated within the actor's taken-for-granted assumptions about the world. It is rather that a radical and unexpected change occurs. The change is one that serves to shatter the structural underpinnings of the everyday world. Normally that world is relatively unchanging because it is validated by parameters that likewise are unchanged and unchanging. What we are talking of here, a radical power dislocation, is where solutions are no longer typical and unproblematic, and experiences cannot be subsumed beneath the stock of knowledge at hand. New perceptions, cognitions and evaluations of the world are now appropriate.

I must emphasize that it is not simple discrepancies between the power-rankings which are important, most significantly because there is a continuous strain to interpret them as part of an everyday world. It is changes within them which are crucial since they serve to dislocate the customary allocations of power which are part of the actor's world as taken-for-granted. But surely, it may be objected, is it not part of the experience of most actors that there is dislocation and change? Although this is correct, what I am arguing is that the changes I am concerned with here are those so acute and unexpected that customary accommodative mechanisms are ineffective (see Sampson, 1966). Thus the degree of power dislocation is a variable, the criticalness of value depending upon the particular actors within the given society. Most actors place a high emphasis upon their ranking along all three dimensions, but it is characteristic of very particular subcultures that no subjective meaning is accorded to certain of the dimensions. I am now going to outline the three forms of power dislocation. Although I shall confine my attention to the analysis of the situation of actors who highly value all three dimensions, it takes no great intellectual gymnastics to extend the analysis to the two and one dimension cases.

The first situation is one where there is a radical and acute transformation of the customary relationships which have been established. This transformation may be due to either an increase or a decrease of power along one or along two dimensions. What is important is not the average, or overall, bundle of power possessed by an individual but whether the effect of the changed relationship is to upset his accepted world. This point is more clearly seen when one considers the second type of power dislocation. This occurs when an actor's ranking along all three dimensions changes; again, it does not matter at this stage in the analysis of dissent whether there is a generalized increase or decrease. But it should be noted that such changes may relate to other stages of dissensual development and so one cannot presume that the same outcome necessarily follows from a generalized and radical increase as from a similar decrease. The third form of power dislocation is more specific and complicated. It results from the actor's passage from childhood to adulthood. The degree to which this is problematic depends on the environing society. It is characteristic of certain societies that for those within specialized educational organizations, there is a long period of transition by which an actor's childhood power rankings, based on his parents' power and on his own educational progress, are transformed into adult rankings. When one talks of the high power of the student, one is essentially speaking of his high potential. If there is a failure to realize this potential then there is intense power dislocation. In the first two situations, what produces dislocation is a gap between expectations and reality. What is distinctive about the genesis of expectations in this third case is that they do not derive from actual power rankings in the past and the present, but rather, from the rankings of others (i.e. his parents) and from his idiosyncratic educational development. The world-as-taken-for-granted of the student is one premised upon this transformation. Thus the significant inconsistencies will be those arising only from the *failure* to realize one's expectations, along one, two or three dimensions.[22]

There are a number of points to note about this account. The first is that the discontinuity has to be substantial because once adulthood has been reached most experiences can be located adequately within the interpretative categories of one's accepted world (see Brim, A1966, p. 37). The second point is that such discontinuities are relative to the assumptions made within that society, or subsociety, about the passage of time. This is crucial to the analysis of this sort of experience which can only be seen as discontinuous for actors if one knows beforehand their assumptions relating to the amount, the rate and the probability of temporal change. Third, and most crucially, this account of power discontinuities relates to the discussion above of self, identity and career. An actor's identity is invested in certain career experiences, which vary, both as to the degree to which they are perceived as a single process which gives meaning to one's life, and as to the degree to which, as a matter of fact, the various experiences are integrated. Different careers exhibit different necessary changes and experiential discontinuities, different relationships between the past, the present and the projected future, different sets of objects of audience reference, which validate the actor's long-run self-conception and identity. Furthermore, various cooling or marking out processes serve to prevent certain unexpected discrepancies from proving psychologically dislocative for the actor. The analysis of power emphasizes the social base of an actor's career and identity. The notion of power discontinuity shows the way in which such established and validated identity may be fundamentally upset because of the dislocation of the actor's self-conceptions relating to his major social positions.

The analysis at this point has to move ideally in three directions at once. First, I need to give an account of the objects of normative reference to which particular actors have related, are relating and will relate. Second, I need to show the consequences of power discontinuity for the actor and the possible outcomes that may follow. Third, the actual structural configurations which realize such dislocative experiences should be detailed. The first of these was outlined in chapter 3, the second is detailed in the rest of this chapter and the third will be briefly mentioned now.

I have shown that a major variable in the analysis of society is that of the contradiction. But I did not indicate the way in which such contradictions may adhere together to realize situations of dissent. What is crucial to the perspective here is that dissent is not taken to follow automatically from the existence of contradictions, or of their particular aggregation. Nevertheless, I do want to argue that there are specific additions of contradictions which produce situations highly problematic for those with power within the given society. But why, it can be asked, may dissent follow? The answer is that the existence of particular contradictions which coalesce together

105

have certain consequences both on the ability of the powerful to exercise their power and on the less powerful since they produce situations of power inconsistency. As Lenin famously says:[23] 'Only when the "lower classes" do not want the old way, and when the "upper classes" cannot carry on in the old way – only then can revolution triumph.'

In this book we are mainly concerned with why the 'lower classes' do not want the old way, although we should point out that the two aspects mentioned by Lenin are interconnected and that at the end of this chapter we will very briefly discuss a few simple points relating to why the 'upper classes' cannot carry on. Thus mainly we shall be concerned to specify whether the contradictions aggregated together do or do not realize situations of power inconsistency for significant numbers of actors. I want to make the following distinction: contradiction(s) that do realize power inconsistent situations for significant categories of actors – and contradiction(s) that do not realize such situations. I will term the latter a 'single-bind' contradiction(s); the former 'double-bind'.[24] I think that the phenomenological psychotherapeutic analogy is justified because in the case of dissent the 'bind' refers to the degree to which the situation of the powerful is problematic. Thus a 'double-bind' situation is a set of 'unresolvable sequences of experiences' (see Bateson, 1956, p. 253) in which no matter what the powerful do, including no change of policy at all, they cannot avoid disrupting the everyday world of significant categories of actors. This also follows whether or not the centre perceives this to be the situation, since even if it does there are still inherent constraints upon the powerful resolving it (see Laing, 1967, p. 95; Kaldor, 1964, p. 265). There are two differences between the 'double-bind' situation of the schizophrenic and of the powerful in society. The first is temporal. In the former, there is a long-run persistence of an insoluble 'can't win' checkmate situation. In the latter, there is an aggregation of contradictions at a point in time. But although this makes the latter less problematic because the situation of the powerful is likely to improve in time if it can maintain at least some of its power, its position is more difficult in other ways. This is because the notion of 'double-bindness' is based upon the prohibition of the victim's escape from the field (Bateson, 1956, p. 254). Yet it is precisely the making of such an escape that resolves the impossible for many in schizophrenic situations. But this is not a feasible solution for the powerful if they are to remain in power.

A 'single-bind' situation, on the other hand, occurs where the existent contradictions do not adhere together to produce power discontinuities in themselves for significant numbers of actors. To the extent to which such discontinuities occur they result from the powerful inappropriately responding to the 'single-bind' situation and they do not follow necessarily from the nature of the contradiction(s). The importance of the notion of 'single-bind' is in showing that contradictions do not necessarily produce power inconsistency, let alone dissent or revolution. After all, as Howard Parsons points out (1965, p. 100), contradictions explain nothing in themselves since they merely set the stage and provide the framework for the events that follow. The first part of the explanation of such events has been outlined above. Particular configurations of contradictions lead to particular situations of power inconsistency such that there may be a dislocation of an actor's taken-for-granted world. The second part, the specification of the meanings that actors give to these experiences, is what follows.

Comparisons

If we are to provide a theory of comparative reference we must first of all develop an explanation of social perception.[25] This is simply because a particular social phenomenon cannot be an object of comparison unless it is perceived by the actor in question. There are many reasons why the patterns of social perception are not necessarily isomorphic with the underlying social reality. There is a high degree of selectivity because of the unstructured, ambiguous and wide-ranging set of options involved. No actor could or would want to perceive the entire structure of reality. He is necessarily selective both in terms of his own notion of self-esteem and of the structured context within which he acts. Further, the relationship between these is historical so that various sorts of selectivity are precluded because of acquired patterns of perceptual experience. The contextual constraints may be divided up into those derived from intellectual facilities, those derived from social organization, and those derived from the value system. They are differently relevant depending upon whether the actor in question is a member of or has some contact with the potential object of perception. Where he is so implicated then the most persuasive constraints are organizational and intellectual. The latter, incidentally, is clearly related to the level of education enjoyed by the individual in question, although even where this is high, there are still certain perceptual constraints that may be salient.[26] Where, on the other hand, the possible social object of perception is one with which the actor has no immediate contact the constraints are even more considerable. Thus the following all reduce the possibility of perception: social and physical distance between the actor and the object; low saliency of a particular dimension to the actor concerned; and the paucity of a precise distinctiveness of specific social objects.[27] Runciman neatly summarizes these points by maintaining that in his study 'a correspondence with the facts is least likely of all among those who are in fact most unequally placed' (A1966, p. 210).

It is now necessary to consider the relationship between such patterning of perception and the social comparison processes which follow. Initially I will concentrate on two studies of comparative reference processes (although only one makes this explicit) which do attempt to explain actual historical dissent rather than to plot certain a-structural, a-historical reified configurations of social comparisons. Rosenberg adumbrates three sets of conditions which minimize the chances that a deprived actor will perceive and compare himself with those less deprived (see Rosenberg, 1953; Williams, 1963). First, the hierarchical character of the modern large-scale workplace heightens the probability that aggression will be focused upon the immediate personal source of frustration, while its multifunctionality promotes a sense both of idiosyncratic diversity rather than unity and of the possibility of satisfying inter-class interpersonal experience. Second, there are similar political constraints (mainly applicable to the USA): territorial political representation, the competition for votes among all classes and multiple group affiliations. Finally, there are various other conditions related mainly to the USA: the lack of clearly visible life-style differences, the homogeneity of mass communications, the pursuit of individual goals which may lead to intra-class enmity, and identification with a past, a future, or a distorted present self. Thus following this analysis it is not surprising that there has been only limited dissent in the USA. Lipset and Trow (A1957), on the other hand, argue very differently. First, they note that the nature of a particular social structure induces the making of some comparisons rather than others. Thus, the more rigid the structure, the more likely it is that comparisons will be intra-class rather than inter-class, and the less rigid, the more the discontent that will result. Therefore they maintain in the 'open-class value system' of the USA with its 'egalitarian ideology', workers will more probably define inequalities between themselves and others as illegitimate and will thus dissent *more* than workers in Europe with their 'more rigid systems of stratification' (ibid., p. 401).

I think the apparent contradiction between these two arguments can be resolved by noting Lipset and Trow's conclusion (ibid., my emphasis): 'An egalitarian, "open class" value system with its less rigid social structures may actually engender *more immediate discontent* among low socio-economic groups, than does a more rigidly stratified structure.' In other words, one set of structural conditions (as in the US) leads to high short-run discontent à la Lipset and Trow, and low long-run dissent à la Rosenberg. The alternative set realizes low short-run and high long-run dissent.[28] This is a very significant argument which relates both to Schutz's claim as to the incoherence, partial unclarity and contradictory quality of man's knowledge for acting in the world (1944, pp. 500–1), and to the suggestion above that a single actor can exhibit a dual consciousness. He may possess two or more sets of attitudes and given the particular situation, one rather than another may be manifest in action. The argument derived from the previous section of the chapter is that it is a radical power discontinuity which brings about this attitudinal substitution.[29]

Thus if there are two sorts of dissent, one short-run and immediate, one long-run and more status group or class conscious, there is an implication that there will be two sorts of comparative reference. That this is so can best be shown by turning to Merton's analysis of the comparisons made by non-combat men overseas in the American army (see Merton and Rossi, A1957, pp. 241–5). He maintains that although attention was directed towards the way they compared themselves with combat men overseas and non-combat men at home, this does not mean that the latter pair (ibid., p. 243):

> constituted the *only* ones with which *any particular individual* among the overseas combat men [should be non-combat men] compared himself. He may indeed have compared his lot with that of numerous and diverse others – a civilian friend in a cushy job back home, a cousin enjoying life as a war correspondent, an undrafted movie star whom he had read about in a magazine. But such comparisons by an individual, precisely because they involve personal frames of reference, might well be idiosyncratic. They would not provide contexts *common* to (many or most of) the individuals in the status of overseas noncombat men. To the degree that they are idiosyncratic, they would vary at random among the various categories of soldiers.

Although this is an interesting argument it is unsatisfactory since no reason is given as to why personal comparisons should be necessarily idiosyncratic. And although it is clear that the object of personal comparison differs (brother, friend, brother-in-law and so on), the very similarity in form suggests that there is some common sociological mechanism involved. If so, such comparisons should not be dismissed summarily but must be explained in the same way as the other forms of comparison that interest Merton. Thus it is plausible to distinguish between types of comparative selection.

Two forms are identifiable; they are 'conventional comparisons' and 'structural comparisons'. The former are the customary, day-to-day comparisons by which the actor interprets and evaluates his own position within his everyday world. The latter delimit the feasible range of comparison that an actor may make once that world has been radically dislocated. The explanation which follows is in terms of this distinction. I think that explanatory inadequacies in the past have partly resulted from the failure to distinguish these types. To fail to recognize the difference between the taken-for-granted world and its radical dislocation compresses into one, two ways of being within the world which have different meanings for the actors concerned. Initially and very briefly, I will explain the selection of conventional comparisons.

I provided some evidence to show the significance of propinquity in the selection of comparisons. This is relevant here since I wish to argue that the overall pattern of comparisons will be determined by the actor's social network, that is, all those other actors with whom the individual believes regular interaction occurs.[30] This pattern of comparisons depends upon the closeness or looseness of this particular network.[31] The closer the network, the more limited the conventional comparisons and the looser the network, the wider the comparisons. It is important to note that comparisons do not extend outside the network. Given the fact that self-evaluation is necessary, the individual's objects of comparative reference will be selected in terms of the desire to maintain a harmony of social relations with other actors within one's world. It is when one considers the social meaning of such comparisons that one can appreciate their significance for maintaining the nature of the actor's world as taken-for-granted.

Structural comparisons have a very different meaning for actors since they delimit the feasible range of comparisons that an actor makes given a dislocation of his world.[32] They are not normally made since they are unnecessary for day-to-day existence. They are termed 'structural' because their form is dependent upon the basic structure within which that actor is implicated. Their activation depends upon the radical and acute transformation of the established relationships between the power dimensions in the way set out above. It is this dislocation which upsets the actor's world and which leads to the making of comparisons beyond those normally made in that world – comparisons which are typically unnecessary and psychologically disturbing. Usually there is a continuous readjustment of expectation and reality such that psychological dislocations are minimized. But here what happens is that the incongruence between expectation and reality can no longer be accommodated within customary comparative categories. Further, the process of disjunction itself makes available a new set of comparative categories, the predominant environing structure. It is this which becomes clear to the actors experiencing the disruption and which provides the structuring of their comparisons. This situation cannot persist indefinitely without

the unlikely occurrence of the continuous reproduction of dislocation. Apart from this, there are two resolutions of this situation. The
first is a movement of dissent which is successful in eliminating the
cause by a wide range of policies which dissipate the significance of
the exacerbated contradictions. The second is that as a consequence
of the disturbing character of structural comparisons there is a
gradual accommodation to the power dislocation. The new allocations of power gradually become part of the actor's everyday world,
a world admittedly changed but within which he strives to interpret
and evaluate himself. Thus structural comparisons are brought
about by the dislocation of an actor's world which means that it is
necessary to seek new objects of self-evaluation. What are the
considerations which will determine the way in which such objects
arc chosen? There are two: first of all, the form of stratification
within which the individual acts and second, some similarity of
ranking along at least one dimension between the actor and the
object of reference.

The second point is explicitly supported in the literature. Hyman
and Singer (A1968), summarizing, distinguish between propinquity
and similarity, the former being relevant to comparisons made within
the actor's everyday world and the latter being relevant to the
selection of comparisons in the situation where that world has been
dislocated and the comparison-object is located outside. Thus in the
second case, as Turner (A1955) maintains, the objects that are
taken as bases of comparison will be those which are in some way or
other relevant to a particular aspect of self-evaluation. Hence, even
where there is a radical dislocation of an actor's world, the consequential comparisons will be selected in accordance with the fact that
they are meaningful to the actor concerned. Thus where such dislocation occurs, there are only a limited range of objects with which
the actor may compare himself. There is, however, some dispute within the literature as to whether these bases of similarity have actually
to exist. Hyman argues that the similarity must exist and be perceived. Merton and Rossi (A1957, p. 242) maintain that it must be
perceived or imagined (see also Hyman, A1968, p. 357). In the
latter, the similarity may only be a figment of the actor's imagination.
Although this is tricky it is probably fairly unimportant since the
dimensions we are considering are the three bases of power rather
than, say, notions of personal worth. Nevertheless, I do not wish to
deny that in very a-typical situations, a category of actors may quite
falsely believe that they are the equal of another category, and where
this is unusually the case it will require explanation. Normally, I
want to argue the basis of similarity both exists and may be perceived. There are three other points to make. First of all, there are
only three bases of such similarity (political, economic and cultural

power), that are relevant to the sorts of comparisons I am considering here. Second, I think it reasonable to suggest that within each dimension there are fairly wide bands of similar ranking. Finally, these sorts of processes are only possible in societies characterized by a certain differentiation such that the rankings of an actor may be partially independent of each other.[33]

So far I have argued that for an actor to compare himself with a specific object of structural comparison the following conditions have to be met: power discontinuity as a result of the particular aggregation of contradictions; perception of that object along one or more dimensions; and perception of a similarity (normally real) along one or more of the other dimensions. But even though the environing structure is a crucial determinant in the realization of the patterning of comparisons that follow these points, this structure is crucial in another sense as well. This was suggested above when in considering the nature of comparisons it was observed that following the upsetting of an actor's everyday world, in terms of which self-evaluations are customarily realized, the environing structure presents to the actor a new set of comparative categories. It is the nature of this environing structure, and particularly the nature of its stratification, that is crucial to the formation of such categories. It is at this point that the earlier discussion of stratification is relevant to the analysis.

The first point to note is that since these structures apply on either the societal or subsocietal level, there may be sectors of a society, which is broadly distinguished by one structure, where another predominates. Capitalist society, for example, although mainly characterized by dichotomized work and market structures, contains sectors of multiple status grouping, as in local status systems or even among the entire 'upper' class. A second point is that the notion of class has been used in two ways; on the one hand, as specifying all members of a category in a similar relationship to the economic facilities, irrespective of the nature of the work structure; on the other, that category of actors in similar and overlapping work and market situations. In the following both usages will be maintained. Finally, it is possible to criticize these notions of class and status groupings because they are reified. It could be argued that I am deriving class consciousness simply from the actor's objective position in the economic system. But this is incorrect. First, the notion of a work structure is emphasized specifically as accounting for the way in which the organizations of work are *experienced* and carried within one.[34] Second, I am not arguing that a certain degree of class consciousness follows precisely from a particular configuration of the work and market structures since that would make redundant the theory I am at present developing. What is important

112

is that, *ceteris paribus*, the form of the stratification structure does impose certain significant constraints upon the nature of the comparisons that can be made.[35]

The stratification structure which presents the most dissensual comparisons is that of similar and overlapping work and market structures so that there are two classes in opposing relations to one another. There is a paucity of status differentiation within each class. Once structural comparisons are articulated they are made across class lines and what typically materialize are them and us comparisons. Few total societies have approached congruence with this paradigm but within societies various sectors have show approximations to it. This argument can be illustrated further by noting the similarity between these sorts of comparisons and the way in which, it is argued, society is often seen as a two-class power model.[36] Since I take the development of class consciousness to be processual, one doubts whether even the most class conscious proletarian operates *continuously* a two-class power model within his everyday world. I want to argue that such a model is only salient when the actor's everyday world has been dislocated, when he perceives the other class in a superior position of power and when he compares his situation with theirs.

Lockwood, after his elaboration of the image of society corresponding to the traditional proletarian worker, proceeds to outline the images of society of two other types of worker, the deferential and those living on new estates. The former has a hierarchical image roughly corresponding to the nature of his implicating stratification structure. This consists of a hierarchy of more or less well-defined status groupings within relatively isolated and autonomous communities (see Lockwood, 1966, pp. 254–6; Plowman, 1962). Thus, even if structural comparisons are made here the likely comparison objects will be status groupings just above and below within that particular hierarchy. However, where the nature of such status groups is caste-like it is probable that because there is no basis of similarity between the different castes, comparisons will be intra- rather than inter-status group. This is enhanced by a caste-system which significantly precludes the perception of the attributes of status groups other than one's own (see Sowa, A1962, pp. 58–9 and 63). The importance that status differentiation has in precluding the selection of profoundly dissensual structural comparisons has been noted above. Within the contemporary workplace, intermediation and multifunctionality dissipate potential class consciousness. Further, where a high valuation is placed upon competition between the members of the same class (defined in terms of market situation alone) this tends to produce intra-class enmity; structural comparisons are intra- rather than inter-class, although, it should be noted, this sort of achievement status system is likely to produce more wide-ranging comparisons than the status system within which the deferential worker finds himself. A further point made above is that consumption patterns in the USA do not yield clearly visible and unequivocal differences between the classes. This relates to Lockwood's third type of worker, those living on new estates, whose work and non-work structures do not realize well-defined status groupings but a rather vague and indistinct hierarchy providing only approximate status allocations for most actors. Lockwood suggests that they will manipulate a money-model image of society, that is, diamond-shaped, the only characteristic distinguishing people being the amount of money they possess or earn. Although the structural comparisons within such a structure may be quite broad it is not clear that they possess important dissensual implications. This is because of a failure of the structure to make explicit real distinctions of status groupings or of classes. The resulting comparisons will simply be with categories such as those 'much better off' or 'considerably better off' and not with that status grouping or that class.

One consideration found in the discussion of stratification is that particular categories of actor are in a necessarily contradictory structural location – a well-known example being the non-combatant troops stationed abroad as described in *The American Soldier* (Stouffer, *et al.* A1965). Structural comparisons could be made in two directions at once. Thus the explanation of the political response of, say, the blackcoated worker is complex. If they are to ally with the proletariat it is at least necessary both that the social structure should appear dichotomous and that only one-dimensional upward comparisons are made. The importance of such structural ambivalence will be well seen in chapter 6.

I also want to consider two points that relate to the situation of the powerful within society. First, they may be differentiated in two different ways: there may be either a number of different actors within a single organization, as in the Chinese agrarian bureaucracy, or a number of different groups and collectivities within different workplaces, as in contemporary capitalism. In the former case, although the work structure is differentiated, there is the possibility of the single bureaucracy being taken as the object of comparison. In the latter case there is a high probability of managers *or* landowners *or* technocrats being taken as the comparison object. The second and related point to consider is the degree of cohesion shown by the powerful. Do they self-consciously act together (this is enhanced by a high degree of overlapping membership), or is there a high degree of conflict between the different élites (that is, those with power in each dimension)? Two conditions favouring the former possibility are common processes of socialization and some collective, shared experience prior to and during the acquisition of power.

Three final points should be made about such comparisons. First, I think it plausible to argue that there is a process of learning that is involved in the making of structural comparisons. Thus, each time an actor makes such a comparison the level of object with which it is made will be higher as the various constraints are overcome. Second, it is necessary to consider how easy it is to generalize the comparison from one dimension to another. This is best explored in later discussion, but for the moment we can contrast the situation within a two-class structure, where generalization is relatively unproblematic and the comparison is with another class as a concrete and explicit historical phenomenon, with a highly differentiated status system, where the consequence of multiple group membership is radically to preclude such generalization and status groups are not clearly distinguishable at all. Two implications of this follow. The first is that there is some validity in the cross-pressurization literature but that it is limited is shown by the fact that generalization is only one stage in the genesis of dissent. The second is that in the two-class structure the status congruence of the 'lower' class is much higher, although dissent is also more probable. The third point to be made here is that not only may the form of stratification vary but so also may its scale. The effect of the evident increasing nationalization and internationalization of stratification is to widen the potential object of structural comparison. This has already been seen with respect to the élites of the developing countries who increasingly compare themselves with the élites of the more industrialized societies. In chapter 6 the former stage, that is, the effects of the development of national rather than local systems of stratification will be analysed.

The interpretation

So far it has merely been shown why it is probable that particular actors will compare themselves with particular objects within their social environment and why such revealed deprivation may be generalized. But it will also be remembered that there is a fallacy in much writing on the comparative reference group concept. This is the presupposition that to specify a comparison is to specify a condition of relative deprivation. It was pointed out that the latter does not follow necessarily but depends upon how the actor concerned interprets his experience. Thus Martin Patchen in his study of the response of different groups of schoolchildren to the imposition of various job assignments concludes that although deprivation in comparison with one's fellows may lower personal enjoyment, it does not necessarily lead to dissatisfaction with the existing rules of the group. Consequently, the critical factor is not how one stands relative to others but 'how legitimate (according to certain values) one considers the rules which placed him in that position' (see Patchen, A1968b, pp. 336–7). Whether or not an actor transforms an upward comparison into a condition of relative deprivation and corresponding action depends both upon his interpreting the inequality as unjust and on blaming for this either those more favourably placed or the environing structure and not blaming himself.

Three things can be said about the actor's interpretation of a conventional comparison. First of all, the greater the unfairness in the specification of the values predominant within a network, the greater the sense of injustice and the more likely the occurrence of relative deprivation. Second, the greater the intensity of interaction within the network (that is, the smaller the numbers and the greater the regularity of contact), the less the blame of oneself and of these members. Finally, since these conventional comparisons are part of the actor's everyday existence he will not blame the environing structure for the revealed deprivation. Thus, where there is high interaction intensity, the actor will not hold himself responsible for the inequality since that would be psychologically damaging; he will also not blame his network members since that would produce intense interpersonal conflict within his network; and he will not blame the environing structure because that lies beyond his immediate experience. Where he persists in evaluating the revealed deprivation as unjust, the actor is most likely to conclude that it is all a matter of fate, perhaps supernaturally ordained.

The first point to note about interpretations that follow structural comparisons is that they are not normally evaluated as unjust. Indeed I think it reasonable to argue that there is less probability of an actor evaluating a structural comparison as unjust than is the probability in the case of conventional comparisons. This is because in the latter the intricate patterns of inequality within an actor's network will not be legitimated in detail. In the former there is a continuous attempt to legitimate the organization of any society. Consequently, many of the comparisons that are made are dissensually insignificant simply because the actor interprets the deprivation as more or less justified. To say that is not, it must be emphasized, to say that there are no contradictions between the components of action but only that the values specifically relating to power-legitimation are often not inconsistent with the social organization of the power relationships. I would now like to list certain mechanisms that various writers have suggested which help to legitimate different societies. Perhaps one should begin by Pascal's general comment that: 'Not being able to make that which is just strong, man has made that which is strong just.' As a consequence, Erikson (1968b, p. 59) points out that 'in any system based on suppression, exclusion, and exploitation, the suppressed, excluded, and exploited unconsciously accept the evil image they are made to represent by those who are dominant'. Specific mechanisms which dissipate potential dissent are drama; Aristotle (1968, ch. vi, lines 4–11) says: 'Tragedy ... is presented in dramatic, not narrative form, and achieves, through the representation of pitiable incidents, the catharsis of such pitiable and fearful incidents'; psychedelia, as Theodore Roszak (1969, pp. 176–7) argues, this 'has nothing to do with radical social or cultural attitudes. The practice is simply another safety-valve. If anything, it allows one to bear up under any grim business-as-usual with a bit less anxiety'; the unconscious, which provides, according to Peter Berger (1965, p. 40) a "scientific" legitimation to the adjustment technology without which such a society could hardly get along'; and the dance, of which Frantz Fanon (1967, p. 44) says: 'The native's relaxation takes precisely the form of a muscular orgy in which the most acute aggressivity and the most impelling violence are canalized, transformed and conjured away.'

But for all this, some relationships are judged to be unjust and so it is necessary to indicate who or what will be blamed for the revealed deprivation. That even this may not imply dissent can be seen if we consider the nature of a traditional status system (see Lockwood, 1966, pp. 254–6). Normally, the power inequalities within such a system are legitimated by the society's values. As Sorokin (1964, pp. 534–5) says of immobile societies: 'Since the social position of every individual is predetermined before his birth, the individuals accept this predestination as a kind of necessity. An individual quietly occupies that "box" in the social building in which he is born.' Normally comparisons are not evaluated as unjust. However, even where they are it is probable that blame for any inequality will be attributed principally to the actor himself (there may be a related blame of one's family for not endowing one with culturally empha-sized status signs), or to one's god (since the basis of the systemic legitimations is likely to be religious values, the placing of blame on one's god or gods may be an indirect and culturally permitted way of expressing dissent), or to mankind in general (the outcome of such universalization of guilt being to rule out the possibility of effective action).

Two objects within such a system which are unlikely to be blamed are those who have superior power and the environing structure. Nevertheless, because there is often a high degree of ambiguity, ambivalence and conflict between the values of different collectivities and groups within a society, certain subcultures may provide, in general, counter-definitions of reality, and in particular, alternative criteria for the evaluation and interpretation of inequalities (see

Rodman, 1963). Such socially meaningful counter-definitions are validated by distinctive social processes; and it may not, however, be a simple conflict of values but a different world with a different reality. There are two possibilities; the first is that such a counter-definition remains merely subcultural so that there is only a certain stretching of the societal value system. Marcuse (1969c, pp. 128–9) points out that this may have the consequence, similar to the phenomena described above, that 'it encourages non-conformity and letting-go in ways which leave the real engines of repression in the society entirely intact, which even strengthens these engines by substituting the satisfactions of private and personal rebellion for a more than private and personal, and therefore more authentic, opposition'. The second possibility occurs where the element of conflict *per se* is central to the subsociety. There is a contracultural definition of social reality.[37]

The development of the latter is problematic. One context in which it more easily develops is among the young in an industrial society where the disjunction between the kinship and occupational systems enables experimentation in roles other than family and firm, both of which are for a time implausible objects of identification (see Abrams, 1970). A separate identity can here be validated within the potentially conflictful world of youth, although the alternative identities are often not fully dismissed and merely subcultural interpretations of social reality are found. In adulthood, there is a much greater fixity of one's identity or identities. Probably they can only be changed within an alternative social reality in some way resembling childhood – the idea of revolution has nothing like the pure identity-supporting strength as has the actor's identification with the conventional roles of the existing society (see Abrams, 1968). There are three reasons for this. First, effective revolutionary identity must often be exhaustive and exclusive and may not efficiently entertain accommodation with orientations to other objects of identification. It alone must exercise the total specification of the patterning of an actor's normative reference. Second, a contraculture cannot develop in certain physical or social conditions because either or both the explicitness and the attractiveness conditions of role-taking are not realized, one factor being that sustained social interaction is for some reason impossible. Finally, there are many defences, strategies, consolations, mitigations and compensations which cool out most potential contracultural members. Most importantly there is mobility or the belief in mobility.[38] Thus the higher the actor's expectation that his present deprivation will soon be mitigated through mobility, the less likely is he to combine with others to seek to eliminate its causes.[39] Thus *ceteris paribus*, the less dissent is probable, the greater the overall rate of mobility, including the possibilities of passing;

the degree to which it is generalizable from one dimension to another; the overall rate of geographical mobility, the pervasiveness of the belief in mobility; the probability of individual as opposed to group mobility; the significance of achievement as opposed to ascriptive mobility; and the degree of vagueness of such criteria. It is crucial, however, if we are explaining the interpretations made by particular actors, that these overall features of the environing society are made precise and specific to their idiosyncratic situation. It is irrelevant to talk about the overall rate of social mobility, if, as a matter of fact, these particular actors accurately perceive the impossibility of *their* mobility. A final consideration here is whether or not the potential comparison object is in a constant sum relationship with the particular category of actors being considered. If they are, then the constraints upon perception, comparison and the attribution of blame are less persuasive and may be temporally compressed.

So far I have concentrated on the conditions which increase or decrease the possibilities of blame being placed on either the object of comparison or the environing structure. I now want to indicate the conditions which facilitate escalation, that is, the placing of blame solely upon the environing structure.[40] Two structural conditions are crucial here. Thus the more the relationship between the powerful and the powerless is both interdependent and impersonal, the greater is the degree of escalation. The justification for selecting these two dimensions is that they relate respectively to the form and content of the powerful–powerless relationship. The capitalist workplace, by way of example, is characterized by a significant impersonal interdependence between the proletariat and the bourgeoisie, and it is not surprising that systematic and comprehensive escalation has there materialized. As Marx and Engels (1888, pp. 61–2) say:[41]

> Masses of labourers . . . are organized like soldiers. As privates of the industrial army they are placed under the command of a perfect hierarchy of officers and sergeants . . . they are daily and hourly enslaved by the machine, by the onlooker, and, above all, by the individual bourgeois manufacturer. The more openly this despotism proclaims gain to be its end and aim, the more petty, the more hateful and the more embittering it is.

It should be noted, first, that the explanation here is not of the degree of dissent but of the potential for escalation; and second, that the heightened interdependence of a *personal* nature will customarily lower and not heighten the escalatory potential. The latter point bears out the observation that close, personal relations between the employer and the worker tend to minimize both dissatisfaction and escalation.[42]

Thus far escalation has been explained in terms of a high degree of

119

impersonality and interdependence; I now want to consider the actor's possible responses. He may escalate his dissent through the application of his intellect and through the practice of dissent; as Lefebvre (1968, p. 63) says: 'The opaqueness or transparency of society is thus a social, or rather, socio-economic fact. Only revolutionary praxis by articulating the (true) theory and furthering (practical, verifying) modes of action restores the conditions of transparency.' Of course, most actors most of the time do not realize such innovatory, creative praxis; they live out their lives in terms of what Lefebvre calls repetitive (cyclical repetition of the same acts) and mimetic (in terms of models) modes of praxis. Escalation to a more correct interpretation is highly problematic both through theory and practice. The latter depends on the continuous reproduction of the conditions productive of relative deprivation and dissent. The latter is related to the distribution of intellectual resources. But even if certain actors have escalated their interpretation, is it not likely that they will conclude that since the structure is to blame there is nothing that can be done about it. There is considerable probability that in the face of these man-made phenomena the actor will fail to acknowledge their humanness and hence their changeability. Why some men at some moments of history have not done so is a most significant question. Its answer, I think, lies in two directions; on the one hand, the inexorability of the *status quo* is upset and questioned; on the other, man does not necessarily stand alone against this world but gains in acting in concert with others.

I will very briefly discuss the second point here. I want to introduce the notion of universalization. This is simply the degree to which it is possible for an actor to generalize his situation of relative deprivation to that of others. Thus Lukacs (1923, p. 211) says:

> The individual can never come to be the measure of things, because the individual necessarily confronts objective reality as a complex of inflexible things which he finds ready and unchangeable. . . . Only the class . . . can practically, transformatively, relate itself to the totality of reality. . . . For the individual, objectification and thus determinism . . . are insurmountable;

which is to amplify Marx's claim that: 'The class making a revolution appears from the very start . . . not as a class but as the representative of the whole society' (Marx and Engels, 1965, p. 80). Thus Marx advocates trade union activity because, although it cannot alone remake the world, it can create the basis for social, other-directed proletarian activity. But Marx lays too much emphasis upon organization among the workers as constituting on its own the basis for changing their situation. Brian Barry (1970, pp. 28–9) maintains that it is doubtful whether joining in collective action aimed solely at the benefit of the working class as a whole would ever be in the interests of a single individual. Thus two points need making. First of all, universalization and organization among the workers is only one stage involved in the genesis of dissent; second, Marx elsewhere emphasizes the contribution which intellectuals can make to the leadership of dissent. Given the latter, it is necessary to consider the conditions which not only promote a high degree of working-class consciousness but also those which facilitate universalization between the proletariat and the intellectuals. Thus a general distinction can be made between in-category and other-category universalization. Each of these forms raise an important theme; these can be seen by considering Runciman's distinction between two types of relative deprivation (A1966, pp. 33–5). Egoistic deprivation results from the actor's position within a group; fraternal deprivation from the group's position within society. The first objection to this distinction is that, besides the failure to indicate what constitutes a group, it is presumed that if an actor is deprived in comparison with other groups within society, this must necessarily be a fraternal form of relative deprivation. That is to say, the reification of the notion of the group leads to the presumption that in-category universalization is unproblematic and is assumed automatically. The second objection is that Runciman does not consider whether there is possibility of a temporary or permanent coalition between members of different groups. But that there are such possibilities does not mean that other-category universalization is unproblematic. Indeed, it may well be the case that the conditions which render this more feasible are the very conditions which would weaken the degree of in-category universalization.

Examples of dissent

I want to try initially to substantiate the argument so far by indicating how dissent or the lack of dissent in a number of different social contexts can be explained by application of the previous theory. Very briefly I should say that my intention here is not to derive certain propositions from the theory, to test them in the real world and then to argue that the theory is verified or refuted. My procedure is different from this in two main ways. First, because of the problems of verification, falsification, operationalization and so on, I do not think that this does provide a test of the theory concerned. Second, I think that this account minimizes the importance of theoretical terms in the process of knowledge production. What I wish to argue is that there are two stages in such production. The first is the elaboration of a systematic theory, a full working through of the

121

relationships between the theoretical terms. The second is the use of such theory so as to describe and explain events and phenomena in the real world. My aim is not to develop a general theory which is then (hopefully) verified by the apparent features of the real world. It is rather to explain the nature of that world by recourse to the theoretically established relationships. I will begin by showing how we can more adequately understand the lack of revolutionary consciousness among American workers.

Thus Bendix and Lipset (1963, p. 81) claim that the majority of Americans believe in the 'rags-to-riches' myth. Mizruchi (1963, p. 83 and *passim*) maintains that there is both a belief in the American Dream of equal opportunity for all who have ability and that the lower classes fairly accurately perceive the obstacles to their own mobility. Chinoy (1955) similarly argues that the automobile workers that he studied both had not given up the value of success but had reinterpreted it in terms of the search for security, the accumulation of personal possessions and the success of their children (see also, Keller and Zavalloni, A1964; Rodman, 1963). There is a lower-class value system (see Hyman, 1966) in which they '*insulate themselves*, limit their outlook and range of comparison' (Lane, 1959, p. 38). Without the upsetting of the world there is no reason for actors to compare themselves with those more distant. This point is emphasized both by Mizruchi who finds that the underprivileged American has low aspirations, and by Reiss and Rhodes who conclude that only a very small percentage of working-class adolescents ever compared themselves with those with a more affluent life-style.[43] Furthermore, even if such comparisons are made, the resulting interpretations need not be dissensual. Robert Lane (1959, pp. 42–5) finds prevalent the sentiments that the upper classes deserve to be upper even if life is a lottery, and that the lower classes deserve no better than they get because of their lack of education. He makes three further points. First, the underprivileged generally find it less punishing to consider themselves correctly placed by a just society than to see themselves as the victims of an unjust society. Second, most people are much less interested in the existence of equality for all than they are about the existence of *some* opportunities for mobility. Finally, an emphasis upon consumption channels discontent into intra-class consumption rivalry, into conflict within the everyday world of the acting American: 'The Great American Medicine Show creates consumer unrest, working wives, and dual-job-holding, not antagonism toward the "owning classes"' (Lane, ibid., p. 50; see also, Potter, 1954; Williams, 1963).

One sector of American society, the American Negro, has been generally excluded from such consumption rivalry. I want to consider one explanation of the growth of Negro dissent which uses the perspective of relative deprivation. Pettigrew contrasts the 'actual gains' of the Negro since the war with his 'psychological losses' and explains the resultant dissent in terms of the differential.[44] One point to note is that this account focuses on changes in the short-run situation of the Negro and not upon processes inherent within the structure and long-run development of American society. Most especially it neglects the contradictions between the caste status system of the south and the developing capitalism of the north, and between the value systems of black and white America. I think that it was the consequence of such an aggregation of contradictions that realized a significant power discontinuity for very many Negroes, especially after the end of the Second World War. Pettigrew notes two features, a massive migration from the south to the north and from the country to the towns, and a fairly radical improvement in economic rewards.[45] Such dislocating experiences increased the probability that Negroes would come to compare themselves with the whites in general. This was also helped by the easy visibility of the white American because of his skin colour, and by the clear-cut inequalities along at least two dimensions between the white man and the Negro.[46] Martin Luther King realized the force of such comparisons made by the Negro: 'The Negro lives on a lonely island of poverty in the midst of a vast ocean of material prosperity . . . and finds himself an exile in his own land' (quoted in Pettigrew, A1968, p. 348).

Regrettably, Pettigrew does not explain why this comparison should be interpreted as unjust. On the one hand, there are the values of American society which are not totally implausible for many Negroes and which provide some legitimation of power inequalities.[47] On the other hand, social mobility, including both passing and sexual mobility (that is, attainment of a highly valued white woman) is highly improbable for most, geographical mobility from the ghetto practically impossible, the existence of the southern Negro subculture may provide the basis for contracultural definitions of social justice, and the high level of Negro education (except in comparison with whites) provides the intellectual facilities for escalation.

Whether or not Negro dissent will transform itself into Negro revolution remains to be seen. That working-class dissent did not bring about revolution in nineteenth-century Britain is still puzzling to some commentators. Although we cannot provide a full explanation of this I think that certain interesting points emerge from considering why there was prolonged working-class dissent in Oldham in the early nineteenth century. It was the very a-typicality of the situation there which shows how improbable was a working-class revolution in Britain.

First, we should note that periods of power dislocation were significant for most urban dwellers and industrial workers over this period.[48] Second, John Foster (1967, pp. 20–20a) suggests two crucial considerations related to the patterning of structural comparisons; whether or not there were a resident bourgeoisie and a unitary labour subculture.

On the latter point, Engels (1889, p. 568) argued that even within capitalist society there is 'the social division of society into innumerable gradations, each recognized without question, each with its own pride, but also with its inborn respect for its "betters" and "superiors"'. More specifically, Foster says of comparisons within such a partially legitimated status system (1967, p. 3 and *passim*):

> This type of reaction . . . protected people from irrelevance
> within society at large by allowing them to build up smaller
> subcultures with their own small-scale versions of success.
> Consequently, to avoid disruptive comparisons, the members
> of each sub-group had to have roughly the same lifechance, and
> thus, the same type of job, income, and pattern of expenditure.

Oldham, on the other hand, was quite different from this. Here there was practically no segregation and sub-grouping; one indication of this being the fact that marriages between the families of labourers and high-paid craft workers were far more frequent than in Shields (where there was no class conflict) and a little more frequent than in Northampton (where there was some conflict).

Of the bourgeoisie, Foster says of Northampton (ibid., p. 9):

> As a community, therefore, Northampton had none of the tight
> completeness of Oldham; ultimately almost everyone's boss
> lived over the horizon. Nor had it the simplicity. The three
> sectors produced tory hoteliers and lawyers . . .; whig dissenter
> corn and wool dealers; and radical garret masters.

In Shields there was no resident bourgeoisie and it appeared that entry to the élite in the town was easy (ibid., p. 13, see also Robbins, 1965, pp. 48–9). By contrast, Foster says 'while mid-century Shields and Northampton each had less than a dozen men who would leave £25,000 or more personally, Oldham had over seventy; and many of these would leave a great deal more than £25,000' (ibid., p. 19). The consequences of such a 'resident bourgeoisie' were that they were much more easily seen and compared with. Also, the fact that their origins were local meant that there was a similarity of cultural power. Generalization to the political dimension was unproblematic. The high degree of impersonal interdependence between capitalist and worker heightened the probability of escalation. The perceived lack of mobility prospects closed off one way of overcoming a situation of relative deprivation.[49] Finally, all these considerations heightened the probability of in-category universalization.

In the nineteenth century it was thought that part of the basis for radicalism was the fact that workers were extremely poor. We have seen though that poverty is not a sufficient explanation of radical political and economic attitudes, although this book is based upon the premise that 'relative poverty' is a necessary condition. That a certain wealth is in fact the basis for developing radical attitudes among workers is the surprising argument most systematically developed by Andre Gorz. I want to consider here just one aspect. This is the claim that the wage demands of semi-skilled highly paid men working in large-scale factories are 'more frequently motivated by *rebellion against working conditions* than by a revolt against the economic *burdens of exploitation* born by labour' (1965, pp. 334–5; 1967). But Gorz himself details reasons why this is unlikely. He talks of 'the opaqueness of the productive process as a whole, and the worker's ignorance of the economic and technical decisions which determine their conditions of work' (1965, p. 324); '[the] extreme differentiation of working conditions and wages within the same industry and for the same work' (ibid.); and through consumption mobility 'the assertion of the possibility of a purely individual liberation by the acquisition of the means of escape'.[50] This last point is particularly relevant and relates to the importance which Alberoni (1946) attaches to the 'powerless élites', those who constitute objects of popular admiration, imitation and collective attachment, yet who are not themselves at the apex of the national status system, do not constitute a class, and do not possess significant power themselves.[51] Thus, if comparisons are made with the powerful, it will be this 'powerless élite' who will be the object of comparison, yet, as Alberoni points out, they are not objects of envy or resentment. And even where this does not occur, simple consumption competition is very much conflict between actors in their daily worlds: 'that powerless, anarchical solitude of separated individuals ... manipulated in their individual behaviour-patterns by the technicians of "hidden persuasion"' (Gorz, 1965, p. 346). Finally, I want to consider dissent among the peasantry, both to elaborate the argument here and to provide a basis for discussion in part 3. Again I want to focus upon specific aspects. Marx's classic statement on the French peasantry (Marx, 1926, pp. 132 and 133) is highly limited because it is relevant only to a specific configuration of relationships between the peasant and the wider society. There are two aspects.

The first is very well brought out by Hamza Alavi's distinction between three types of rural economy: non-cultivating landlords and cultivating sharecroppers classed as *poor peasants*; independent small-holders who own the land they cultivate themselves as *middle peasants*; and capitalist farmers, *rich peasants*, who employ others, namely, agricultural labourers, or *poor peasants* (1965, p. 244). In other words, he does not concentrate solely upon the obvious class interest of different categories of peasantry and deduce their degree of dissent simply from that but rather, he locates each type within their local economic structure. He concludes that it is not the poor peasant who is initially the leading force of the peasant revolution with the middle peasant coming in later when its success is guaranteed, but rather the reverse. It is the middle peasants who are initially more revolutionary, their objects of comparison being either richer peasants or urban capitalists. The poorer peasant is much more dependent upon his paternalistic master, especially in times of crisis; even where he may murder his master under exceptional circumstances it is unlikely that he will dissent with the system itself.[52]

The second aspect I want to consider is Barrington Moore's analysis of the relationship between these various rural economies and the wider society (1967, p. 459).[53] First of all he maintains that:

> A highly segmented society that depends on diffuse sanctions
> for its coherence and for extracting the surplus from the
> underlying peasantry is nearly immune to peasant rebellion
> because opposition is likely to take the form of creating another
> segment. On the other hand, an agrarian bureaucracy, or a
> society that depends on a central authority for extracting a
> surplus, is a type most vulnerable to such outbreaks.

This argument can be re-expressed. An agrarian bureaucracy is more prone to dissent because the relative lack of differentiation of the powerful means they are more visible to the periphery and more likely as an object of comparison, the high degree of interdependence and the lack of 'religiously tinged caste codes' (ibid., p. 458) means that there is a probable evaluation of the inequality as unjust and the outcome of the structure, rather than say, one's god, and the lack of a high degree of segmentation increases the probabilities of universalization.

A further point appears contrary to the theory here. Moore says that 'where the links arising out of this relationship between overlord and peasant community are strong, the tendency toward peasant rebellion (and later revolution) is feeble' (ibid., p. 469). Thus the links were tenuous in both China and Russia and peasant upheavals were endemic. But for Moore, the argument that the links are strong implies two further points. The first is that there should not be resource competition between the overlord and peasant; the second is that the overlord and/or priest should be members of the village community for which they perform services and for which they are fairly remunerated (ibid., p. 471). Thus the argument that strong links between lord and peasant do not produce dissent is an argument that there is no double-bind situation and that the power relationship is legitimate. Further the corollary of this argument, namely that where there are weak links, more dissent results, surely relates to the previous point. Thus in China and Russia much dissent resulted from the strong links between the central bureaucracy and the peasantry. It is because this bureaucracy is an object of comparison for the peasantry that there has been persistent peasant dissent and it has nothing directly to do with the weakness of the links on the local level. Moore himself almost reaches this conclusion since he points out the significant contradiction implied for the local lord–peasant relationship by the spread of the state and the intrusion of the market.[54] The first factor meant that the overlord lost his function of protecting the peasantry and so would appear illegitimate; the second factor meant an increase in the lord's need to squeeze the peasantry (Moore, 1967, p. 473). The disturbing nature of the power dislocation brought about by the latter is seen clearly by Moore (ibid., p. 474):

> Economic deterioration by slow degrees can become accepted by its victims as part of the normal situation. Especially where no alternative is clearly visible, more and more privation can gradually find acceptance in the peasants' standards of what is right and proper. What infuriates peasants (and not just peasants) is a new and sudden imposition or demand that strikes many people at once and that is a break with accepted rules and customs.

The similarity between Moore's argument and the theory above is also seen if we consider the process of universalization. He points out that it was necessary to have an approximate minimum of property to be a full member of the Chinese village and hence to be subsumed beneath the conservative influence of kinship and religion. Modernization processes served to increase radically the numbers below this minimum, within which there were no significant constraints upon in-category universalization. No such categories were excluded in this way in Japan and India. Similarly, he points out that the contemporary peasant village is essentially competitive rather than co-operative and that as a consequence, as Marx described, universalization among the peasantry is problematic.

Dissent and revolution

So far we have mainly concentrated on the genesis of dissent among groups of actors. We have ignored certain aspects of the society in which that dissent occurs, and the conditions that would transform a movement of dissent (what we will call a dissensual movement) into a successful revolutionary movement. To a significant extent I shall not be concerned here to fill these lacunae. For example, I will not define revolution, or criticize the formulations provided by others, although it is clear that I follow the tradition that sees revolution as an 'object overturned' rather than as a 'revolving wheel', as revolution starting history anew as opposed to it re-cycling the same historical spectacle.[55] I wish merely to emphasize three features of revolutionary change.

The first is that it has something to do with changing the power relationships within a society. Thus in the following we will distinguish between the centre and the periphery of any society. The former comprises all those actors who at any time wield power; the latter those actors who do not. We should emphasize that any particular form of society will be characterized by a certain configuration of power relationships (ruling class, or caste system, etc.). The centre–periphery distinction is simply a shorthand way of helping the general argument here. One further point is that the orientation of the centre to dissensual movements will both vary and have consequences for their development. Reformist and revolutionary dissent can thus be distinguished not only from the point of view of the dissenters, but also from the way in which the centre classifies and treats such dissent.

A second point about revolutionary change is that although it may occur quite briefly, it is the outcome of a long process of dissatisfaction, dissent and organization. Thus its explanation requires outlining not simply the factors operative at the time of revolution but rather the complex of conditions responsible for bringing about each stage which is then one condition for the development of the next stage. Two points follow. First, since the dissensual movement is one which develops and operates within the pre-revolutionary society, the changing reaction of the society and especially of its centre to that movement will importantly relate to development through the different stages. Second, the form of explanation implied is what Becker characterizes as sequential rather than simultaneous (1963), pp. 22–3; see also Glaser and Strauss, 1968, pp. 93–4). The latter assumes that all the factors which operate to produce the phenomenon in question occur simultaneously and the preferred explanation consists of that factor or set of factors that best 'predicts' the behaviour one is studying. But as Becker effectively points out, all causes do not operate at the same time and a satisfactory explanation must take as crucial the fact that patterns of behaviour may *develop* in sequence, each stage of which requires explanation. Furthermore, each of these separate explanations is a necessary

128

condition of the particular outcome; and, analogously with Smelser's process of value-addition (1962), that variable which predisposes an actor to take a particular step may not operate because he has not yet reached the stage in the process where it is possible to take that step.

The third point here is that it is necessary to specify the conditions under which dissent and revolution are minimally possible. Willer and Zollschan (1964, p. 133) suggest that there must be something approaching a nation-state with a centralized government for a revolution to occur. This condition could be weakened by maintaining that the centralization need only be regional but this still means that revolution implies both a particular inequality of power which is the focus of dissent and something approaching a society. There are two further threshold conditions which are suggested by Willer and Zollschan's unitary–plurality continuum. A unitary society exists when an élite holds a monopoly of all significant power positions, their legitimation, and the means of access to them. In such a society, they maintain, existing exigencies are easily recognized and controlled. It is only with increasing complexity that there is a highly differentiated complex of exigencies and the establishment of new modes of channelling and controlling their articulation is problematic. Thus dissent and revolution can only result when there is a certain degree of differentiation. There seems to be two relevant dimensions: first, it is necessary that there is a minimum differentiation of Parsons's and Smelser's components of action, and second, the centre of the society must be minimally differentiated.

So far I have talked only vaguely of revolution itself. It is now necessary to outline very briefly certain conditions which will be likely to transform a dissensual movement into a revolutionary movement. A first point to note is that any such movement may be categorized both into whether its desired change is on the level of values, organization or facilities, and into whether its focus is political, economic or cultural. A second point is that any movement is limited organizationally. Where dissent is solely peripheral, the level of dissent will typically be low and the focus non-crucial. Examples are *jacqueries* and expressive movements of facility-destroying violence. Dissent within the centre is crucially affected by the fact that on the one hand, they gain from being members of the centre, but on the other they possess the intellectual and organizational facilities crucial to high-level, escalated, organized dissent. Normally where members of the centre do dissent, it tends to be affirmative of the overall structure, yet may suggest that the societal values are partially inoperative with respect to the other components of action or that changes should be brought about congruent with such values. Such movements tend to be high-level but traditionalistic, or low-level progressive, such as palace or military coups and minor reforms. There are, of course, both solely peripheral and solely central movements that espouse significant non-affirmative dissent. Customarily they tend to be unsuccessful because medium and high level dissent within significant societal areas demands both leadership by the centre and the organization of the periphery.

All such movements may be unorganized, informally organized, or formally organized. By informal organization is meant a movement based on personal confidence; by formal organization is meant the full institutionalization of the dissensual movement *vis-à-vis* its own value system such that there is regularization and regulation according to formal procedures. The degree of organization of any movement depends upon: its ends; its size, its heterogeneity; the inclusion of central categories which both possess more abundant organizational facilities yet because of a greater sense of personal affinity have less need of formal organization; the direct influence of the environing structure, where, for instance, secret societies are a patterning conducive to cell-like organization of dissent; and the reaction of the centre including the possibility of infiltration.

This last point, the reaction of the centre and its capacity for institutionalizing movements has a more general significance. The more movement is likely to be institutionalized, the greater the differentiation of the components of action and of the centre and the less radical the movement in terms of both content and method. An organized radical movement with non-displaced ends is unlikely to be institutionalized. While if organization leads to goal displacement (because of the preclusion of a contra-culture), then the greater the degree of organization, the greater the degree of institutionalization. While the more institutionalized it is, the greater the likely degree of organization and possibly of goal displacement. It follows that a necessary condition for the maintenance over time of a movement espousing fairly radical, non-displaced goals is the persistence of a significant contra-culture.

A further point relates to the question of leadership, most especially of central leadership of a movement with peripheral membership. First of all 'the shaping of belief systems of any range into apparently logical wholes that are credible to large numbers of people is an act of creative synthesis characteristic of only a miniscule proportion of any population'; second 'to the extent that multiple idea-elements of a belief system are socially diffused from such disruptive sources, they tend to be diffused in "packages", which consumers see as "natural" wholes' (Converse, 1964, p. 211).[56] Furthermore, such leadership will be most successful when, other things being equal, its 'style', that is, its approach, stance and behaviour, is congruent with existing value-orientations within that society. Thus, as Marx (1926,

p. 23) says generally of revolutionaries: 'they are eager to press the spirits of the past into their service, borrowing the names of the dead, reviving old war-cries, dressing up in traditional costumes, that they make a braver pageant on the newly-staged scene of universal history'.[57]

Lastly, it is necessary to consider why the revolutionary movement is finally successful. There are two considerations, a failure of social control and the existence of an appropriate precipitant. The first refers to an ineffectiveness of 'codes, courts and constables' or of law enforcement in general and not to all aspects of the social structure which increase or decrease the potential for dissent. Certain sociologies of revolution have neglected this consideration, the importance of which is seen by Arendt, who maintains that 'no revolution is even possible . . . where the armed forces can be trusted to obey the civil authorities'.[58] The second consideration, an appropriate precipitant, is required to explain when and not why revolutions occur.[59] The appropriateness of the precipitant relates to the fact that in some broad way it must be congruent with the nature of the movement which is thought to follow. Thus it is unlikely that a street demonstration can be interpreted by the members of a high-level movement seeking radical social change as indicating that the *status quo* is so dislocated that it will be successful in seeking such social transformation.

Conclusion

There are a number of criticisms that may be levelled against the argument developed in this chapter. I want to consider briefly what these might be and whether they can be refuted.

First of all, it might be said that this chapter is merely speculative since there is little effort to operationalize the terms that I use. But what I have been concerned with in this chapter is the development of theory. I do not claim that the theoretical terms *necessarily* correspond with empirically observable objects in the real world. Rather, I wish to argue that knowledge of the observable contours of that world results from developing and then applying the sort of theory developed here. Thus in part 3 I shall be concerned not to verify the theory but to show how it enables substantive phenomena in the world, specifically, events in Indonesia in the first fifty years of this century, to be adequately explained.

Second, it could be argued that there is very little relationship between parts 1 and 2 of this book. In the former I was concerned with emphasizing how neither the individual nor the society should be seen as superior, and especially with showing how much reference group analysis is reified and neglects the meanings that actors place upon their experiences. In the latter, I have been developing a theory of reference group processes in which a concern with structure appears as primary. But there are two reasons why there is in fact no real disjunction. First of all, I also elaborated the a-sociological, a-structural character of normal reference group analysis. So in this chapter I have attempted to explain certain events and processes by reference to such sociological and structural concerns. But in this I have made it quite clear that the outcome of dissent does not follow simply from the contradictory nature of the social structure. It depends rather upon a number of stages in which actors come to interpret the character of their experience with such structures. Second, we have analysed in this chapter the way in which actors come to respond to the objective reality of society, a reality which is itself the product of the way men have previously acted together. I have outlined how men act in relation to such structures and how they may develop ways of thinking and acting that serve to modify, reform or transform their structurally defined world. The reality of social structure is the unintended product of men acting intentionally together. The way in which such intentionality of acting occurs is through the processes described by the interactionist tradition. The unintended consequences of such acting have been elaborated in the first part of this chapter. The later parts show the importance of the meaning that actors themselves place upon their experience of acting in that world. It is thus to follow the interactionist position that action is not simply released by actors but arises through a meaning-ful, interpretative and intentional relationship to the physical and social objects within their environment. The interactionist tradition is, I tried to show, one in which human activity is seen as social, in which there is no individual or society reductionism, in which some forms of conflict may occur, and in which social phenomena are seen as man-made and consequently delicate, tenuous and changeable.

A third criticism is that the theory is historically unspecific. It is like much of the rest of the sociology of revolution in attempting to derive certain general properties of revolutionary social change and not to provide analysis specific to particular forms of society. Is there any such thing as *the* sociology of revolution? Rather, should we not simply develop different theories specific to different types of society? Now although I agree with the spirit of this argument I do not think that the theory above need preclude such considerations. On the one hand, although I would argue that it is an appropriate framework for explaining mass revolutionary consciousness in most contemporary forms of society, I do not think that it will have been appropriate to all pre-capitalist societies, or that in the future (with the abolition of scarcity?) it will necessarily still be appropriate. On the other hand, the very analysis of structure above is one where it is intended that the explanation of dissent is situated within an analysis focused on the characterization of the form of that society (through contradictions, the analysis of power, stratification and so on). This will be well seen in the next chapter.

The final criticism that I want to mention here is that if I am claiming this to be *the* basis of the sociology of revolution then I am wrong, while if I say that it is merely systematizing and elaborating our way of thinking about certain limited aspects of the theory of revolution, then I have not said anything very important. Now as I said earlier, my aims here are modest ones; but this still might not satisfy the critic who could point out that I never specify whether the stages of dissensual development are necessary or sufficient for revolutionary consciousness. Specifically he might claim that my analysis of contradictions never states quite how many and how intense these must be before they produce a situation of double-bind. I am afraid that I do not have any clear way of resolving the latter problem, although what substantively I see as constituting a double-bind situation can be seen from the next chapter.

My account of the stages of dissensual development provides, I think, a set of necessary conditions of mass revolutionary consciousness in specific types of society and a set which although not sufficient could be the basis for developing such a set. But a critic might go further and point to my failure to describe fully what it is I am trying to explain, what *is* mass revolutionary consciousness? What are the specific types of society in which I try to explain the genesis of such consciousness?

I do not intend here to answer these questions. Rather I shall turn to my attempt to explain the development of the revolutionary consciousness of specific groups of Indonesians during the early part of this century.[60]

part three

The sociology of Indonesian dissent[1]

It should be noted that the following chapter should not be read as a general history of Indonesia up to 1945. There are a number of quite useful and interesting books, such as Kahin (B1952), Palmier (B1965) and Wertheim (B1956) which in different ways give such accounts. Neither is it intended to provide any new information about *particular* events in Indonesian history. In no way does it attempt to do for the twentieth century what Kartodirdjo (B1966) does for the nineteenth century in Bantam. Rather, this chapter should be viewed as an exercise of how one should go about providing an explanation of dissent based upon chapter 5. It is, therefore, a different way of approaching what many historians have already described. But apart from one or two articles by van der Kroef, the account here is, I believe, the only systematic attempt to *explain* why this dissent occurred in the form that it did and why it was at different times successful or unsuccessful. Finally, since I rely mainly on secondary materials, it is perhaps not too presumptuous to quote Weber's justification of the use of such materials in his own comparative studies (1930, p. 28). He says:

> The Sinologist, the Indologist, the Semitist, or the Egyptologist, will of course find no facts unknown to him. We only hope that he will find nothing definitely wrong in points that are essential. How far it has been possible to come as near this ideal as a non-specialist is able to do, the author cannot know. It is quite evident that anyone who is forced to rely on translations, and furthermore on the use and evaluation of monumental, documentary, or literary sources, has to rely on a specialist literature which is often highly controversial, and the merits of which he is unable to judge accurately. Such a writer must make modest claims for the value of his work.

6 Of Indonesian dissent

There are two important points to note about the last few centuries of Indonesian history. The first is that the principal holders of power were mainly members of another society, the Netherlands, and only secondarily, often through representatives, members of Indonesian society. The second is that the primary and continuous basis of this outside domination was economic (see Thompson and Adloff, B1950, p. 165; Furnivall, B1939, p. 449). We can see the importance of these two features in the bureaucratic form of rule found in the archipelago which was continued by the Dutch East India Company and later by the Dutch administration.[2] The stability of these bureaucracies rested upon the allegiance of the periphery to local rulers and of these rulers to the centre proper. Tithes and services were extracted by these local rulers, of which part was rendered in the form of tribute to the centre. This two-tier system resulted in the contradiction suggested by Weber and made explicit by Lockwood between the economic facilities of a patrimonial-type bureaucracy and its social organization and values. Lockwood (1964, p. 254) summarizes the basic contradiction as:

> one of maintaining a taxation system that can effectively
> meet the material needs of a bureaucracy in the context of a
> subsistence, or near-subsistence, economy. The centralising
> goal of bureaucratic institutions is constantly liable to sabotage
> by the potential social relationship structure of the subsistence
> economy which favours the decentralisation and 'feudalisation'
> of power relationships.

Lockwood characterizes the focal point of contradiction in such bureaucracies as 'taxation capacity relative to bureaucratic needs' (ibid.). But there was an immensely added strain when the purpose of that bureaucracy was to meet the interests of the economically powerful outside that particular society. In other words, 'bureau-cratic needs' in the Dutch East Indies were not derived simply from internal interests but were determined externally. This heightened the basic contradiction since the central government was only able to increase its amount of tribute with very great difficulty through suppressing the opposition of local power holders.[3]

There are a number of points to note about dissent within this period. The first and most important was that peripheral dissent was 'endemic in rural Indonesia' (Benda, B1958a, p. 18; see also Benda and McVey, B1960, p. xi): that anarchic protests against the Great Tradition have been 'a continuum in Southeast Asian history';[4] second, on occasions there were temporary coalitions between members of the periphery and local Regent(s); third, dissent was informally organized; fourth, its level and focus was normally restricted; fifth, by the early nineteenth century Indonesian society possessed the structural conditions generally conducive to dissent (Van Mook, B1958, p. 311).

The last point can be seen more directly by considering the idiosyncratic history of the Indonesian archipelago over the last two thousand years. This embraces a subject-matter of profound controversy mainly centred on the degree to which the autochthonic forms of social life had been transformed by the various socio-cultural invasions. The problems involved in characterizing pre-Indic society arise both from enormous variations at any point in time, and from significant changes over time. Nevertheless the following seems reasonably, although over-sympathetically, to encapsulate this history (Alisjahbana, B1966, pp. 3–5):

A belief in spirits and supernatural powers pervaded all aspects of individual and communal life. Thought and action centred round the question of how to get help from the good spirits and how to avert the influence of those that were mischievous or obstructive . . . [in consequence] Economics, law, government and the arts were not isolated human activities; in fact they were so closely interwoven that it is almost impossible to say where one began and another ended. . . . Furthermore . . . all human aims and actions were seen simply as parts of one grand natural process – the cosmic order. . . . Such knowledge could not be gained by instruction [but was] subsumed in the intellectual legacy received from his forefathers, and which he called *adat* . . . communal life was inevitably static and deeply conservative . . . social structure [was] typified by small-scale communities of people in villages or of nomads wandering over a specific area. . . . Really important decisions were taken by collective deliberation.

138

In these circumstances the predominant religious belief-items had the consequence of sacralizing and rendering as unalterable the traditional practices; pre-Indic Indonesia was characterized by Weberian traditional religion where all branches of human activity were drawn into the circle of symbolic magic (see Weber, 1965, p. 71). The fundamental problems of meaning were met in a piecemeal, discrete and irregular way. There was a multitudinous and untidy agglomeration of rituals, entities and images all inextricably inter-dependent with secular custom.

I now want to consider, by contrast, two of Weber's world religions (these are more abstract, logical, general and less interdependent with everyday life) (ibid.; Bendix, 1966, pp. 87–97; Geertz, B1964, pp. 282–7) which have had particularly profound consequences for Indonesian society. The first is that of Hinduism which provided the spiritual base for the great kingdoms of Indonesia which dominated the archipelago for over a thousand years.[5] Geertz (B1968, pp. 36–8) summarizes the tradition of these centres into the doctrines of the exemplary centre, the dissemination of civilization by its display, of graded spirituality, the interchangeability of prestige and sanctity, and of the theatre-state, the extension of power by dramatization. The effect of such Hinduization upon the Indonesian *tani* (peasant) was not so significant as one might think.[6] Thus van der Kroef, (B1951a, p. 30) talks of the 'continuity of native forms of civilisation', and argues that the introduction of Hindu was an attempt to provide legitimation for the dominance of courts and rulers (see also Kerstiens, B1966, p. 33; van der Kroef, B1954a, pp. 98–9). There is a Javanese saying which symbolizes the socio-cultural dichotomy between court and village:

Nagara mama tata desa wama care (the court has culture, the people have their customs).

The main significance of Hinduism was to increase the differentiation of the centre and the distance between central élites. But this was not of major significance for dissent until further changes had occurred which were to transform devastatingly what Geertz (B1968, p. 38) calls the 'magical circle' of 'quietism, ceremonialism, and hierarchism'.

It is important to note that it was not just the intrusion of Islam which was to break through this 'magical circle'. Rather, it was the growth of a trading bourgeoisie who were unassimilable to the Indic world-view; Geertz (ibid., p. 39) says:

The trading groups, organised into separate ethnic quarters centred not upon the local court but on mosque and market, moved easily from one town to next and in and out of the

139

archipelago, and, too busy with commerce to be much concerned with either rank or ceremony, upset the status hierarchy, disrupted the theatre-state, and ignored the exemplary center.

Islam then spread to much of the Indonesian peasantry for two main reasons. First, it became a point of identity which symbolized separateness from, and opposition to, foreign Christian domination (Benda, B1958a, p. 13). Second, such Shiah-infected Islam was not only the easiest religion of conversion but was also not incompatible with existing Indonesian religious beliefs and practices, most especially because there was a considerable mystical component within each (see Landon, B1949, pp. 135 and 138–9; Drewes, B1955). Nevertheless, although Indonesian religion is intensely syncretic, there is much controversy as to the proportionate significance of *adat* and Islam. Van der Kroef characterizes it as 'folk Islam', while Geertz (B1968) describes Indonesian Islam as adaptive, absorbent, pragmatic and gradualistic; never striving to be pure, only comprehensive (see also van der Kroef, B1954b; Landon, B1949). The effects of Islam were, first of all, that it threatened the traditional, hierarchical nature of the village community. This is because in Islam each man is separated from Allah and in this private relationship is given the opportunity to build his own world directed and controlled by himself. Islam is thus more individualistic than *adat* (see van der Kroef, B1954a, p. 76). Second, since it led to the growth of the *kiaji* and *ulama* (religious teachers) Islam introduced a religious élite who challenged the traditional national local holders of secular power (see ibid., p. 195; Benda, B1962a, p. 124). Finally, because of the association of Islam with the growth of trade there was the development of an indigenous bourgeoisie and this enlarged the distance and differentiation between central élites. By the early nineteenth century, Indicism was still predominant among the aristocrats, Islam among the traders, and the syncretic hotchpotch among the peasantry. Islam, which customarily fails to differentiate, here magnified and amplified differentiations which were a potential for dissent.[7]

Similarly, for all van Leur's strictures it is clear that Dutch colonial rule was very significant for the ultimate development of dissent (see van Leur, B1955, pp. 150 and 289). For almost two hundred years the archipelago was ruled by the Dutch East India Company whose principal interest was in the maximization of long-term profit. And although the Dutch, because of mercantile, Calvinistic and republican values, disliked the ostentation and arbitrariness of the rule of the *kraton* (court centres), they soon reached a *rapprochement* with these aristocratic elements (see van der Kroef, B1963c, pp. 77–9). Further, since the influence of the Dutch did not extend beyond the traditional élite, they did not directly affect the 'village sphere' (see Burger, B1957). For example, practically no money at all circulated within the eighteenth-century village since native products were procured from the chief and not by payment to the villagers themselves (see ibid., p. 1). The consequence of Dutch domination[8] was first, on the old Mataram empire which crumbled and culturally turned inwards – Burger (B1956, p. 13) summarizes such introversion: 'the refinement of court life to a high degree, the splitting of language into "high" and "low", the exaltation of etiquette, the refining and stylization of the aristocratic way of life' (see also, van der Kroef, B1958a, p. 357). Second, Dutch domination precluded further development of an indigenous bourgeoisie and of urban trading centres. Finally, as the Company's power grew even more secure, the regents became increasingly regarded as mere officials (see Palmier, B1960b, p. 207).

The exaggeration of the contradiction between bureaucratic needs and taxation capacity reached significant proportions by around 1800. Contributing factors were the growing demand for income from the Netherlands, the increasing cost of policing and administering the archipelago, and the need to reverse the trend of declining native welfare. In response the centre, represented first, by Daendels under the Dutch and second, by Raffles under the British, attempted limited defeudalization.[9] This served to heighten both the fundamental facilities–organization contradiction and to realize another between defeudalization at the organizational level and feudal collectivism and communality at the value level. The best evidence for the latter was that although a number of private estates developed during this period (non-feudal), they acquired both their land and labour by collective contract with indigenous chiefs or nobility (feudal collective values) (see van der Kroef, B1963c, p. 17). The former contradiction, that between the facilities and social organization, was of more dynamic significance. This is because the very reason why defeudalization was initially necessary was because of the increasing inefficiency of the subsistence-based tax-gathering facilities in relation to the needs of the central organization. But this very inefficiency however following Lockwood sabotaged the centralizing goal of bureaucratic organizations by favouring the potential social relationship structure of a subsistence economy, that is, decentralization and feudalization. Thus the response of the centre in asserting defeudalization was to attempt to reverse this at the organizational level – however, to the extent that this was realized, there was an exacerbation of the initial contradiction. Clearly, different categories were differently affected by the defeudalization necessary to re-establish a balance between the demands of the central organization and the capacity of a taxation system, based within a subsistence economy,

141

to meet them. In the pivotal position were the Javanese Regents who had gone through a process of intense charismatic routinization implied by the policy of defeudalization. As a consequence their ranking along all three dimensions was radically lowered and since for them the other conditions of dissent were operative they were able to ensure that 'a radical defeudalisation was still quite impossible' (Burger, B1957, p. 2). The Java War of 1825–30, which although lost by the Regents, led to their regaining former rankings along all three dimensions of power.

Dutch policy radically changed in 1830. Their attempt to break out of the patrimonial bureaucratic-type contradiction had been a failure; not only because of the feudal reaction of the Javanese Regents but also because of the ever-growing deficits of the Indonesian budget.[10] These deficits arose both because of the inefficiency of the tax structure and because of the increasing pressures for more effective Dutch exploitation of the resources of the archipelago (see Day, B1966, p. 244; Geertz, B1963a, p. 63). In consequence, the possibility of strain of 'taxation capacity relative to bureaucratic needs' was minimized by the financial success of the refeudalization of 1830 known as the Culture System (see Day, B1966, pp. 259 and 309–10; Geertz, B1963a, p. 53f; Gonggrijp, B1949, p. 111) – the Regents were given land grants, their office was made hereditary, and in common with lesser native and new European officials, were given a percentage of the crops collected by the peasantry. The consequence of this for future agricultural–industrial development within Indonesia was a rigidification of the existing structure. This finalized the contrast between Java and the Outer Islands, accentuated the dual economy pattern of western and eastern economic enterprise, and prevented indigenous agricultural modernization (see Geertz, B1963a, pp. 52–82; Gonggrijp, B1949, p. 111; Day, B1966, p. 259; van der Kroef, 1963c, p. 25). All of this resulted from the fact that, although the Culture System helped to launch the estate sector in significant form,[11] the peasantry were not part of it. Estate-working was just something they were obliged to do in their spare time. In their own time, they multiplied and 'take-off' was into rapid and sustained population growth (see Geertz, B1963a, p. 69). Thus the particular nature of the mutualistic relationship between indigenous and estate production had the consequence of presenting the Javanese *tani* with but a single set of alternatives in view of the rapidly expanding population (ibid., pp. 79–80):[12]

> Driving their terraces, and in fact all their agricultural
> resources, harder by working them more carefully. There was
> no industrial sector into which to move and . . . none
> was developed. . . . The Javanese could not themselves

become part of the estate economy, and they could not transform their general pattern of already intensive farming in an extensive direction, for they lacked capital, had no way to shuck off excess labour, and were administratively barred from . . . the so-called 'waste lands' which were filling up with coffee trees. . . . Wet-rice cultivation, with its extraordinary ability to maintain levels of marginal labour productivity by always managing to work one more man in without a serious fall in *per-capita* income, soaked up almost the whole of the additional population.

Thus the effect of the system was a quantitative intensification of the existing socio-cultural structure. Wertheim (B1956, p. 289) talks of social ossification and petrification and says that although there was 'an intensive exploitation of the Indonesian labour force . . . the social structure was artificially preserved by the colonial policy in its original state'. The essential 'corporate communalism' (Wolf, B1957, *passim*) of the Indonesian village, where responsibility was shared, where *gotong rojong* expressed the common responsibility of the members towards each other, and where things were done for the whole community by the whole community, was intensified rather than reduced. Simultaneously, the peasant was increasingly precluded from gaining contact with the market economy. Van der Kolff (B1936) talks of how this system 'does not promote the development of a strong farmer class within its sphere of influence' (p. 123); hence 'no prospect exists for the development of a strong and prosperous peasantry' (p. 124). One final effect was that there was an increase in the inequality of political power within the village coincident upon such relationships assuming a substantially more authoritarian character (see Wertheim, B1956, p. 140; Kahin, B1952, p. 13).

Contradictions were thus building up during the period of the Culture System but they had not yet realized a situation of 'double-bind'. This was only to develop with further economic changes that began in 1850 and were significant by 1870.

Pre-war dissent

Multiple contradictions

It has already been seen that the primary objective of Dutch colonial policy was the economic exploitation of Indonesia. This had the corollary that Indonesian economic development was harnessed almost solely to the interests of those with economic power in the Netherlands (see Geertz, B1963a, p. 141). Nevertheless as Boeke

143

(B1942, p. 181) shows the form which this demand took has varied considerably over the period of Dutch rule:

In the beginning it was the trade capital of the mother country, then its industrial capital, and finally – recently – capital invested in the economy itself. . . . The aim of trade capital was to bring and sell goods; that of industrial capital to sell its own products; that of colonial capital to produce colonial products. The first kind of capital made use of the population mainly as suppliers, the second as purchasers, the third as labourers . . . the third and most recent, colonial-capitalism . . . has chiefly determined colonial policy since about 1860.

The development of the last policy came about for two sets of reasons. On the one hand, external demands in general and Dutch demands in particular radically increased. This was so, first, because of a rapidly growing demand for various raw materials and food-stuffs exerted by the European countries undergoing their capitalist industrial revolution. Further, Dutch interest was heightened by the increasingly acrimonious division of the non-European world into antagonistic spheres of interest. And third, there was the rapid development of the steamship and the opening of the Suez canal which significantly enhanced the potential economic importance of the archipelago to both European and North American markets.[13] On the other hand, there were certain factors related to the internal development of the Indonesian economy. As Reinsma points out (B1955, p. 157), the rise of the Corporate Plantation System was largely self-generated since the Culture System had been only too successful in transforming the critical sector of the facilities component, that is, for economic export. Similarly, Geertz (B1963a, p. 83) maintains that at least in terms of sugar production, colonial management became very much less of a matter of mobilizing labour than of regulating the symbiotic relationships between the highly capitalized sugar 'factory', or other such enterprises, and the Indonesian *desa* (village) (see also Burger, B1957, p. 7). In pursuance of this objective the Dutch passed the Agrarian Land Law in 1870, which, with ancillary enactments, made possible the rapid expansion of private enterprise while at the same time prevented the outright alienation of land to foreigners (Geertz, B1963a, pp. 83–4). Thus Callis shows that these nineteenth-century changes in the Indonesian economy had the effect of increasing investment in the years 1900–37 from 318 million US dollars to 2264 million dollars. In the same way, Thompson and Adloff have pointed out the fact that during the pre-war years the Indonesian economy supplied one-sixth of the national income of the metropolitan society.[14]

The external imposition of this capitalist transformation of the Indonesian economy realized a double-bind situation by the end of the century. This was because of the exacerbation of the contradictions of a patrimonial-type bureaucracy and that within the value system between the West and Islam. But it also led to 'the gigantic contradiction between the stage of development of capitalist methods of production . . . and the medieval state of the country' (Althusser, 1967, p. 20).[15] I must explicate all this in detail.

The first consequence was that the economic power of the Dutch was now derived from the profits of private development rather than from public levies. Thus taxation capacity was lowered at the same time that there was added expenditure needed for communication and policing especially within the Outer Islands (see Vlekke, B1959, p. 313). Thus there occurred 'a vicious decentralisation of power' (Lockwood, 1964, p. 254), the most significant consequence of which from the viewpoint of the Dutch administrators, was the increasing inefficiency of the native administration.[16] Prior to the nineteenth century any incompetence had been less important because of the essentially charismatic rule of the Regents.[17] However, as a result of the long period of routinization, the criteria of evaluation were rational-legal rather than personal, and signs of inefficiency were grounds for questioning the legitimacy of the administration (see Schrieke, B1955, pp. 193–4). The Dutch had two main alternatives. The first was to replace the indirect by a direct system of administration; to some extent this occurred but it could never be a *general* policy. The second was to improve present and future indigenous administrators, both by greater encouragement of their participation within certain consultative bodies, and by improved education. This strategy was the basis of the Ethical Policy during the first quarter of the twentieth century.[18] There were two further implications of the shift from product levies to regressive taxation.[19] It was a very significant and more easily perceived burden placed upon the periphery;[20] and it implied the necessity for more efficient administration.

The second contradiction exacerbated during this period was that within the value system. Although there had been various Islamic led revolts in the eighteenth and nineteenth centuries, these did not exhibit unified opposition to the Dutch, mainly because of a lack of interdependence between the Dutch centre and the Islamic periphery. As a consequence of this, although the centre and the periphery lived within the same society, they adhered to different and potentially conflictful value systems. With the late nineteenth-century expansion of the economic facilities, there was a highly significant increase in centre–periphery interdependence, both within Java and in the Outer Islands.[21] The reaction of Islam to this multidimensional expansion of Dutch power was threefold. First of all, both trading and peasant

145

Muslims coalesced in at least temporary coalitions against the Dutch; Islam was beginning to function as a pre-nationalist ideology (see Wertheim, B1956, p. 88; Vandenbosch, B1952, p. 182). An interesting example of such Islamic inspired dissent was the Saminist movement which began in 1890 in Central Java; there are two points to note about it. First, it was partly an expression of the peasantry wishing to lead their lives unmolested and to return to a communal form of organization (see Kahin, B1952, p. 43). Second, its millenarian and messianic characteristics very clearly show how it was a pre-political response to the intrusion of the West.[22] The second Islamic reaction was the gradual shedding of some of its more mystical syncretic characteristics (see Benda, B1958a, p. 17; van Niel, B1960, p. 43). Finally, many Muslims became increasingly devout and interested in Islam and pan-Islam, evidence for this is provided by the growing numbers making the pilgrimage to Mecca (see Benda, B1958a, p. 17). Although these latter two responses were not unique to Indonesia, they were particularly significant because of the colonial situation and the enormously widespread commitment to Islam.

The Dutch were increasingly worried by such developments. By 1899 and the appointment of Snouck Hurgronje as Adviser on Arab and Native Affairs, they believed that pan-Islamism was the most serious threat to the continuation of their rule.[23] Hurgronje partially moderated these fears by denying that the 'priests' in Indonesia were members of a religious hierarchy and executors of the Caliph's will, by emphasizing the non-fanatic quality of Indonesian Islam and by stressing the continued importance of *adat*.[24] He thought the dangers of Islam for Dutch rule could be minimized by two policies. The first was to separate the religious and political aspects of Islam. Towards the former the Dutch would practise neutrality, towards the latter, increased vigilance (see Benda, B1958a, pp. 23–4; B1958b). The second and more significant policy was to try and associate Indonesians with Dutch culture – an inevitable development if Indonesia was to become part of the modern world (see Benda, B1958a, pp. 26–7). Thus again, as an outcome of an exacerbated contradiction, a great stimulus was given to the expansion of western education.

A further contradiction heightened during this period was that between the highly capitalized colonial enterprise and the communal forms of indigenous production (see Godelier, 1967, p. 104). I mentioned above that the Culture System rigidified the already existent corporate communalism of the Indonesian village. To some extent changes in this period altered this on the facilities and organizational levels of action. This had two consequences. On the one hand, there was a growing contradiction between the communal nature of the values and the increasing individualism of the other components.

This showed itself to the Dutch administration in the fear that the level of native welfare was diminishing (see Burger, B1961, p. 321). On the other hand, because of the increasing symbiotic relationship between the indigenous peasant and the foreign capitalist it finally became evident that no large-scale indigenous bourgeoisie was going to develop – that is, although there was some development of private property relationships,[25] the owners of property were not going to be indigenous. No such bourgeoisie developed because the Javanese nobleman in general would not, and the Indonesian *tani* could not, take part in economic life on a significant scale (see Burger, B1956, pp. 22 and 24). The lack of such development by around 1900, coupled with the clear fall in native welfare since the onset of the liberal period, led to a significant change in Dutch colonial policy. They now maintained that the centre should interfere in village life not to protect the individual freedom of the villager against the village government but to strengthen corporate village life and build up the village community through the care of public welfare (see Furnivall, B1935, p. 48; Wolf, B1957). But it is important to emphasize that if a group of dynamic native entrepreneurs had developed, the centre would not have gone nearly so far with their welfare policies as they did (see Burger, B1961, p. 329). Thus it was as a direct result of the contradiction between foreign capitalism and small-scale indigenous production that the development of a significant Indonesian bourgeoisie was entirely prevented. And it was precisely because of this that the Dutch had to interfere to a far greater extent in the internal workings of the Indonesian *desa*.

Power dislocation

I have outlined the 'double-bind' contradictory situation which had developed by the end of the nineteenth century. The Dutch policy pursued for the first twenty years of this century was based upon the following policies: increased taxation, because of the reversal of the Culture System; the encouragement of participation, because of increasingly evident native inefficiency; religious neutrality, so as to combat pan-Islam; vast educational expansion, because of native inefficiency and to combat pan-Islam; and the strengthening of the village community, because of growing capitalist intrusion. Such policies, combined with previous social processes, had three effects: the lack of an indigenous bourgeoisie, the expansion of Dutch power at the village level, and the development of capitalist facilities and organization. The first four policies and the last two effects relate to changes in the actors' power rankings (the other points relate to further stages of dissensual development). Thus, increased taxation led to intermittent reductions of economic power, greater political participation increased political power without any rise in other dimensions, and religious neutrality raised the cultural power of the *kiaji* and *ulama* without any necessary rise in other dimensions (see Kartodirdjo, B1966, p. 61).

The expansion of education brought about profound and complex consequences.[26] First of all it acted to change the primary means of attaining cultural power for the Indonesian and especially for the Javanese *prijaji* (gentry). Previously within Java, an actor's cultural power had been dependent upon the degree to which he appeared Javanese, the degree to which he appeared pure, refined, polished, polite, exquisite, ethereal, and civilized (see Geertz, B1955-6, p. 153). But now an increasingly important criterion of cultural power was the attainment of certain degrees of western education. However, that radically reduced the cultural power of already established *prijaji* and semi-*prijaji*. Their response was the *Budi Utomo* movement designed to advance Javanese people and culture.[27] Yet it was clear that it had little chance of success because the criteria for the attainment of cultural power would be increasingly western.

The effects of this can be more explicitly expressed. Thus the nobility, previously high ranked with respect to all three power dimensions (although all had been similarly diminished in the nineteenth century), experienced, first, a diminution in their cultural power (this led to the *Budi Utomo*), and second, a new basis of cultural power, western education. Thus the nobility now had to share such power with the Dutch as well as with the *kiaji*. And the previous quasi-automatic coincidence of their power rankings no longer existed: or more specifically, there was a failure of economic rewards to rise coincidentally with the rise in cultural power dependent upon western education. The last point resulted from the structure of realistic possibilities open to the newly educated *prijaji*. A career in trade was prevented by the lack of industrialization, the control of big business by the Dutch, the control of small business by the Chinese, and by the Indic world-view which derogated trade and emphasized state service.[28] The effect of western education in no way undermined this world-view. Rather, it significantly increased the numbers wishing to undertake state employment. Two consequences followed: very great unemployment,[29] and intense economic discrimination, the native being paid less and having much lower chances of promotion than a corresponding Dutchman (see Kahin, B1952, pp. 33-5). Thus the effect of Dutch economic, political and cultural predominance was that its values were pre-eminent. Yet even if the Indonesian fully adhered to them he was still partially excluded, he could not transform an object of identification into an object of membership. Most importantly, within this period there was the failure to maintain previously realized levels of economic rewards. This was important because the increasing development of a two-class structure placed the *prijaji* in a singularly ambivalent position. As the lowest status group within the 'upper class', any fall in the relative economic position threatened their entire situation as members of that class, especially as their position there was not validated by the possession of any productive property. Two factors in this period heightened the probability that there would be a fall in their economic rewards. The first was a decree issued some time after 1910 which specified that senior administrative positions should be filled only by Europeans and Eurasians, and that Indonesians should be restricted to the Indonesian Civil Service. The latter 'did not include, nor with rare exceptions lead to the senior administrative positions' (Palmier, B1962, p. 20). The second factor was the non-existence prior to 1921 of Connecting Schools. This meant that graduates of Second Class Native Schools were unable to make the transition to the regular, westernized, secondary school system. Thus of the thousand or so who were interrogated after the Communist dissent of 1926–7, three-quarters were literate, none had been to college, four-tenths had been to Second Class Native Schools, and over a tenth claimed to have suffered lengthy unemployment.[30] The decline in economic rewards in the 1920s is shown specifically by the importance of elementary school teachers in the West Sumatran dissent who had not been paid for five or six months, and generally for the periphery by the rising import prices, falling wage-rates, falling indigenous prices, declining welfare expenditure and rising land and income taxation.[31]

Perception

It is evident that by 1900 the limitations upon perception were being radically reduced. This was so both because of structural changes and because the expansion of education weakened intellectual limitations.

Clearly, among the aristocracy the Dutch were visible and there were no important perceptual constraints upon the formation of *Budi Utomo*. *Sarekat Islam* (SI) is more interesting here. It was formed by Javanese merchants undergoing a diminution of economic rewards that was brought about by the activity of Chinese merchants in the archipelago who in 1901 formed the *Chuang Hua Hui Kuan* and upon whom internal travel restrictions were gradually lifted from 1904–11 (see Wertheim, B1964, pp. 39–82; Purcell, B1951). Vishal Singh (B1961) maintains that as a consequence they clashed with the status group with whom they were in closest contact, the Indonesian batik traders, especially in Central Java where there was a long-established trading community (see also Benda, B1958a, p. 47).

Thus as a result of 'the suddenly increased impingement of aggres-sively competitive Chinese entrepreneurs upon the interests of the vestigial Javanese merchant class' (Kahin, B1952, p. 67), the former were perceived as a status group with superior economic rewards. The membership of *Sarekat Islam* grew rapidly after its foundation in 1912. One reason for this was that the Chinese were very important in the villages as professional moneylenders, shopkeepers and traders, and were thus easily perceived by the Indonesian *tani*.

But there were certain structural changes occurring that increased the likelihood of the Dutch being perceived as the main constituent of the centre. Before I outline these it is necessary to emphasize the conditions that still hindered such perception. First of all, there was the fact that only an infinitesimal percentage of the population had experienced even three years primary education. Furthermore, Gillin (B1952, p. 197) talks of how 'the Indonesian universe is spatially limited and its horizon typically does not extend beyond the limits of the local community or region' (see also, Wolf, B1957). There is thus a high degree of local-centrism in the Indonesian village. Another point is simply that there were a relatively small number of Dutch-men in the archipelago. Even by 1930 there were only 100,000 and this again reduced the likelihood that there would be perception of the Dutch by the Indonesian peasant (see Smail, B1961, p. 89). Finally, an important structural consideration was the high degree of independence between the Dutch centre and the Indonesian periphery. Although the notion of a plural society is somewhat misleading, the fact that the interdependencies which did exist were between the Chinese and the periphery economically, and the indigenous aristocracy and the periphery politico-culturally, emphas-izes the high degree of Dutch centre-Indonesian periphery inde-pendence.

To an important extent the lack of interdependence between centre and periphery was the result of involution, of what Geertz (B1963a, p. 90) calls 'the shared poverty system'. But this process was in itself a reaction to 'the impingements of high capitalism'. Thus, the growth of such capitalism could not but bring about some increase in the degree to which the Dutch were perceived by the Indonesian as a significant possessor of political, economic and cultural power. Burger (B1961, p. 328) summarizes: 'around the year 1800 the eco-nomic policies of the Dutch authorities had exerted an influence on the upper strata of Native society, during the period of the Culture System on the village headmen, and with the advent of the modern colonial society on the masses'.

Economically, this arose out of two processes: cash crop produc-tion and the growth of estate and quasi-estate employment. Generally speaking on Java (or more correctly on Inner Indonesia) (see Geertz,

B1963a) quasi-estate employment and cash crop production were most important, while on Outer Indonesia, estate employment was most significant, although there was some development of cash crops (ibid., p. 103). In the latter case, one would have dramatically affected the indigenous *swidden* producers such that they would have perceived the power of the Dutch.[32] It was really only amongst the coolies on the estates, who were imported from Inner Indonesia, that such perfection would be clear. Geertz (ibid., p. 103) summarizes this development: 'There, the enclave, not the mutualistic, pattern was flourishing, a true proletariat was being forged from a mass of imported coolies.' There were also points within outer Indonesia where 'peasants moved towards agricultural specialisation, frank individualism, social conflict, and cultural rationalisation' (ibid., p. 123) – the best example of this was in Menangkabau in western Sumatra where the peasant became an 'acquisitive business man fully enmeshed in a pecuniary nexus' (ibid., p. 122), although this was a-typical (see also, pp. 116–23 in general). Within Java, apart from employees in new technical industries (see Tedjasukmana, B1959), and among individualistic peasants as in Bantam (see Benda and McVey, B1960, p. xx), the Dutch were improbable objects of perception. This was so even where there was a symbiotic relationship between the estate production of sugar and indigenous rice production. This was because of the idiosyncratic involutional response of the Javanese village; the Javanese cane worker 'remained a peasant at the same time that he became a coolie' (Geertz, B1963a, p. 89). The 'communal ownership' of the village was strengthened since this enabled the mill to treat it as a whole through its agent, the village headman. It is because of this indirectness of economic power that the average Indonesian *tani*, even where he was part of the rice-sugar symbiosis, did not clearly perceive the economic predominance of the Dutch. It was far more likely that he would perceive the village headman and the local aristocracy as economically predominant. Yet, on the other hand, perception of the Dutch was even less likely among *sawah* cultivators non-symbiotically related to sugar-estates. In their case, involution resulted in a productive system of 'a dense web of finely spun work rights and work responsibilities spread, like the reticulate veins of the hand throughout the whole body of the village lands' (ibid., p. 99). Geertz lists the following sorts of labour agreements that were found: sub-contracting, renting, pawning, jobbing, work exchange, collective harvesting and wage work. In this 'advance towards vagueness' the likely object of perception would be other members of the village, perhaps the village head, but certainly not the Dutch who were ultimately responsible for the oddness of their agrarian development.

Political and cultural perception derived largely from the increased intrusion of the Dutch in response to certain of the economic consequences outlined above. Again, however, we must not overestimate the significance of this. Burger (B1961, p. 323) argues that a large part of the Ethical Policy was effected through intermediation by the village authorities and by means of the traditional village structure. If anything, the policy simply seems to have increased the visibility of the indigenous rather than that of the Dutch political power structure. Wertheim (B1964, p. 214) suggests that the new welfare innovations were mainly introduced in the conventional, aloof and authoritarian way by means of *perinteh halus* (gentle commands). Thus the experience of the Indonesian *tani* was predominantly to increase the visibility of the village headman, whose enhancement of political power acted as a buffer between the Dutch civil service and much of the agrarian population (see Kahin, B1952, p. 57). Of course, certain actors in certain structural locations were able to perceive the Dutch as politically predominant; but this was much more probable among the centre. Here it tended to result from the widening gap between what the Dutch promised and what was actually fulfilled. Thus van der Kroef (B1951b, pp. 375–6) writes of the *Volksraad*:

> The long series of conflicts with the government, the
> absence of more fervent nationalist leaders (like Soekarno),
> the constant abridgement of the *Volksraad's* authority
> with respect to the rights of investigation, interpellation,
> and petition – these resulted in a growing conviction in many
> political circles that the *Volksraad* was but an outlet for the
> relief of excess oratorical or administrative 'steam'.

Similarly, conclusions could be presented with respect to the other quasi-representative councils initiated by the Dutch.[33] In general, the gap between promise and fulfilment made it clear to the Indonesian centre that their political power was, relative to the Dutch, profoundly chimerical.

The perception of Dutch cultural power was probably only possible for the Muslim leaders and for those members of the centre who had highish cultural power. This was so, first, because such power implied that they were educated alongside the Dutch both in Indonesia and especially in the Netherlands (see Kahin, B1952, p. 50); and second, because the perception of such Dutch power necessitated a highish degree of intellectual understanding. It should also be noted that the cultural power of especially the local Dutchmen was extremely limited and so it is probable that if a comparison was made, it would be the cultural dimension that would be the basis of similarity. It is now necessary to consider the making of comparisons in more detail.

Comparison

Although there is no necessary isomorphism between the patterning of perception and the patterning of social comparisons, it would be reasonable to argue that the perception by the Javanese merchants of the economic superiority of the Chinese was accompanied by the making of comparisons with them. This was because the radical and acute diminution of economic power of these merchants was sufficient to bring about structural comparisons, and that because of their implication within the particular status system where the Chinese were closest to them, that is, equal in political and cultural power and superior in economic power, they were the obvious object of comparison. A similar analysis can be applied to the comparisons being made by the periphery; thus it was the Chinese moneylenders and small traders who constituted the initial object of peripheral comparison, brought about by the decline in their economic rewards from 1913 onwards. The comparison was possible because the Chinese were similarly ranked in terms of political and cultural power and only enjoyed superior economic rewards, and arose because it was the Chinese and Indian partners of the colonial system who more directly interfered with the life of the peasant than did the western authorities or entrepreneurs (see Jacoby, B1948, p. 247).

There was not, therefore, a perfect two-class structure in Indonesia; in particular the foreign orientals reduced the probability of comparisons with the Dutch since they acted as 'a buffer between Europeans and the Natives' (Furnivall, B1935, p. 33). But apart from this the essential feature of the overall structure was that 'the social classes tend to coincide with racial lines and that the social mobility from class to class is very low ... a society characterised by vertical stratification rather than vertical integration' (Emerson, B1942, p. 30). Wertheim (B1964, p. 220) consequently characterized it as a 'colour caste' system of stratification (see also, pp. 39–82). Although he acknowledges that among the natives there were both landless labourers and medium-sized landowners, the isolation of the whites at the top meant that the rest could be considered as the 'mass of the population' (see ibid., pp. 220–2). Part of the reason for this was that the internal function of the 'closed corporate community' was 'to equalize the life chances and life risks of its members' (Wolf, B1957, p. 12). This increased the likelihood of the Dutch being taken as the object of structural comparison. But, on the other hand, the Indonesian did everything possible to avoid becoming a full-time wage-earner, largely because this involved leaving his village community. Thus in the depressions of both the

1920s and 1930s, most of the economically destitute were supported by their village (see Thompson, B1947, p. 131). This is specifically confirmed by a government survey which found that between 1913 and 1924 there had been such a sufficient expansion of arable land that the *per capita tani* holding remained the same.[34] Of course, some peasants did compare themselves with the Dutch: where this was so it was due to the growing intrusion of money into the everyday world of the Indonesian *tani*. Van der Kolff in his 1922 study of five *sawah* complexes in Southern Java (see B1936, p. 25) maintained that the general development lay in cash transactions playing the main role in the tilling of the soil. But even this effect should not be overemphasized since during the depression, for example, the rural economy was able to revert to barter at very short notice (see Thompson, B1947, p. 131).

Thus for most Indonesians (at least within the periphery) the predominant stratification structure within which they were implicated was a local one in which the Dutch were not normally an element. They were thus not comparison-objects, except where Indonesians were located within very distinctive stratification structures in which there was an adjacent class or there were reasonably adjacent status groups comprised predominantly of the Dutch. The main locations were those of coolies, workers in modern industry, especially transport, the *prijaji* and semi-*prijaji*, and the small indigenous, commercial bourgeoisie. Apart from these, however, when structural comparisons were made they would probably be made with richer peasants, the Chinese, or local aristocrats.

Most of this discussion has concerned itself with comparisons along the economic dimension. But there was a significant change within the structure of political–cultural power which rendered comparisons along these dimensions as also possible; but this was only so for those who had perceived the Dutch as here predominant. The change resulted from the fact that the new guiding principle was that of welfare, and that this was to be realized not indirectly but through the giving of a greater freedom of action and autonomy to the Dutch government in Indonesia (see Furnivall, B1935, p. 34). That is to say, since there was a radical shift of political–cultural power from the metropolitan to the internal Dutch centre, comparison might now be made with the major holders of such power. Previously, when the locus of such power was in the metropolitan society, comparison with the predominant holders was highly improbable.

Generalization

Where the object of comparison was the Chinese, because of the roughly coincidental ranking of both the Indonesian *tani* and the

Chinese trader along the political and cultural dimensions, there was a high probability that there was no generalization of the economic deprivation experienced by the Indonesian. But where, on the other hand, the Dutch were the object of comparison, both the two-class structure and the non-differentiating Islamic heritage facilitated the probability of generalizing the deprivation to another dimension. Paradoxically, this was more probable among the periphery where the lack of intellectual resources prevented them from distinguishing between the Dutch government and Dutch economic interests.

Interpretation and escalation

Wertheim (B1964, p. 35) criticizes the application of Furnivall's notion to a plural society of Indonesia by maintaining that: 'The dominating group has called into life a hierarchical system of stratification according to race which it succeeds in imposing upon the social structure, and which has been, to a certain extent, internalised by the members of the dominated groups.' Indonesian culture, in other words, when it was evident that the Dutch were going to remain, reacted by a process of myth creation in which Dutch power (along all three dimensions) was legitimated and integrated within the stories which set out to explain the origin of the Javanese ruling dynasties. Similarly, the Javanese aristocracy rationalized their dependence upon the Dutch by making their king and themselves descendants of the Dutch monarch.[35] Thus there was some legitimation of Dutch power and this meant that it was quite possible for a revealed inequality to be held to be just. But there are three reservations to note about this statement.

The first is that the apparent value agreement at this level did not mean that there were not fundamental disagreements of values, or of world-views, held by different elements of Indonesian society. We have already drawn attention to the contradiction within the value system between Islam and the West. Second, the Chinese were not integrated within this socio-cultural context and as a consequence the Javanese could reach the conclusion as to 'how their own economic progress was being hampered by the Chinese traders' (Singh, B1961, p. 51). Finally, changes were occurring within Indonesian society which were to render the legitimation of the Dutch as less effective. This can be seen first of all on the structural level. There are two types of relevant change; these relate to the degrees of interdependence and impersonality. In terms of the former, the independence of the Dutch centre and the Indonesian periphery has been noted above, but it is clear that the economic and political expansion at the turn of the century increased the degree of centre-periphery interdependence, although perhaps not *pari passu* with the

155

expansion (see Furnivall, B1935, pp. 39–40; Wolf, B1957, p. 7). The change within the quality of this interdependence is easier to judge; there is no doubt that it grew increasingly impersonal. This can be seen first, from the fact that while in 1870 practically all Europeans had been government officials, by 1890 their numerical strength had fallen below that of private enterprise employees (see Vlekke, B1959, p. 314). Second, and related to this, there was in the twentieth century, a highly significant influx of European-born Netherlanders. Vlekke (ibid., pp. 375–6) maintains that:

Most of these immigrants came with no intention of settling permanently in the tropics. They hoped to serve their term (the average was twenty years) and then to return to enjoy their pension for another twenty years or more. . . . From now on, a distinction was commonly made between the 'trekkers' and the 'blijvers' among the Dutch in Indonesia. . . . The 'trekkers' were those who came to serve their 20 years after which they planned to return home as quickly as possible. The 'trekkers' were not interested in colonial politics.

This is emphasized by the decline in the numbers of mixed marriages.[36] Van der Kroef (B1963a, p. 31) summarizes: 'in the opinion of many observers the various component parts of the Indonesian plural society had, in the present century, the tendency to have less, rather than more, informal interpersonal and intercultural contact with each other' (see also. Lasker, B1950, p. 221; Schrieke, B1929, pp. 237–8). We will now consider what was the importance of this for the periphery.

The first point to note is that the peasant takes for granted the arbitrary, unanalysable, and controlling character of the world about him. He presumes that it is natural, given and unchanging, and he does not consider the possibility that it might be transformed, that social phenomena could be different from what they are. The peasant reifies everything that is about him. Therefore, if we are concerned to explain peripheral dissent in the Indonesian archipelago we must commence by asking what it was that ever led the world to be seen in partially de-reified terms. That this is problematic is clear especially when we consider two further aspects: Javanese socialization processes and the all-embracing Islam. We will consider them in that order.

Thus in Java there is a very strong tendency to treat the new born child not as an autonomous human being but as a toy or an automaton (see M. Geertz, B1959a; B1959b; Hagen, B1964). The child is seen as having no inner resources for his or her own development. Socialization thus consists of protecting, restraining and controlling the child so that he or she feels that it is dangerous to use initiative or to

156

rival authority. There are heavy and pervasive sanctions against change and emotion. The child, at least after the age of five, becomes docile, restrained, formal, controlled and most important of all, respectful. The last characteristic is learnt within the nuclear family in relation to the father, or rather in relation to the status of the father. It should be noted that it is utterly crucial that the individual must come to show respect, although, as a matter of fact, he need not feel it at all. Thus *sungkan* is the feeling of respectful politeness before a superior or an unfamiliar equal, it is an attitude of constraint, or the repression of one's emotions so as not to disturb the equanimity of the other. This sort of distanced performance is ideally suited to the colonial situation. But this makes it more difficult to judge the legitimacy of Dutch rule. This emphasis on the *showing* of respect allows for quite pervasive subcultural interpretations and identities to be validated simultaneously within the context of the Dutch belief in the authority of their rule. Thus although the general effect of Javanese socialization was conservative, it also had this important distancing effect. Islam also had contradictory effects.

The content of such Islam was 'a strong other-worldly attitude and political passivity' (Eisenstadt, 1962, pp. 291–2), and its form was of relatively low 'force' and high 'scope'. The last point arises because in Indonesia 'almost everything is tinged, if lightly, with metaphysical meaning, the whole of ordinary life has a faintly transcendental quality about it, and it is rather difficult to isolate one part of it in which religious beliefs, and the attitudes derived from them, play a more prominent part than any other' (Geertz, B1963a, p. 112). But it should be noted, that that does not mean that religion did not have potentially disintegrative effects. Geertz (B1957, p. 49) shows that even in the 1950s in urban Indonesia (specifically in the town he calls Modjukuto), the *kampong* residents shared a common, highly integrated cultural tradition: 'kampong people . . . culturally . . . are still folk'. This has had two rather significant consequences. First of all, there had not been a general disintegration of the communal pattern of social relationships in the countryside or in the *kampongs*. Second, within the latter, and the former to the degree to which capitalist, individualistic changes had penetrated the countryside, there developed 'an incongruity between the cultural framework of meaning and the patterning of social interaction, an incongruity due to the persistence in an urban environment of a religious symbol system adjusted to peasant social structure' (ibid., p. 53). Thus, there was a rather complicated two-pronged effect. On the one hand, there was no significant shift in the structure of values which thus had important organizational consequences. While, on the other hand, there was the development of a marked incongruity between the social organization of rural, folk Islamic Indonesia and the increasingly capitalist urban Indonesia. The second of these consequences meant that the former legitimation of the high power of the Dutch, the *prijaji* and the village headman could no longer be taken for granted. Nevertheless, because of the indirect nature of Dutch rule, for there to be any examination of its legitimacy it was necessary that the legitimacy of the Indonesian representatives in general, and of the *prijaji* in particular, should be questioned initially. The effect of the liberal period was to bring about a considerable acceleration of the process by which the nobility was transformed into a quasi-rational-legal bureaucracy. As a consequence the Javanese nobility now had to share power with four other groups and only the European officials and specialist departments were obliged to go through the Regents and lesser nobility. European planters and the Chinese entertained direct relations with the periphery (see van Mook, B1958, p. 309; Palmier, B1960b, p. 221). Thus the decades around the turn of the century signified the period in which the legitimacy (to the extent that it existed, it should be noted) of the *prijaji* fell critically. And as a result the power of the Dutch that lay behind was more apparent and could now be evaluated. However, it seems reasonably agreed that prior to the outbreak of hostilities in 1942 the legitimacy of the Dutch was not seriously called into question except by Indonesians in rather specific structural locations. Part of the reason for this was the fact that up to the Second World War 'the Dutch had been *effective* on the whole, in their use of force to prevent hostile outbursts and challenges of legitimacy' (Smelser, 1962, p. 369).

But beyond this there were two major factors which tended to minimize the Dutch being the object of blame. The first was the existence of certain alternatives available for the actor making a structural comparison, the second was that escalation could only result from practice and not in general through the application of a trained intellect. In terms of the former point, it should be noted that two alternatives were closed to the Indonesian: these were, first, the deprived Indonesian 'passing' himself off as a white man, and second, hyper-identification with the Dutch. The former was precluded because of the racial character of stratification; the latter could not occur because of the great physical distance between the Dutch rulers and the Indonesian periphery (see Hagen, B1964, p. 419). But there were other alternatives available to the deprived Indonesian. First of all, there could be further involution (see van der Kroef, B1965a, p. 9); second, he could move either to a town or to an estate on the outer Islands; and third, the persistence of the traditional communal values permitted the ready return of many urban or plantation workers at times of acute power dislocation (see Lasker, B1950, p. 226). The second problem for peripheral escalation mentioned above was that it could normally only result through the practice of dissent. This was for a number of reasons. First of all, the religious problem-solving framework heightened the probability that the relatively deprived actor would blame either himself or his god for his particular situation. Further, since most of the periphery had not experienced western education, they lacked the cognitive apparatus for systematic escalatory interpretations of dissent. Finally, the nature of colonial rule and of the ecosystem precluded the development in Java, certainly of contracultures, and probably of significantly deviant subcultures (apart from Islam). Thus we can see the importance of *Sarekat Islam* which did provide some such locus for dissent and peripheral escalation. But there is no doubt that mass dissent depended very heavily upon central leadership.

There were fewer constraints upon the centre. First of all, the Indonesian members of the centre were generally not actual or potential members of a commercial bourgeoisie and thus there were no significant economic interests which mediated against escalation to the environing structure. Second, the vast expansion of western education provided, superficially at least, the tools for an intellectual analysis of the reasons for their deprivation in comparison with the Dutch. This was assisted by the lack of control exerted by the Dutch on whom they imported to teach in Indonesia. Finally, and related to this, the Netherlands were important in providing for the few Indonesian students who studied there a subculture in which it was possible to derive alternative criteria of what was just. Students who went to the Netherlands found particularly significant a greater degree of personal freedom as compared with the archipelago, an enthusiasm in academic circles for a united Indonesia, an awareness of Indian and Irish non-co-operation and civil disobedience, and the acquisition of intellectual techniques in terms of which the nature of the colonial society could be more effectively analysed. There was, of course, something paradoxical about the Indonesian centre being able to criticize the West in terms of a conceptual framework that was itself western and which was acquired through the policies of the colonial centre. Wertheim (B1956, p. 137) talks of how in the late nineteenth and early twentieth centuries there was 'a marked increase in the social standing of the whites, and a high social regard for all the outward characteristics, such as language, dress and skin colour, which symbolized the white race'. That is to say, the West was a highly significant and increasingly pervasive object of identification for the Indonesian centre (see Hagen, B1964, p. 419; Mannoni, 1964, p. 11); and at the same time it was an object of structural comparison. It was in terms of the former that there was escalation within the latter. We will consider below the importance of western education for the processes of universalization.

159

Universalization

But first we will consider certain other factors. Thus initially there was the inherent contradiction of colonial rule brought about by the Dutch belief in racial superiority (see Mannoni, ibid.). As a consequence the Dutch normally did not communicate with the Indonesian except in the old *lingua franca* of the archipelago, bazaar Malay. This heightened the distinctiveness of the status divisions based on colour and helped the growth of universalization.[37] A second factor was the steady growth of towns in the late nineteenth and early twentieth centuries. By 1920 7·63 per cent of the population were urban dwellers and this had risen to 8·7 per cent by 1930. The effect of this is difficult to interpret, both because even by 1930 there was still an overwhelming predominance of agricultural employment (see Jacoby, B1948, p. 54), and because movement to the towns was one important way in which the relatively deprived actor might avoid expressing dissent within his rural locality. Finally, Islam might well have acted as the basis of universalization but its effectiveness was limited both by the urban-rural and *santri-abangan* splits.[38] Both of these were related to the gradual development of an unambiguously Islamic small bourgeoisie who began to found co-operative societies, savings banks, education funds and the like, and whose motto was as much self-help as 'Indonesia Merdeka' (see Smail, B1961, p. 76). Furthermore, Islam exhibited two overwhelming disadvantages as a means of mobilizing an effective centre-plus-periphery movement. The first was that it was, as Benda says of *Sarekat Islam*: 'a reaffirmation of something traditional' (Benda, B1958a, p. 43); the second was, as a consequence, that it had to be accompanied by non-Islamic beliefs which heightened the probability of ideological fragmentation. This can be seen from the experience of *Sarekat Islam* where there were not only three different leadership groups, but the support gained within the periphery had practically nothing to do with the politics and the demands advanced by the central leaders (see van Niel, B1960, p. 157). The importance of the cultural orientation of the centre can also be seen from Sjahrir's characterization of the PKI (Indonesian Communist Party) (B1949, p. 74) as 'a strange sort of communism indeed, a mystical Hinduistic-Javanese, Islamic-Menangkabau, or Islamic-Bantam sort of communism, with definite animistic tendencies. There are not many Europeans who could recognise anything of their communism in this Indonesian variety.'

It is evident that there was no plausible identity of interests between the peasantry and the PKI leaders; thus especially the aristocratic antecedents of certain of the leadership made a thorough identification between them and the peasantry extremely unlikely.

A good example of policy failure was the way in which land reform was omitted as a major component of PKI ideology in a society where 30–50 per cent of the peasantry was landless.[39] The failure of Indonesian trade unionism to provide really effective organized dissent even among the industrial proletariat magnified the problems for the PKI leadership.[40]

So far we can see that the conditions which favoured universalization were less persuasive than they might have initially appeared. Normally, the factor which intruded to weaken this universalization was western education. As dissent developed through the *Muhammadijah* movement, the *Sarekat Islam* and the PKI, the universalization through cultural deprivation (which led to *Budi Utomo*) was dissipated because of the contradictions implied for any movement. Western education brought about a reasonably coherent and consistent world-view among the centre where it acted as a source of in-category universalization; it did nothing to increase universalization with the periphery. Thus the inherent contradiction was that it only aggravated the dilemma summarized by Kartodirdjo (B1962, p. 84): 'The conception of the idea of unity was hampered by the basic problem regarding the leading ideology in the independence struggle, that is, the alternative between a religious nationalism and an Indonesian nationalism.'

Outcome

I devote more specific attention below to the 1926–7 communist dissent. For the moment, I want to provide a brief account which will explain the failure of both the PKI and *Sarekat Islam* in general. There were two conditions of any movement that was to be successful. It should contain peripheral and central members; and it should be formally organized, a necessary condition of this being other-category universalization. Furthermore, the latter is dependent upon some congruence between the style of dissensual leadership and existing cultural patterns. There were two main patterns in Indonesia: Indic theatre-state with Islamic overtones; Islamic tradition with acknowledgements to *adat* (see Geertz, B1968). Examples of movements in the latter tradition were *Muhammadijah* and the SI, both of which drew upon the Islamic tradition of local leadership. Thus *Sarekat Islam* was not much more than an agglomeration of local branches.[41] The problem with this was that it tended to preclude high level political change. The alternative tradition above, examples of movements here being the PI and PNI (nationalist movements), did permit a combined organization of the centre and the periphery. However, its content was in contradiction to communist interpretation, both because of its conduciveness to charismatic rather than rational–legal leadership, and because of its emphasis upon cultural rather than economic or political resources which made escalatory interpretations less likely. Thus the only form of dissensual leadership by the centre which appeared culturally plausible was based on the Indic theatre-state tradition which did not attempt to provide complex political-economic escalatory interpretations for the periphery. In this light, therefore, it was not surprising that the only organizations led from the centre to gain mass support from the periphery were those led by Sukarno in the late 1920s, as Clifford Geertz (ibid., pp. 74 and 86–7) says:[42]

> With Sukarno the theatre-state returned to Indonesia.
> Sukarno, less plebeian than he imagined and less radical
> than he sounded, was the historical heir of the Indic tradition.
> This tradition had been maintained . . . by the bureaucratized
> gentry of the Colonial Period. And it was from this class –
> or, more accurately, the lower revolutionary edge of it
> that Sukarno emerged and to which, for all his attacks on
> feudalism, he never ceased to belong, for which he never
> ceased to speak.

It was noteworthy that none of these movements was in any significant sense institutionalized, although specific groups and individuals were regularly attracted away to practise co-operation with the Dutch. The main reason for the lack of institutionalization was that since the organization of a movement did not lead to goal displacement (partly because the movements were so short-lived), the greater the degree of organization the less was the degree of institutionalization. Two other considerations should be noted. The first was that there was no appropriate precipitant for medium and high range dissent, and thus, any dissensual movement had to create its own conditions of precipitation; which is thus a major reason for the total fragmentation of the 1926–7 dissent. Admittedly, by the end of the decade the depression had created a precipitant that could be meaningfully interpreted as representing a considerable breakdown of the colonial structure. By then, however, the second factor here, namely social control, had become so effective that dissent in the 1930s was minimal. The main point to note about such control was that in the ultimate analysis, the power of the Dutch centre within Indonesia was maintained by the political power of the metropolitan centre. Van der Kroef (B1965a, p. 20) thus maintains that the Dutch centre was never in real danger from even communist dissent. Smail (B1964, pp. 12 and 60–3) lists the techniques that were used: political banishment, preventive arrest, restrictions on political meetings, after-publication censorship, and the encouragement of moderate debate within the *Volksraad* and the like. After 1926–7 the degree of social control was noticeably tightened, the Ethical Policy came to an end, and there was an emphasis upon re-establishing *adat* (see Benda, B1958a, p. 68; Tedjasukmana, B1959, p. 15).

Dissent, 1942–5

Multiple contradictions

After only three years of Japanese rule the Indonesians proclaimed independence and were successful in repulsing two sizeable Dutch military actions aimed at the re-establishment of colonial hegemony. Three years of Japanese rule brought about what three centuries of Dutch rule had studiously avoided. Benda (1962a, pp. 133–4) pleads that:

> The Japanese interregnum be provisionally accorded the status of a distinct historical epoch in Southeast Asian history. It is, indeed, no exaggeration to say that without the Japanese interlude the balance between continuity and change might conceivably still be weighted in favour of continuity, or at best of more gradual, evolutionary change.

The archipelago was undoubtedly Japan's 'richest prize in terms of natural resources' (Elsbree, B1953, p. 22).[43] The essential basis of the Japanese interregnum was to effect the maximum exploitation of the economic resources of the archipelago. A Japanese official declared:[44]

> For the military administration, the most important thing is winning the war and all its efforts go into this. The greatest of the present efforts towards winning the war is economic reconstruction. Political and cultural considerations cannot weigh very heavily with the present military administration in the Southern Areas.

It will be remembered that economic exploitation was also the basis of Dutch colonialism, but there is no mistaking the profound difference between the nature of the economic demands made by the different metropolitan centres. In the Dutch case the aim was the long-run maximization of the profit of various individuals and firms located within both Indonesia and the Netherlands. In the case of the Japanese the primary objective was to secure the immediate resources necessary to pursue a world-wide war, to establish an autarchic east Asia, and to develop the economic strength of the Japanese empire (see Benda, B1962a, p. 234; Benda, *et al.*, B1965, p. 17). Such short-run maximization implied the mobilization of very large numbers of the Indonesian population (see Smail, B1964, p. 12).

It is not surprising that such mobilization produced dissent. The response of the Japanese faced with such growing dissent, the continually increasing economic demands and the failure to gain satisfactory economic benefit,[45] and the worsening military situation, was to offer escalating political concessions which culminated in that of independence. Elsbree points out the very strong correlation between a fall in military fortunes and the development of pro-independence attitudes, and the explicit emphasis upon the giving of concessions to the nationalists as a minimum price for co-operation. It was also significant that the first concessions came from the army in Java where there was most dissent and were most opposed by the navy in the Celebes where there was least dissent.[46] As a result of these factors we can identify four periods of Japanese rule. The first was from the invasion in March 1942 until March 1943; attention was devoted almost entirely to economic exploitation and only two political organizations were set up. The second period lasted until the latter half of 1944, the policy within this period resulting from the fact that Japan's expansion had reached its outer limits and so her latest acquisitions were no longer stepping stones but the outer perimeter of defence. Since the problem now was to consolidate and protect the gains already made, political concessions became more probable. Symbolic of this policy change was Premier Tojo's speech in June 1943:[47] 'It is our intention to go further and, in pursuance of the aspirations of the natives, to take measures step by step envisaging the participation of the native populations in government to the extent commensurate with the degree of their ability.' The final major shift in Japanese policy occurred in September 1944, when President Koiso made his pronouncement that Indonesian independence would be sanctioned in the near future (see Elsbree, B1953, pp. 88–9). Aziz (B1955, pp. 231–2) maintains with some justification that it was only in the second half of 1944, when Japan lay wide open to Allied attack that she first seriously considered independence for the Indonesians, and thus Koiso's pronouncement in September can be seen as the direct result of the defeat at Saipan in July. A fourth period lasted from the announcement of the Japanese surrender on 16 August 1945, until the arrival of the British on 29 September of the same year.

There was, therefore, a further contradiction over and above those manifest during Dutch rule. This arose from the 'illegitimate' character of a Japanese rule where full-scale mobilization was necessitated by its very *raison d'être*. The only way by which this mobilization could be attained was through the promising of political concessions, but for such promises to be at least minimally plausible there had to be a certain realization of what was expected. As a result of this mobilization and of its consequences, important changes were brought about in the economic, political and religious subsystems. All of these had important consequences for the power rankings of specific categories of actors.

Power dislocation

The occupation had undoubtedly profound consequences upon the Indonesian *tani*. The first effect was a major reduction in the agricultural production of rice: it fell from 4061 to 2855 thousand metric tons between 1943 and 1945 (see de Vries, B1949, p. 130, n. 1). At the same time though, this falling agricultural production had to meet an expanding demand, most especially from the Japanese troops stationed in the archipelago. One obvious consequence was a very rapid rise in food prices particularly during and after 1944 (ibid., p. 132). Japanese rule also led to the requirement that each island had to become self-sufficient in both food and clothing (see Thompson, B1946, pp. 201–2). Third, about half a million villagers were distributed as forced labourers throughout Japanese controlled South-east Asia (see de Vries, B1949, p. 132). Finally, the periphery experienced significant political and cultural deprivations because of the high degree of mobilization resulting from Japanese rule. Sjahrir (B1946, p. 11) summarized the nature of their generalized diminution of power along all three dimensions:

During the three and a half years of Japanese occupation, the foundations of rural society were shaken and undermined by forced regulations, kidnapping from homes for conscription as labourers abroad or as soldiers, compulsory surrender of harvested crops, compulsory planting of designated crops – all imposed with unlimited arbitrariness.

The Indonesian centre did not suffer from the same generalization of deprivation. It will be remembered that the Indonesian 'degree holder' felt deprived because there was little or no congruence between his relatively high cultural power and his low political and economic power. But the onset of Japanese rule and the removal of practically all Europeans and Eurasians from positions of political power both increased the political power and economic rewards of already established administrators and increased the number of natives employed within the Japanese administration. It is important though not to overemphasize the significance of this experience; de Weerd (B1946, p. 12163) said that 'leading positions remained in the hands of Japanese and if an Indonesian held an important post there was always a Japanese who was the real executive'. But clearly this experience was of some importance, perhaps most significantly in re-establishing congruence along the power dimensions. To a certain extent, this category of Indonesians must be distinguished from the traditional rulers of Dutch colonialism, the *prijaji* proper. Their rankings of political power and economic rewards were reduced because many members of central and local councils, *Peta* (see below) officers, certain Islamic leaders and many administrators 'became equals, if not superiors, of the *prijaji* in rank, and in several instances, also in pay' (Benda, B1958a, p. 164). Thus, although it was improbable that the *prijaji* would dissent, there was a heightened possibility that they would not oppose dissent mobilized against the Japanese.

Two other categories of the centre experienced very marked changes in their situation. On the one hand, the nationalist politicians were released from prison and joined various political organizations, although they did not in fact enjoy very significant political power and might have at times suffered power dislocation (ibid., p. 170). On the other hand, the *kiaji* became members of the centre for the first time. This resulted from the Japanese need to mobilize the population and from the fact that Islam rather than secular nationalism could command a real following (ibid., p. 92). The Japanese quite early on allowed the Muslims to reopen their schools with modified curricula, while organizational changes resulted in a much reduced separation between the church and the state and a general enhancement of the religious apparatus within the political system.[48]

Finally, we must consider briefly the fourth period of the occupation since radical changes occurred there which help to explain the generally high degree of commitment to the revolution. Smail points out that although a political vacuum had been developing during the previous three or four months this had been almost entirely confined to Jakarta. But the effect of the surrender was that (Smail, B1964, p. 20):

> At one stroke . . . the surrender removed the *raison d'etre* of
> Japanese rule. . . . The country was thus suddenly left
> without a real government. The depth of the political vacuum
> was accentuated by the fact that the Allies were unable for
> some time to replace them in Indonesia.

From 14 August to 29 September 1945, when the first British troops arrived, the political centre consisted of a demoralized Japanese administration and army, who were far less enthusiastic about preserving the *status quo* so as not to displease the Allies than they had been in ruling in the name of Japan. Smail (ibid., pp. 21 and 37) summarizes the effect: 'to the majority of Indonesians – not only the peasant masses but most of the educated class as well – the news of mid-August came as a great surprise, a break in the continuity of their lives'. In other words, although the distribution of economic and cultural power remained approximately the same, there was a radical increase in the political power of each Indonesian. There was a process of political power diffusion resulting in power inconsistency. Importantly, this now affected practically all categories of Indonesians and especially those administrators and nationalist politicians who had been participating within 'a "dual apparatus" of government at the highest levels' (Anderson, B1961, p. 12). The result of the Japanese surrender was that 'the baton of power was finally relinquished to the Indonesian leadership' (ibid.; see also, Elsbree, B1953, p. 59).

Perception

There is no doubt that the Japanese were clearly visible to the Indonesian centre. There is also little question that the nature of Japanese rule made it likely that they were perceived as economically and politically powerful by the Indonesian periphery. Sjahrir (B1949, p. 249) says: 'To the Japanese, governing ... consisted only of the bayonet, propaganda, seizure of food and other goods, force, and conscript labour' (see also, de Weerd, B1946, pp. 12167–8; Aziz, B1955, pp. 166–82). To this list may be added the Japanese penchant for creating new organizations, most of which were intended to mobilize different categories of the centre. The main exception to this was the *Tomari Gumi* (neighbourhood associations) which were intended to organize the periphery in small groups within the villages and townships; these associations then became the lowest units in the government pyramid. This organization was the first instance of a centralized system of administration within Indonesia, and the first time that the *tani* had been subjected to direct organization by the centre. Clearly, its effect was to heighten the perception of the centre in general and of the Japanese centre in particular.

Comparison

There was a high probability that various actors would compare themselves with the Japanese. The first reason for this was that the Japanese were not ranked more highly than even the Indonesian *tani* with respect to cultural power. Second, de Weerd (B1946, p. 12189) suggests that the new stratification structure introduced by the Japanese was the following: (1) Japanese; (2) Indonesians; (3) other Asiatics; (4) mixtures of Indonesians with other groups; (5) Europeans. This seems somewhat questionable. What was distinctive about the pre-occupation structure was its division into two status groups – what seems particular about this wartime structure was its overwhelming similarity. As Wertheim (B1955, p. 43) says: 'Indonesians might hold positions much higher than those held under Dutch rule but a son of the gods could never be an inferior of any Indonesian.' As a result, the Indonesian, when making a structural comparison, would compare himself with the Japanese. There were two reasons why this was more likely than in the case of Dutch rule. The first was that Orientals and Eurasians were less important and thus less likely to act as comparison objects. The second was that because of the Japanese mobilization on to the level of the individual *tani* 'never had the distance from central authorities to village communities seemed so short' (Elsbree, B1953, p. 127). Thus peripheral perception of and comparison with the Japanese centre was increasingly probable. Two points should be noted about the comparisons made by the Indonesian centre. First, such Indonesians were implicated within the stratification structures of the Japanese centre (for example, administrative hierarchies); second, they were partially excluded from positions of power by identifiable Japanese. Again, therefore, comparison with the Japanese was probable.

Generalization

I have suggested above that there were no significant cultural limitations upon generalizing from one dimension to another. Lasker says, for example (B1950, p. 171):

When Japanese occupying forces in Southeast Asia compelled the inhabitants to construct vessels for them as well as roads, or to grow and deliver cotton as well as food for the occupying forces, the simple countryman did not ask whether perchance his involuntary labour really served the state – or whether . . . it was used to pile up profits for business firms and corporations. For in the historic experience of his own people, the two kinds of purpose have never been clearly kept apart.

Now, furthermore, under the simpler more transparent conditions of the Japanese occupation, this cultural confusion of the economic and political served to heighten the sense of relative deprivation experienced by the Indonesian *tani*. He could now generalize his sense of deprivation compared with the Japanese from the political to the economic or vice versa. Previously, both the high degree of power localization, and the way in which the Chinese and the Orientals served as intermediaries, had acted as significant structural constraints on such generalization. To an important extent, these were no longer that significant.

168

Interpretation and escalation

The continued existence of some sort of dissensual subculture maintained the possibility of escalation by the centre throughout the 1930s. There were three sources of such dissensual interpretation: the large numbers of so-called wild schools, resulting at least in part from the lack of official employment opportunities for those with western education;[49] the National Education Club founded by Sjahrir and Hatta which, despite official sanctions, remained in existence until the occupation (see Kahin, B1952, p. 93); and the common prison experience of the many Indonesians who were put in jail by the Dutch (see Sjahrir, B1949, *passim*).

This meant that when the occupation began there were a number of leaders of dissent who were willing and able to provide escalatory interpretations to the periphery. That these would appear plausible was radically enhanced by the further increase in the degree of impersonal interdependence experienced during the course of the Japanese rule. The increase in interdependence is quite clear, economically, because of the *raison d'être* of Japanese rule, politically, because of the organization of each village within the central administration, and culturally, because of the demand for spiritual unity with *Nippon*. The increase in impersonality should also be evident; as Sjahrir says (ibid., p. 249): 'Under the Japanese, the people had to endure indignities worse than any they had known before; bowing before people for whom they had only contempt in their hearts, bearing physical abuse, and being treated as though they were wholly unfeeling beings.' The result of the initial stage of Japanese rule was to make clear the fact that the Dutch were no longer the legitimate rulers. It should be noted that prior to the arrival of the Japanese there was considerable sympathy for them on the part of many Indonesians. Reasons for this were the supposed Japanese tolerance for Islam, her significance as a leading Asiatic power since 1904–5, her potential for providing liberation from western imperialism, the popularity of well served Japanese imports sold in Japanese shops in the archipelago, and the version of the *Djojobojo* legend where the restoration of Javanese freedom was said to follow a short period of oppression by a yellow race from the north (see ibid., pp. 112 and 136; Aziz, B1955, pp. 147–8). The main evidence for the last point is provided by Sjahrir (B1949, p. 187) who quoted the myth in 1937 and said 'now the people say, "It is the Japanese who will come"' (see also p. 218). It is this which explains the lack of sympathy for the Dutch in 1942. Why, we may now ask, did the Japanese lose this initial authority?

The first reason was that Japanese rule set out systematically to destroy the traditional bases of authority, and especially that of the *prijaji*. This meant that the legitimacy of the Japanese was the next in line to be questioned. Sjahrir says (ibid., pp. 248–9):

> As I look back at the Japanese period it is clear to what
> extent everything in the Indonesian community, spiritually
> as well as materially, was shaken loose from its old moorings.
> The fall of the colonial regime was in itself a cause but
> what the Japanese showed our people afterwards dealt the
> decisive blow to the old standards and norms. The Japanese
> gave the people a surprise that was widespread and general. . . .
> What people saw were barbarians who were often more
> stupid than they themselves. . . . The old, experienced Indonesian
> administrators of the colonial service felt only contempt for the
> political ignoramuses who were placed over them. As a
> consequence, all layers of society came to see the past in
> another light. If these barbarians had been able to replace
> the old colonial authority, why had that authority been
> necessary at all? Why, indeed, hadn't they handled the affairs
> of government themselves?

But even so it is wrong to suggest that this experience fully destroyed the legitimacy of Japanese rule. Antoine Cabaton pointed out in 1911 (p. 133) that the Javanese native had been exploited for centuries by various rulers, and Bruno Lasker (B1950, pp. 248–9) maintains that the incredibly oppressive demands of the Japanese administration represented 'a familiar exercise of power'. This point, combined with a chronic lack of intellectual resources and of recent practice of dissent, explains the very limited peripheral escalation.

Thus it is not surprising that no important peripheral dissent occurred until the second period of Japanese rule. The potential for such dissent was aggravated here because in response to the fear of outbursts of religious fanaticism, there was an increase in courses for Muslim school teachers, and religious leaders were now largely freed from the direct control of administrative officials (see Benda, B1958a, pp. 158–60). But the former further heightened the intrusion of the Japanese on the local level, while the latter served suddenly to limit the power of the administrators. There was a growing expression of dissent, generally low level, activated by widespread power dislocation, and led on the local level by either *kiaji* or one of the undergrounds. Sjahrir (B1949, pp. 250–1) summarizes this experience:

> Not the least attention was given to old customs and
> village habits. . . . The existing pattern of relationships was
> discarded and no constructive new pattern was substituted.
> The situation clearly became more revolutionary as time went

on. Everywhere unrest grew. The Japanese military were obliged to act against the simple people.

In itself, such dissent could not actually eject the Japanese; but this experience was important in two ways. First, through the practice of dissent, some escalation was realized; second, through contact with the underground movements, a certain cogency was given to the development of a contraculture.[50]

For some time it appeared probable, since Sukarno and Hatta were so well institutionalized within the centre, that dissensual leadership of the periphery would be provided by one or more of the various youth groups that had grown up during the occupation. Their development resulted from: power dislocation because of the inadequate educational facilities provided in Japan, and the lack of political power that they gained when they returned; comparison, because of their continuous mobilization and organization by the Japanese; escalation, because of their possession of intellectual facilities and from the practice of dissent; and in-category universalization, because of their collective withdrawal from their birthplaces and the political activity within the towns.[51]

Universalization

Before showing the development of the relationships between the *pemudas* (youth groups), the nationalists, and the *kiaji*, it is necessary to note certain factors that would tend to increase universalization. These were the creation during the depression of a sizeable rural proletariat (see Anderson, B1961, p. 45); the emphasis placed on national unity at least within the third stage of Japanese rule (see Elsbree, B1953, p. 168); the reorganization of education into standardized and uniform national schools (see ibid., p. 130; Aziz, B1955, p. 181); the banning of the Dutch language which led to the use of bazaar Malay as the official language of administration and senior education (see Alisjahbana, B1949, p. 390); and, as a result of increasing military worries, the establishment of *Peta* in late 1943, which, although Japanese trained, was Indonesian officered (see Elsbree, B1953, pp. 129–30; Pauker, B1962). Both *Peta* and many civilian organizations (*Putera, Hokokai*; youth, women, Islamic organizations, etc.), increased the potential for central leadership, propaganda, and infiltration – by 1945: 'for the first time in Indonesian history there were political organisations continuously and fairly effectively connecting the rural family to the centres of political power and decision making in the capital' (see Anderson, B1961, p. 46). There were thus half-a-dozen factors that were tending to increase radically the degree of universalization. At the same time, however, there was a high degree of competition between the different élite groups, partly as a result of two contradictory pressures. First, the mounting dissent of the periphery which needed central entrepreneurship to be effective; second, the split within the Japanese centre and the consequential gains to be derived from institutionalized political action, as well as the dangers of goal displacement.

Initially, the group best able to resolve the contradiction was the newly significant *kiaji*, whose connections with the *desa* were strengthened; but who, on the other hand, would be unlikely to mobilize for dissent (see ibid., p. 41; Benda, B1958a, pp. 135 and 176). Only during the latter half of the third period, that is, from March to August 1945, when power was slipping away from the *kiaji*, did they show any sympathy at all for anti-Japanese dissent. It was in this period that the nationalists were for the first time placed in any position of power. And although there was increasing dissent among both the peasantry and the youth, these older nationalists still hoped to gain independence through institutionalized political activity, especially through using the divisions within the Japanese administration.[52] It was only when they discovered that under the terms of the surrender the Japanese were merely agents of the Allies that Sukarno and Hatta were willing to proclaim independence. The reason why the revolution did not occur without waiting for the leadership of Sukarno and Hatta seems to be that while many Indonesians had escalated their dissent on to the structural level they had not formulated this within a reasonably coherent and consistent belief-system which facilitated other-category universalization. Thus Palmier (B1955, pp. 119–20) maintains that 'the allegiance of the mass of their [nationalist leaders] followers would appear to have been to them as personalities, rather than as representatives of a cause; in other words the peasants saw as their guides and saviours certain individuals who formed a common group'. This was very clearly perceived by the *pemudas*, since as Hatta put it 'they had no leader of stature' (quoted in Anderson, B1961, p. 70); they needed the leadership of Sukarno and Hatta (ibid., pp. 70–1). On 31 August a national ministry was created under President Sukarno. Anderson points out that with the exception of Amir Sjarifuddin, all members of it had worked with the Japanese and were of the older generation.[53] Two further conditions of revolution did not exist in the 1920s but were operative now. The surrender of the Japanese meant that there was both a precipitant that could be meaningfully interpreted as representative of a major failure at the value level within important societal areas, and that there was a cataclysmic breakdown of social control. The inability of the British troops to arrive for six weeks meant that on their arrival 'they found the Indonesian government more or less firmly in power' (Pluvier, B1968, p. 6). Thus, by late

September the revolution had more or less established itself over much of the archipelago. The centre of Indonesian society was now comprised predominantly of Indonesians.

Outcome

Ideally a satisfactory account of revolutionary change would explain two further features of Indonesian dissent: the ability of the Republic to repulse two considerable Dutch invasions; and the inability of the Republic to establish a social reality in any way congruent with its apocalyptic vision. Neither of these will be discussed here; the only point I want to consider is why the content of dissent that was ultimately successful was nationalist rather than communist. Already, various suggestions have been made in this direction; but there are two factors which have been implied yet not amplified which do seem pertinent. Specifically, I want to suggest that the lack of an indigenous bourgeoisie and the existence of a prior sense of nationality increase the probability that if dissent occurs it will be of a higher level and relate to more profound societal areas than if one or both these conditions do not apply. The second condition is one which minimizes the problems of universalization between socially distant actors, as well as providing a social identity in terms of which radical social transformation can be envisaged. Where the first condition is found, there are a number of consequences. On the one hand, if the bourgeoisie is foreign, the deprived actor is more likely to compare himself with that bourgeoisie because they are easier to perceive, the comparisons are more wide-ranging, and the deprived actor is likely to conclude that he cannot easily become a member. On the other hand, where the indigenous élite is not commercial, universalization with the periphery is more probable and there is a greater likelihood of escalation and of a sub- or contra-culture. In Indonesia where there was no such indigenous bourgeoisie (except of very small entrepreneurs) all these phenomena were found. But the lack of any nationality rendered the content of revolution here, as in much of the rest of the third world, more a search for the nation-state than the attempt to transform revolutionarily an already existent Indonesian nation and validated Indonesian identity. Further discussion of why Sunan Kalidjaga rather than Karl Marx was the spiritual ancestor of the early Indonesian Republic will be seen below.[54]

Dissent, 1926–7

One criticism of the sort of explanation provided above is that it is not delicate enough to provide a satisfactory account of precisely why different actors at different times in different places should undertake any particular action. It cannot, in other words, explain not the broad generalities but rather the complex minutiae of social relations. That this claim is ill-founded is the presupposition of this section in which I will try to explain in general the variation in dissensual response between different areas within Indonesia in the 1920s and specifically why differing actors in Bantam as opposed to Menangkabau were more dissensual.

Two sets of factors explain the failure of dissent in Bali. First, since the Islamic, colonial and capitalist intrusions were very much less profound than elsewhere, the resulting contradictions were far less significant. Second, although structural comparisons may have been made, the meaning given to them was probably one where blame was placed upon foci other than the dominant power holders or the environing structure. Geertz (B1964, p. 289) talks of 'the sanctification of social hierarchy' being the basis of all supra-village organization. G. W. Skinner finds Hildred Geertz's term 'centripetal' particularly apt in characterizing the social organization both of Bali and of central and east Java. But there were certain differences between Bali and Java; in particular, there was enormous variety within the latter due to variation in external influence, traditional social structure and religious belief system. The area most closely approximating to the paradigm customarily presented of Javanese life was that of central Java, followed closely by east Java and at a greater distance by west Java. Dissent within the former two areas was improbable because of the persistent communalism of the village and the legitimation of the social structure through the aristocratic cultural élite.[55]

West Java, on the other hand, was a centre of dissent; PKI-led uprisings occurred in November 1926 in Bantam. There were similar risings in 1927 in Menangkabau in western Sumatra which I will discuss below. The main feature of Bantam was its individualism. The population consisted mainly of Javanese who had moved west in search of more land but who had not taken their communal village organization.[56] They were principally small landowners who operated their own moderate holdings, there was a lack of over-population and of European plantations, the only source of cohesion was an unorthodox and fanatical Islam,[57] and there was a sharp fall in the peasant's economic rewards in the 1920s – this is shown by the decrease in the consumption of 'luxuries' such as salt, travel and so on, by the growing shortage of arable land which because of the smaller opportunities for involution was more important here, and by the sharp increase in taxation from 1921–6 (see van der Kroef, B1965a, pp. 9 and 19). Further, because of the primary emphasis placed upon economic exploitation, there was a lack of legitimation

174

of the powerful. This meant that comparison with the Dutch was probable and implied a lack of legitimation of their power. But escalation of this was, I think, unlikely. It was more probable that there would be both blame of oneself and of one's god for any revealed deprivation.[58] Thus, the dissensual entrepreneurs were significant in Bantam. The possibility that they would bring about successful other-category universalization was enhanced by the cultural tradition found among the Sundanese which (Palmer, B1959, pp. 42–3):

> traditionally emphasises loyalty to superiors. . . . To-day the villager fears his superior's anger, he fears being ashamed, and fears losing the advantages which his superior's favour can bring. Those who join political parties and organisations still tend to do so through ties to an individual, usually a superior, rather than through loyalty to a group with a given ideology.

Typically these superiors had been independent religious teachers as opposed to civil and religious authorities appointed by the centre. Moreover, these Islamic teachers were still important in dissensual entrepreneurship – that is to say, although the contact at the centre between the *Sarekat Islam* and the PKI had been broken, at the level of the periphery in Bantam 'communist leaders had been able to elicit widespread Islamic support, particularly among the less sophisticated orthodox village scribes' (Benda and McVey, B1960, p. xvi). Conversely, though, as a consequence of the fact that the fundamental framework was an orthodox Islam the form of dissent was a 'bigoted, fanatical variety of the Islam faith' (Hurgronje, B1924, p. 255). To some extent this was true of the Menangkabau dissent although the conditions that produced dissent there were very different.

Two contradictions were of particular relevance. The first was that between Islam and *adat* which was especially intense. This was because of the distinctive communalism of social life within western Sumatra (see van der Kroef, B1954a, pp. 194–5), an example of which was the Menangkabau family system and law of succession. The degree of conflict can be seen from the fact that some orthodox Muslims proclaimed that all property inherited under the succession law was in fact plunder (see Drewes, B1955, p. 293). Further conflict arose because although western Sumatra was the 'supreme seat of civil and religious authority in this part of the East' (ibid., p. 292), the number of theologians who could be satisfactorily incorporated into the structure of Menangkabau society was extremely small. The second contradiction, and one which critically exacerbated the first, arose from the sudden intrusion of capitalism, which Schrieke dates

175

from 1908–12 when various government restrictions were abolished and export demand expanded (see Schrieke, B1955, pp. 84–166; Geertz, B1963a, pp. 118–19). The results were 'the pledging of land, the slackening of family ties, the weakening of the authority of the *adat* leaders in the community, all of which combined to provide a ready environment for the growth of mass movements or resistance to Dutch authority' (Legge, B1964, p. 116). To some extent the 'centrifugal' (see Skinner, B1959, p. 7) character of the Menangkabau social system militated against dissent since at least the lower middle class, the officials and the small traders who experienced relative deprivation over the period 1921–4 could move away to Java.[59] But clearly this was impossible for many.

If one considers the nature of the peripheral commitment, especially among the peasantry, one finds an interesting difference between the two areas. In Menangkabau, those most involved were 'the poorest strata of the peasant population in the over-populated areas (such as Pariaman, Old Agam) and the poorest, economically most backward districts (Sawah Lunto sub-division, the territory east of Lake Singkarak)' (Schrieke, B1955, p. 133; see also, n. 20, p. 269). The Government Report on Bantam, on the other hand, claimed that 'it is the Lebak district, where the protagonists of the PKI have failed to gain a hold on the population, that there is least prosperity and in some districts even poverty'.[60] Given that these relationships were not the result of erroneous interpretation, it can be asked whether the theory here can help to elucidate this finding.

During this period Menangkabau was characterized by the rapid growth of both the selling of land formerly held by the family and by the pledging of it to others in circumstances unspecified by *adat* (see Schrieke, B1955, pp. 107–8). Thus, for example, in Sawah Lunto 'which was poor in rice, the valid motive for the pledging of family land was recognized as being "an urgent lack of the necessities of life"' (ibid., p. 102). But this was not to resolve power dislocation since (ibid., p. 112):

> those who had pledged their rice fields or clearings as security for debts are even worse off. The land is soon sold and if there are no buyers it brings very little in. Since the capitalists are always supported from above the little man declines into poverty. And as the government assists the capitalists invest their money in the village, those who as a result are plunged into misery also regard the government as their enemy.

Thus, not only did the peasant in these areas experience power dislocations but it also facilitated the comparing of the self both with peasants within the same area and with specific capitalists in the towns or perhaps with representatives of the political centre at times of significant tax increases (see ibid., pp. 113–14). Comparisons with such capitalists were permitted since their cultural power was probably as low as the Indonesian peasant, both because they had no influence upon the determination of non-western values and because they had only moderate power with respect to western values. Furthermore, a certain degree of escalation would have resulted from both the questioning of the traditional legitimacy of the *penghulus* (village heads in Sumatra) and the radical increase in both impersonality and interdependence that characterized the selling of land and the intrusion of the capitalist. Schrieke (ibid., p. 112) says: 'Thus it was the effects of the penetration of money economy which opened the minds of people to the doctrines of communism. It was "capitalism" that created the troubles which harassed their daily lives.' The Bantamese, on the other hand, did not experience the intrusion of capitalism in this markedly discontinuous form. As a consequence, the peasants in poor areas did not compare themselves with the capitalists but probably with the slightly richer peasants in their own locality or the local administrator. The peasants in richer areas probably made similar comparisons, while the richer peasants in the richer areas who came into contact with capitalists will probably have compared themselves with them. Generally we can see that the structural context mediated against the peasantry making highly distant structural comparisons. This therefore meant that dissent was rendered less probable in the poorer than in the richer areas – this was the opposite of the situation in Menangkabau.

There was also a further and related difference between the dissensual movements between the two areas. The Sumatran rebellion, although more geographically limited, was far longer, more violent and required pacification by the military (see Benda and McVey, B1960, p. xx). I have already shown that there were a number of important reasons for this: in Menangkabau, the sudden coalescence of two major contradictions, the marked increase in interdependence and impersonality, and the major questioning of the economically powerful; in Bantam, less probability of escalation, the necessity for Islamic mobilization of the periphery, and the marked individualism which rendered universalization as less probable.[61]

I hope that this brief account will support my claim that the theory as developed in part 2 is adequate in explaining small-scale variations of dissent and change. I want in conclusion to consider not any general features of Indonesian history but the implications that this sort of analysis has for the sociology of revolution and for social theory in general.

Conclusion

Hannah Arendt (1963, p. 112) says 'revolutions can break out and succeed only if there exists a sufficient number of men who are prepared for its collapse and, at the same time, willing to act together for a common purpose'.

I have been concerned in the second and third parts of this book to provide an explanation of why in some societies at some times there have been a large number of men preparing and organizing both consciously and collectively for the ending of the *status quo*. I take the explanation of that to be immensely difficult. But further, it should be clear, although this is often left implicit, that I consider that many of the existing attempts to account for revolutionary action are miraculously feeble. What then is my argument and what are the advantages that it has over the other accounts that are given?

Let me try to answer this in a roundabout way; by considering the criticism of my explanation which states that what I have in effect done is to take some aspects of a watered-down Marxism (contradictions, power and class), added to this a number of terms from bourgeois social science (reference groups, identity, self), and claimed that some significance should be attached to the synthesis. My first response to this criticism would be to argue that the account of recent Indonesian history does provide some support for my general argument. Specifically, I argue that it is only through the use of the concept of the contradiction, of how these contradictions develop and are generated particularly through the relationship between the colonial society and the metropolitan centre, that we can see how the everyday situation of very many Indonesians was dislocated in the early part of this century. But further, I then show that the outcome of dissent was only realized when people perceived, compared and generalized their deprivation with first, the Chinese and second, with the Dutch; when they interpreted it structurally;

and when they universalized their situation with that of other categories of Indonesians. The key process is that of the contradictory objective structure of the society creating the possibility that people may make structural comparisons. I outline both the conditions that had prevented this and what was occurring to change this. I finally show the conditions in terms of which the Indonesian who is viewing himself in comparison with others may interpret the revealed deprivation, of how the relationship between self and other may be judged. What part 3 is therefore dependent upon is a theory of social justice, a theory of how different categories and classes come to develop different conceptions of what is just and unjust. It should be clear that I argue that such conceptions result from the interaction between the objective structure and the subjective orientations of the actors involved.

After all, it is this which I am concerned with detailing in part 2. Let me thus return to the criticism that I am attempting to synthesize what cannot be synthesized – that Marxist and bourgeois social science cannot be added together simply and unproblematically. Now I am unable to answer this in any way adequately here; specifically, I am not going to discuss the most articulated version of this doctrine.[1] I wish rather to consider two criticisms that Robin Blackburn makes of the bourgeois sociology of revolution (see Blackburn, 1969, pp. 182–8). First of all, such sociology fails in general to use the concept of contradiction, replacing it with the less satisfactory notions of strain or dysfunction. The second is that it neglects the conscious element in revolution, the fact that modern revolutionaries do not act blindly, irrationally, but base their activities on careful analysis and rationally planned strategy. Revolutions are not taken, he says, to be sensible, coherent and planned attempts by people to make and remake their own history.

I am very sympathetic to Blackburn's position on both of these points. But where he does not come clean is in failing to indicate what an analysis would look like which incorporated these two aspects. Thus he says of a structural contradiction that they carry with them the possibility of a new social order, that is, they can only be overcome if that very form of society is somehow overturned. Any particular contradiction will always remain where the society retains the same form. Contradictions, therefore, do not refer to any strain between the structural elements but only to quite specific, and given the society, irreconcilable antagonisms. My objection to Blackburn's argument is that there are other sorts of contradictory aspects of any society, which are both critically relevant to revolutionary change and which demand analysis. Anyway it is very difficult to know when the fundamental form of any society has changed. As a result of, for example, Marx's inadequate specification of the forms of pre-capitalist society, we cannot know what is an irreconcilable antagonism which contains the possibility of a new social order. Rather, in this book I have explored the various sorts of structural contradiction that exist and how they may develop and accumulate.

Blackburn's second point seems equally problematic. What Marx's analysis does not tell us is exactly how, why and when revolutionary change comes about and this is because of a failure to provide an explanation of mass revolutionary consciousness. There is, of course, a great deal in Marx which provides a *basis* for such explanation – the analyses of alienation, pauperization, processes of social comparison, polarization and exploitation. But I would emphasize two points: first, these arguments partially contradict each other; second, they are not adequately related in Marx to the very nature of the objective structure. They are, to a degree, free-floating and employed in an *ad hoc* manner. We are thus not provided with an adequate account of why some people sometimes develop a revolutionary consciousness and set out to remake their world.

I hope it is clear that my analysis in part 2 is an attempt to remedy these faults and specifically, to link together the study of contradictions and of patterns of social consciousness. Now this attempt is very much dependent upon what I have argued in part 1. I do not here want to outline the significance of chapters 1, 2 and 3 for parts 2 and 3. Rather, I want to consider the central theme of this book, namely, the study of social comparisons. Especially I want to consider some radical criticisms of this notion made by W. G. Runciman in the postscript to the new edition of his *Relative Deprivation and Social Justice*. If his comments were relevant to my argument they would be extremely damaging.

Runciman asks us what it means when we say that my satisfactions depend on my lot relative to those with whom I compare myself. His reply is that this is a ridiculous argument in a strong sense since we compare ourselves with a multitude of other people without it affecting our satisfactions in one way or the other. We are always contrasting our own position, our abilities, or our rewards, with others, but we do not necessarily feel dissatisfied as a consequence. Thus Runciman points out that he often compares his own locomotive capacity unfavourably with that of athletes but he is not upset by the revealed difference. But if we then qualify the statement by saying that comparison leads to dissatisfaction *only* where the comparison is important to one, then our argument is circular. We cannot, therefore, cite the comparison made by an actor as *the* cause of the dissatisfaction he expresses.

Runciman rather indicates two points. First of all, we must ask what was it that caused the person to take *this* particular comparison seriously rather than others. Second, we must never take the identification of a person's comparative reference group as providing in itself an adequate explanation of his resentment at the patterning of social inequality. Now it seems to me that in my discussion of the various analyses of social comparisons in chapter 4 and in my theoretical exegesis in chapter 5 I have been concerned with both of these points. Consider the following three aspects of my argument. First, I distinguished between conventional and structural comparisons pointing out that the failure to make this distinction conflated two different sorts of social comparison with very different meaning and implication. Second, I mainly focused on the social comparisons made in relation to the three dimensions of social inequality and not in relation to all sorts of personal attributes (such as locomotive capacity). Finally, I emphasized throughout that the analysis of social comparisons can only be made plausible where it is merely one consideration or stage within a much longer and more complicated account. My attempt to provide this in part 2 is based on both the necessity of explaining the choice of social comparisons, and on showing that the identification of a comparison implies neither dissatisfaction nor dissent.

Finally, I wish to return to the dialectic between man and society with which I began this book. Now generally it is clear that I have concentrated mainly on showing how men's actions should not be explained as merely the product of external objective forces. Rather, I have been interested in developing an account of revolutionary thought and action in terms of the meanings which actors give to their experiences within various sorts of social structural contexts. But if we consider that further, we can see how social phenomena in general and revolutionary phenomena in particular are irreducibly man-made. Revolution thus exemplifies the general point that social phenomena are, on the one hand, man-made and man-changeable, and on the other, occur within tremendously powerful and pervasive social structures.

Notes

Introduction

1 Other products of this seminar are: Dunn (1972), the influence of which can be seen in the rest of this Introduction; Bob Jessop's *Social Order, Reform and Revolution* (Macmillan, London, 1972); and Dick Geary's book on Karl Kautsky to be published by Cambridge University Press.

Part one, chapter 1

1 Baldwin (1911, p. 28); but even so, his account perpetuates the sociology–psychology distinction, uses the notion of instinct, and emphasizes only mental movements and processes for accounting for the existence and progress of social life.

2 Thus James (1892, p. 176) says both that 'the total self of me ... must have two aspects discriminated in it, of which for shortness we may call one the *Me* and the other the *I*', and that there is 'the identity of *I* and *Me*, even in their very act of discrimination'.

3 See James (1890, pp. 294–5); on p. 295 he quotes John Locke to the effect that:

> He must be a strange and unusual constitution who can content himself to live in constant disgrace and disrepute with his own particular society. Solitude many men have sought and been reconciled to; but nobody that has the least thought or sense of a man about him can live in society under the constant dislike and ill opinion of his familiars and those he converses with.

4 Thus Dewey (1927, p. 191) says 'an individual as a member of different groups may be divided within himself, and in a true sense have conflicting selves, or be a relatively disintegrated individual. A man may be one thing as a church member and another thing as a member of the business community.'

5 Cooley (1966, p. 400): generally, see pp. 397–400, as well as Hinkle (1967).

6 Cooley (1956a, p. 36) says that 'A well-developed individual can exist only in and through a well-developed whole, and *vice versa*' (see also pp. 261 and 423–6).
7 See ibid., p. 92; as well as Cooley (1956b, p. 61) where he tautologically maintains that communication is the mechanism through which human relations exist and develop.
8 See also Mead (1934, p. 224, n. 26) and, for a cognate critique of Hegel, see Marx and Engels (1956, p. 254):

> Hegel makes man *the man of self consciousness* instead of making self-consciousness the *self-consciousness of man*, of real man, man living in a real objective world and determined by that world. He stands the world *on its head* and can therefore dissolve *in the head* all limitations which naturally remain in existence for *evil sensuousness*, for *real* man. Besides everything which *betrays the limitations of general self-consciousness* – all sensuousness, reality, individuality of men and of their world – necessarily rates for him as a limit. The whole of *Phenomenology* is intended to prove that *self-consciousness* is the *only reality* and *all reality*.

9 See Mead (1932, p. 169; 1938, p. 292); generally on Mead, see Pfuetze (1954); Blumer (1966); Chasin (1964); Strauss (1964); Natanson (1956).
10 See Mead (1934, p. 135). That *social* experience is a *sine qua non* for such development can be seen by considering the consequences for the actor when he is deprived of such human intercourse. Some good illustrative material is presented in Sprott (1958, pp. 27–8). It is perhaps worthwhile at this stage to point out the similarity between Mead and Piaget, not only in their common realization that the self is emergent as, in Piaget's terms, egocentric speech develops into socialized speech, but also for their emphasis upon language as a tool, upon dialectical processes, upon an epistemological relativism, upon the interpenetration of genesis and structure, and upon reflection as an 'internalized social discussion'.
11 Thus Morris (1934, p. 78) says at one stage that: 'Language does not simply symbolize a situation or object which is already there in advance; it makes possible the existence or the appearance of that situation or object, for it is a part of the mechanism whereby that situation or object is created' (see also Speier, 1967; Harrell, 1967).
12 See Mead (1934, p. 316 and esp. pp. 221–2) on the liberating potential of civilized society.
13 It is also a highly limited exegesis of symbolic interactionism; see also Thomas (1966); Znaniecki (1967); and the over-brief discussion of Sullivan in chapter 4 of this book. A useful bibliography is in Kuhn (A1964a); three useful readers are: Rose (1962); Manis and Meltzer (1967); Stone and Farberman (1970); and the best textbook is Lindesmith and Strauss (A1968). A contemporary example in fiction of interactionist writing is Mervyn Jones's *John and Mary* (Pan Books, London, 1969). On the ontological similarity of Marx and Mead, see Marx (1956, p. 176; and 1959 in particular).

14 This argument from a distinguished symbolic interactionist is thus of great interest: it is in Strauss (A1959, p. 11).

15 Natanson (1956, pp. 66–8) gives the example at one extreme of the law, or legal institutions, as the generalized other.

16 It is perhaps presumptuous to continue the discussion of groups and conflict any further without mentioning Simmel's contribution. Often he is seen to be important for two reasons: one for his discussion of the possible functions of social conflict; the other for his elucidation of the notion of cross-pressurization. Less often is it noted that he maintains that 'society arises from the individual and that the individual arises out of association' (Simmel, 1955, p. 163); or that 'advanced culture' is potentially liberating because each individual may establish contacts with persons outside his original group-affiliation. Modern man may regain his individuality through his capacity to form for himself a unique constellation of multiple group-affiliations. Yet although that may presage psychological collapse (see ibid., pp. 151 and 154 on early suggestions of the theory of status congruence) as well as a lack of overlapping conflict, Simmel does point out that modern industry is such that thousands of workers are subject to identical working conditions and that their performance is entirely reduced to its monetary equivalent.

One problem of Simmel's group psychology is its predication upon formal membership as providing the essential nexus between the individual actor and the group. It is taken as axiomatic that once such membership has been established there is no question as to the individual's acting in accordance with the group's norms and values. See later (p. 12f.) for further discussion.

17 This discussion is heavily indebted to Natanson (1956).

18 See Schutz (1962; 1964; 1966; 1967); for a recent and related contribution, see Berger and Luckmann (A1967), as well as Light's critique (1969).

19 The argument here is set out in much greater detail in Urry (1970).

20 See the Introduction to Freud, 1960 (pp. xiv–xv); in general, see Holmes (1965).

21 This is realized in the two most popular New Left interpretations of Freud, namely Brown (1968) and Marcuse (1969a). The distinction drawn in the latter between basic and surplus repression, although a travesty of Freudian repression, is just such an acknowledgement that all human action is premised upon social interaction and in this sense upon some degree of repression.

22 See Campbell (1964, pp. 391–6); see also Campbell (A1958) for his contribution to reference group analysis.

23 See Wrong (1966); see also Campbell (1964, pp. 396–8) on why he does not agree with the argument here.

24 This is no sense an adequate account; see Baldwin (1963); Bronfenbrenner (1963), and for a bibliography of relevant writings, see Smelser and Smelser (1963, p. 33).

25 Goffman (1961, p. 140). Two interesting articles have, from opposed directions, criticized Goffman's notion of role-distance. MacIntyre

(1969) castigates Goffman for submerging the human agent beneath the conceptual agglomeration of role-playing and role-performances so that there is no self apart from the parts which it plays; while Rose Laub Coser (1966) claims that there is no reason for not believing that role-distance is normatively sanctioned. It is not possible for both writers to be right. MacIntyre seems to have misunderstood the Goffman of at least *Stigma* (1963) and *Encounters* (1961), since much emphasis is there placed upon an unsubmerged self transcending role-prescriptions. Coser's re-statement of role-distance in terms of sociological ambivalence seems to be a way of emasculating these considerations, of castrating MacIntyre's: 'possibilities of a moral growth beyond mere performance' (1969, p. 447).

Chapter 2

1 See Sherif (A1968a, pp. 85–6); for the best discussion of this see Sowa (A1962) especially for her specification of the inadequacy of the in-group–out-group distinction in mobile societies.
2 As Scott (1958, p. 188) says:

> Man's biological nature equips him for developing a wide variety of complex social relationships. Each of these can be developed with a great deal of individual variability and is subject to all sorts of modification by learning and experience. The ideal human being is one who develops a variety of social relationships suited to his individual needs and capacities, and the ideal human society is one which is based on these relationships.

The distinction between symbol and sign is made explicit by Cassirer (1944, p. 32): 'Symbols ... cannot be reduced to mere signals. Signals and symbols belong to different universes of discourse: a signal is a part of the physical world of being; a symbol is a part of the human world of meaning.'
3 See Newcomb (A1951b); Parsons (A1964, p. 152) for his only statement on reference group analysis; Linn (A1966, pp. 494–5) on the relationship between the reference group and other social psychological concepts; see also ibid., p. 499 where he suggests the possibility that all of social psychology may be submerged beneath the notion of the reference group.
4 See Kelly (A1968); two examples of writers who do not so distinguish are Turner (A1955) and Parker and Kleiner (A1966).
5 See the discussion in chapter 3.
6 Jackson (A1959b) where these are considered as geometric dimensions yielding a nine-section orthogonal space.
7 Merton (A1957, pp. 286–7 and 288 and generally, pp. 284–300).
8 Except, that is, for Cain (A1968).
9 See Child (1941, p. 416); Kuhn (A1964a; A1964b, esp. pp. 12–13 in the latter); and Mannheim (1936, p. 26):

> Knowledge is from the very beginning a co-operative process of group life, in which everyone unfolds his knowledge within the

framework of a common fate, a common activity, and the overcoming of common difficulties. . . . And even this common world . . . appears differently to the subordinate groups within the larger group. It appears differently because the subordinate groups and strata in a functionally differentiated society have a greater experimental approach to the common contents of the objects of their world.

10 He also points out the similarity between the dialectic within Meadian social psychology and a phenomenological sociology of knowledge.

11 See Natanson (1956, pp. 65–6) on 'being-with'.

12 See Shibutani (A1955, p. 566); and Schatzman and Strauss (1955) on middle-working-class linguistic differences; Burns (A1958) on the sociological perspective; Becker and Carper (1956) on identification with an occupation; and Sowa (A1962, p. 46), on detailing the importance of communication for the process of acquiring objects of normative reference.

13 Thus the Sherifs (A1953, p. 161) define a reference group as 'those groups to which the individual relates himself as a part or to which he aspires to relate himself psychologically' (all emphasized in original). This relates to the problem posed by Kuhn (A1964a) when he asks whether the notion of a reference group refers to the attitudes, expectations and norms of existent others, or only to when they have been transmuted to the imagination of the actors themselves, to the 'solid facts' of social life in Cooley's terms. The answer is that even where role-taking occurs (and there is thus transmutation) these refer to the two moments of the dialectical process. See the rest of this paragraph.

14 Thus Nettl and Robertson's discussion (A1968, pp. 77–8) of the way in which the beneficiary both takes the role of the benefactor in the colonial situation and dissociates from his standpoint is, in itself, inadequate since it neglects the identification groups in terms of which that normative reference is specified (see also Diab, A1962).

15 Two exceptions to the very last point are Nettl and Robertson (A1968, p. 78) when they discuss the nature of a validation group; and Kemper (A1968) in the *use* of his audience group.

16 See Gerth and Mills (1954, pp. 94–5); and Wrong (1966), pp. 116–19) for a discussion of the limitations of the maximized self-evaluation approach.

17 See among others, Deutsch and Krauss (A1965, p. 202); Sowa (A1962, p. 41); Gross (A1967); or as Glaser and Strauss (1968, p. 81) say generally of theory through redescription: 'All they have done is to raise the conceptual level of their work mechanically; they have not raised it through comparative understanding. They have done nothing to broaden the scope of their theory on the formal level by comparative investigation of different substantive areas.'

18 Barry (A1966, p. 35); he is referring to Runciman, A1966, for further discussion of which see below.

187

19 See also Kelly (A1955) for a critique thereof.
20 Thus Linn's claim (A1966, p. 494) that there is 'no constant kind of social phenomena [which] has been studied by most of those who have used the term' is similarly predicated upon the erroneous conflation of the dissimilar (see also Shibutani, A1962, p. 133).
21 Kaplan (A1955, p. 14) talks of the difficulty which has been experienced in the attempt to use the concept empirically.

Chapter 3

1 Merton (A1957, p. 350) seems to agree.
2 See Newcomb (A1952, pp. 240-3) for a discussion of this.
3 Although to some extent Hyman (A1942, p. 24) argued the opposite.
4 See, for example, McCall and Simmons (A1966, pp. 7-8); Merton and Rossi (A1957, p. 254); Sullivan (1955a, pp. 18-22) on the significant other; Shibutani (A1962, pp. 141-3).
5 See among others: Bauer (A1968); Riley and Riley (A1968); Katz and Lazarsfeld (1960); Riley and Flowerman (1951); Brouwer (1962).
6 See Hyman, Wright and Hopkins (A1968) who show the significance of encampment as a positive and long-lasting normative reference.
7 See Eulau (A1968); Kaplan (A1955, ch. 5) and Bott (A1957, p. 159). Each bases his ideas of class upon his own experience.
8 Rose (A1962, p. 11); Kuhn (A1964b); and see Dai (1969) on the primary-secondary self distinction, and Brim (A1966, pp. 16-17) on the notion of a reference set, that is, a synthesis of reference group and role-set concepts.
9 See n. 11 below for a brief discussion of Turner.
10 See Bott (A1957, ch. 6) and Strauss (A1959, pp. 148-52) on the symbolic character of group membership.
11 See Kuhn (1964a, p. 70). Turner provides the best illustration of this. Much implicit praise has been bestowed on his article on role taking (A1966) which first appeared in January 1956; yet three months before (October 1955) he published an article in *Social Forces* (A1955) based upon empirical data, which is a systematic denial of practically all that he later argued.
12 The following is the only really clear statement of the emasculation of Mead within contemporary sociology; it is in Strauss (A1964, pp. xii-xiii):

What sociologists – including such widely read functionalist theorists as Parsons, Davis, and Merton – selected from Mead's writings was very restricted and pertained mainly to how culture and norms got 'internalized' into the person, that is, how self-control was a reflection of social control. Mead's treatment of the self as a process was transformed into something much more static, in accordance with the sociological view of internalized social control. The 'generalized other' became just another way of talking about reference group affiliation, and Mead's notion of role tended to be interpreted to fit with the

structural concept of status and its associated role-playing. It is
even possible to maintain that sociologists, who tend principally
to be social determinists, read Mead as if he too were a social
determinist, although his reiteration of the potential influence of
individuals upon society should have warned against any such
interpretation.

13 For example, of friendship: 'nice people, they know how to live';
and power: 'much influence ... everybody listens to them' and:
'they are important. They can get what they want; everybody seems
to obey them.'

14 There are, of course, sociologists in the USA who do not subscribe
to these presuppositions, just as the most extensive attempt to quantify reference group processes has been made by an Englishman,
W. G. Runciman. However, the thrust of American sociology since
the war has been to favour what one might term the Columbia
rather than the Chicago tradition; and it is this, as well as the Rawl-
sian model of social justice, which is the basis of Runciman's work
(see chapter 4 of this book). On quantification, see Stone (A1958,
p. 560); on pluralism, see Rogin (1967, esp. ch. 9) and Wolff (1969,
pp. 46 and 49). In the latter, it is important to note how pluralism
favours groups already established rather than those in the process
of formation.

15 On the distinction between real and referent power, see French and
Raven (A1959).

16 See Lipset, et al. (A1956); also on the notion of an occupational
reference group, see England and Stein (A1961) and Etzkorn (A1966).

17 The last point can be seen in the following cases among others:
coalminers, trawlermen, jazz musicians, policemen, printers and
railwaymen.

18 It should be noted that in Salaman (A1969) the existence of an
occupational community necessarily depends upon the first of these,
plus one or other of the two further conditions.

19 On the last point see Lipset (A1954, p. 102).

20 Some of this is summarized in Salaman (A1969).

21 See Cain (A1968, pp. 195–6); note that she does not *herself* mention
role-taking.

22 See the following paragraph on the same page where Cain argues
the opposite.

23 See pp. 20–1 of chapter 2 for the dimensions of reference groups.

24 Hartley (A1960a; A1960b; A1968a) has also paid some attention to
this problem.

25 See Newcomb (A1968a, p. 385); as well as Lehman (A1966) who
found a Bennington-type liberal movement but emphasized the
increasing use of faculty as an object of normative reference.

26 Among those writers within the field of reference group analysis,
see, for example, Bennis, et al. (A1958); Emery and Katz (A1951);
Haskell (A1960–1); Marsh and Coleman (A1954); Rogers (A1960).

27 See Pollis (A1968); see also Blum (1966), who maintains that there

is less cross-pressurization, the greater the structural differentiation of the social objects involved.

28 See Ehrlich, *et al.* (A1962) and Shibutani (A1962); see also Kaplan (A1955, p. 283) who says that an individual 'probably remains unaware of such potential conflicts to the extent that he refers his specific behaviour or attitude to one or more intimate associates'.

29 See below for further discussion.

30 See Litwak (A1960); Fellin (A1961); Fellin and Litwak (A1963) and Kaplan (A1955, ch. 6) esp. p.163 where he argues that 'potential conflicts between past and present occur with such relatively low frequency'.

31 See Riesman (1951) and below.

32 See Cloward and Ohlin (A1960, pp. 94–5); Kerckhoff and McCormick (A1955, p. 54) and an example of this can be seen in Carmichael and Hamilton (1969, p. 46): 'The black person ceases to identify himself with black people yet is obviously unable to assimilate with whites. He becomes a "marginal man", living on the fringes of both societies in a world largely of "make-believe".'

33 See Strauss (A1959, p. 123). Goldthorpe and Lockwood's specification of the four stages of working-class embourgeoisement (A1963), realizes the first but not explicitly the second of these points. There are two problems raised by their interesting discussion of issues germane here. The first is that it is not obvious that the term 'reference group' adds anything to the account. Second, their discussion in terms of possible movement from a membership to a reference group seems to ignore both that the membership group will have some sort of normative significance, and that middle-class normative reference is, in practice, premised upon white-collar affiliation. The last point is systematically shown in Goldthorpe (A1969a).

34 The exceptions to this are Ellis, Lane and Clayton (A1966); Fellin (A1961); Fellin and Litwak (A1963); Kaplan (A1955); Litwak (A1960); Merton and Rossi (A1957).

35 See Hartley (A1951) on the master-self, and Dahrendorf (A1968) on man's moral, intelligible character.

36 See among others: *Dictionary of Social Sciences* (trans. by Govld and Kolb, eds, Tavistock, 1964) for various meanings of the self; Diggory (1966); Erikson (1969; 1968a; 1968b); Moustakas (1956) Pressey and Kuhlen (1957); Rosenberg (1967); Wylie (1961); Gordon and Gergen (1968) for the best collection of readings. The tradition which rejects the notion of a self is famously represented by Hume (1962, p. 308):

> The identity which we ascribe to the mind of man is only a fictitious one, and of a like kind with that which we ascribe to vegetable and animal bodies. . . . It is evident, that the identity which we attribute to the human mind . . . is not able to run the several different perceptions into one.

Wundt likewise declared for 'a psychology without a soul' (see Allport, 1955, p. 36); Bruyn (1966, p. 196, n. 17) points out that

Brahminism advocates the elimination of the self and of all related desires. See also ibid., p. 33, n. 10, where he advocates the notion of the self (that is, that which can act as an object to itself) because of its possible validation through the sheer act of introspection.

37 See the references for n. 36, as well as Miller (A1963) and Kolb (1967) which criticizes the Meadian distinction between the 'me' and the 'I'.

38 See Miller (A1963) on sub-identities; and McCall and Simmons (A1966) on role-identities.

39 To neglect one or other of these is to posit the individual either as a series of steps along a continuum, or as an unchanging personality laid down in early life.

40 See also the short piece, Lecky (1968).

41 See among others: Heider (1967); Festinger (1953); Miller (A1963); Becker (1964); Moustakas (1956); and the status congruence literature, for which see chapters 4 and 5 of this book.

42 As May (1958, p. 12) says:

> While one should not rule out the study of dynamisms, drives and patterns of behaviour . . . these cannot be understood in any given person except in the context of the overarching fact that here is a person who happens *to exist, to be,* and if we do not keep this in mind, all else we know about this person will lose its meaning.

43 See among others: Becker (1964); Becker and Strauss (1956); Cain (1964); Hall (1948); Hughes (1937; 1958); Strauss (A1959; 1962).

44 For a discussion see Glucksman (1962).

45 See Wilensky (1969) on the empirical extent of career disorganization. In Strauss (1968) certain typically neglected dimensions of careers are indicated: some of these are degrees of regulation, inevitability, desirability, reversibility, repeatability, clarity, centrality to individual, voluntariness, collectiveness and length of time involved. Strauss (A1959, p. 43) thus says: 'Human careers . . . have always an unfinished character, a certain indeterminancy of outcome.'

46 Abrams (1970); Cain (1964); Mannheim (1952); and Zeitlin (A1967), especially p. 230, where he shows how the rebel leaders in Cuba became a normative reference for the whole population.

Chapter 4

1 See also pp. 192 and 199.

2 See also pp. 180–7 and Mishan (1969, p. 27).

3 This account of Kautsky is totally indebted to Geary (1969, pp. 20–30); see also Kautsky (1909, pp. 20–1).

4 He suggests that, among others, the social situations of women, the elderly and the priests are likely to induce sentiments of *ressentiment*.

5 See Schoeck (A1969, pp. 6–22). Some detailed attention must be devoted to this work because there are just so few extended contributions in this field.

6 See ibid., p. 328, where Schoeck seems to acknowledge this possibility. Or, as Daphne du Maurier writes in *The Progress of Julius* (Heinemann, London, 1963):

> It was good to be envied by men, it was good to be feared, it was good to experience deeply the sensation of power by wealth, the power of money tossed to and fro lightly in his hands like a little god obedient as a slave. The voices around him were warm and thrilling to his heart because of their envy. He knew the meaning of the whisper and the glances, 'Julius Levy . . . there's Julius Levy.'

7 It is not surprising in consequence that Schoeck does not quote Francis Bacon (1911, p. 39) that 'those are most subject to envy which carry the greatness of their fortunes in an insolent and proud manner'.

8 See Duesenberry (1967); more generally, of the economics and sociology of consumer behaviour, see Engel, *et al.* (A1968).

9 See Gurr and Ruttenberg (A1967); more generally on 'internal war' see Eckstein (1964; 1965).

10 See Brinton (1953); for a discussion of this see Nadel (1960) and Dahrendorf (1961).

11 Stouffer, *et al.* (A1965, p. 251). For a much extended discussion of these findings see Urry (A1971) as well as Urry (A1972).

12 On the generality of this relationship see Stouffer, *et al.* (A1965, p. 254–8); a cultural explanation is incorrect because morale was found to be *highest* in the Air Corps (see ibid., p. 253 and ch. 7).

13 See Davis (A1959). It should be noted that this theory is used to explain a wide range of empirical findings found in *The American Soldier*.

14 See Blau (A1964, p. 160); Homans (A1961, p. 270); Runciman (A1966). For a longer and more systematic analysis of Runciman, see Urry (A1972).

15 See Runciman (A1966, pp. 6, 7 and 217). Leach (A1966) points out that if the analysis of relative deprivation in 1962 requires the complex paraphernalia of survey technology, then surely this applies to the analysis of the period 1918–62 as well.

16 Other evidence of the restricted nature of social comparisons is provided by Wedderburn (1970); Coates and Silburn (A1967) and implicitly, by Jahoda (A1953).

17 See Urry (A1972) for three other objections to self-rating.

18 See the third section of this chapter on methodology; as well as Westergaard (A1970, p. 122) who challenges some of Runciman's interpretations of his data.

19 But see Runciman (1967).

20 Thus, as Patchen himself says, the necessity of asking for comparison individuals earning either more or less leads to both a choice of persons of differing status, that is, to probable consonant comparisons, and to ignoring possible comparison objects with the same earnings; second, consideration is paid only to reference individuals,

and groups, collectivities, and categories are all neglected; third, no attempt is made to discover whether the respondent *in fact* compares with the comparison person cited; and fourth, no rationale is provided for choosing two rather than one or three or more comparison persons.

21 See Lenski (1954); some of the literature is summarized in various articles in J. Berger, *et al.* (1966); more recent literature is discussed in Box and Ford (1969) and Doreian and Stockman (1969).

22 See Bagley (A1970a) and Geschwender (A1968); there is further discussion of the latter below.

23 See also Runciman (A1967) and Hyman (A1967).

24 These are Anderson and Zelditch (A1964) and Galtung (A1964); see also Bagley (A1970a) and Runciman and Bagley (A1969).

25 See also Hyman and Singer (A1968); Latane (A1966) and *Human Relations*, 7, 1954.

26 On the following page he explicitly points out the significance of reference individuals.

27 See Cantril (A1965) for a discussion of the different techniques of analysing relative deprivation.

28 See Fletcher (1970) for the most extensive discussion of replication.

29 On the interview, see the well-known third chapter of Cicourel (1964).

30 See Urry (A1972) for a brief discussion of the way in which the survey questions asked may structure the responses obtained.

31 LaPiere (1934); or more directly as Jock Macrae, Convenor at Dagenham, asked in the *Black Dwarf* (30 January 1970, p. 7): 'How do you gauge the mood of the men on the shop floor?' replied:

> 'Well, I think it's for the birds, really, this type of question on how you gauge opinion. You have the boys flat to-day and to-morrow they can be raring to go. . . . It's like a bloody barometer you know, day can be fair, the night can be changeable and to-morrow it can really be hard and raining.'

32 This is systematically shown in Brown and Gilmartin (1969); 85 per cent of research referred to the present, very few studies related to the study of change or process, and most research was quantitative.

Part two, chapter 5

1 See Demerath (1967, pp. 502–6) for a summary of such distinctions; and see Gouldner (1967).

2 See Cole (1966) for a similar, albeit less successful, attempt.

3 See Lockwood (1964) on this distinction; see also Nettl and Robertson (A1968, p. 148) on the distinction between two types of integration.

4 See Dahrendorf (1959) and Rex (1961), although this criticism is in fact more relevant to the former.

5 See among others: Lockwood (1964, p. 246); Bruyn (1966, p. 75); Lenski (1966); Rodner (1967).

6 See Moore (1958, p. 138) for a similar advocation from a different political standpoint; and, by way of example, Plato (1955, p. 323).

7 See Firth (1964, pp. 25–6) who similarly misinterprets Marx, although he does distinguish between conflict and contradiction; the latter is, however, seen purely as conflict *within* the value system.

8 See Firth (1964); van den Berghe (1967) and Supek (1967) for various discussions of this contradiction.

9 For its congruence with Marx see Avineri (1968, p. 76); for its relationship with Parsons, see Parsons and Shils (1951); Parsons and Smelser (1956) and Smelser (1962).

10 These are derived especially from Lockwood (1958) and Ossowski (1963).

11 It should be noted that the Weberian category of 'parties' is not considered useful here since it does not seem distinguishable from either a class or status group seeking political power.

12 It should be recognized that the idle/work dichotomy is a split *within* the 'top class'.

13 See Urry (1973) for a brief discussion of some further points raised by the study of power.

14 Note how Ingham (1969) approaches a similar conclusion, as does Runciman (1970).

15 Thus although Lenski (1966) suggests that power is an independent variable more or less determining privilege and prestige, he also points out the various *foundations* of power (pp. 79–80).

16 See Etzioni (1965, pp. 5–6) on the three sorts of power.

17 See ibid., p. 5, n. 4 and pp. 14–16. On p. 16, Etzioni does distinguish between social and pure normative power. This means that it is possible to envisage one power dimension corresponding to each of Parsons's functional problems. However, Etzioni does insist that this division is one within the normative (cultural) dimension and thus does not destroy the argument here.

18 Thus status 'is not a substantial property of the person arising automatically from the possession of certain entitlements but is in fact an element in a relationship between the person deferred to and the deferred person' (Shils, 1968, p. 116); the macro-social dimensions being 'those characteristics which describe the role or positions of persons in the larger society in which they live' (ibid., p. 105).

19 See Hughes (1945) on the notion of master-status.

20 See among others: Leggett (1968, esp. pp. 69–70); Hamilton (1967); Ulam (1960, esp. pp. 58–90); Zeitlin (A1967, ch. 6).

21 See Hoffer (1964, pp. 4–5); see also Newton (1965, p. 198, Diagram 11) on the importance of the disorganization of one's life pattern.

22 See Erikson (1968b, p. 155f) on the psycho-social moratorium.

23 See Kumar (1971, p. 160); see also the Introduction to this book in which Kumar focuses almost entirely on why 'the "upper classes" cannot carry on in the old way'.

24 See Bateson, *et al.* (1956) on the notion of 'double-bind'.

25 See Hyman and Singer (A1968, p. 16); Merton and Rossi (A1957, p. 247); McCall and Simmons (A1966, esp. ch. 5); Rosenberg (1967);

Fathi (1965); Bertrand, *et al.* (A1967); all of which point out how perception is a necessary condition of relative deprivation.

26 See Marsh (1967) and the difficulties that he has as an experienced social scientist in making satisfactory comparisons; I am indebted to Philip Abrams for suggesting this to me.

27 Examples of each of these respectively are the colonizer–colonized situation, the lack of emphasis upon the economic dimensions among the religiously devout, and the lack of clear-cut consumption patterns.

28 This mirrors the sorts of radicalism discovered by Manis and Meltzer (1963).

29 An example of the notion of dual consciousness is found in Blackburn (1969, p. 200) when he says of Luton car workers: 'On the one hand they are quite aware that the owners are profiting from their labour; on the other they know they cannot change the system so they are prepared to go along with it.' Blackburn quotes approvingly Leach's argument that the Burmese that he studied held two world-views simultaneously. This is discussed in Leach (1954).

30 See Barnes (1969) for a recent and comprehensive summary and discussion of the many meanings of the notion of a network. This concept, as opposed to role-set, group, and so on, seems more appropriate to systematizing the reality of the actor's social world for two reasons: one is that it appreciates the segmental and inter-mittent character of self–other interaction; the other is that it focuses upon the way in which the actor constructs his world. Incidentally, that explains the use of the term 'believes' in the text; in other words, a TV personality does not formally interact with an actor but in that such interaction is believed to occur this personality becomes one component of the actor's network.

31 See Bott (A1957) on this distinction.

32 As Lipset (A1968, p. 312) importantly and perceptively says:

The formation of class consciousness may be seen as a process in which members of the lower social strata change their reference groups, while class consciousness is dormant or incipent, the lower-class individual relates himself to various small groups; with the full emergence of class consciousness, he relates himself to aspects of the larger social structure.

33 This seems to be the main significance of the process of structural differentiation so emphasized within functionalism; for an alternative interpretation see Nettl and Robertson (A1968, p. 173, n. 3).

34 As Merleau-Ponty (1962, p. 443) says:

What makes me a good proletarian is not the economic system or society considered as systems of impersonal forces, but these institutions as I carry them within me and experience them; nor is it an intellectual operation devoid of motive, but my way of being in the world within this institutional framework.

35 Zeitlin (A1967, p. 10) says: 'It is the structure of social relationships in which the worker is implicated that determines . . . how he

perceives these deprivations . . . and their objective impact on him.'
The argument here appears cognate with that of Goldmann (1969,
p. 111) on the notion of 'potential consciousness'.

36 See among others: Bott (A1957); Dennis, *et al.* (1956); Hoggart
(1957); Davies (1967); Lockwood (1966); Popitz (1957); Young
and Willmott (1962); Kerr and Siegel (1954); Willener (1957); Oeser
and Hammond (1954).

37 See among others: Yinger (1960, p. 629 in particular); Nettl and
Robertson (A1968, p. 159) on international contra-cultures; Berger
and Luckmann (A1967, pp. 144–5) on revolutionary subsocieties;
and for two presentations of certain components of contemporary
youth–student culture in this light, Roszak (1969) and Berke
(1969).

38 See Goffman (1962) on cooling-out. See Hans Koenigsberger's sympathetic treatment in *The Revolutionary* (Penguin, London, 1970)
on the difficulties of maintaining a revolutionary identity.

39 See among others: Goffman (1968, pp. 92–113); Anderson and
Zelditch (A1964, p. 118); Sorokin (1964, p. 533); Garfinkel (1967,
esp. pp. 116–85); Germani (A1966) for a systematic discussion of
the consequences of mobility.

40 The best elucidation of the meaning of escalation is that of Mills's
'sociological imagination'; see Mills (1967). Also note Adam Ulam's
suggestion (1960, pp. 28–57) that European Marxism leads to reformist trade unionism precisely because it concentrated not upon the
work process as a system but upon the capitalist himself.

41 See also Ingham (1969).

42 This relates to the argument of Zeitlin (A1967, pp. 179–81) that in
Cuba, workers were *less* likely to have been pre-revolutionary sup-
porters of the communists (implication of highish degree of escalation) where there was a high ratio of managerial, technical and
administrative personnel to production workers.

43 See Mizruchi (1967); Reiss and Rhodes (A1962) and Keller and
Zavalloni (A1964) who point out that even where there are lofty
aspirations, these are essentially fantastic (p. 61).

44 See Pettigrew (A1968); see also Bagley (A1968) and Runciman and
Bagley (A1969) for similar explanations of certain forms of racialism.

45 See Pettigrew (A1968, pp. 340–3) for details.

46 See ibid., pp. 345–8, for details.

47 A further consideration is that there are particular phenomena which
serve to obscure the reality of the power structure; see Cleaver (1968,
pp. 133–4) on the nature of police brutality which serves to obscure
the social, economic and political brutality which, he maintains, lies
behind.

48 See Foster (1967, pp. 6 and 15); the discussion here is indebted to
this particularly interesting work.

49 Foster (ibid., p. 19) says: 'If a town's top people were . . . garret
masters who started out (and remained) working-men, then a man's
picture of his own chances in society would not be so unfavourable
(to society or to himself) as it might be otherwise.'

50 Gorz (1967, p. 346); see also Wolpe (1970, pp. 261–3) on all of these points.
51 Also quoted in Burns (A1966b, p. 323).
52 See Alavi (1965, pp. 274–5) the best discussion of the relationship between this and the banditry is Hobsbawm (1959, p. 22f).
53 He further points out how feudal societies lie in between the highly segmented and the unsegmented.
54 It is noteworthy that he does not use the term contradiction, although he had advocated this in Moore (1958).
55 On the concept of revolution, see among many others: Snow (1962); Lasky (1970a; 1970b); Kumar (1971); Arendt (1963); Dunn (1972). My thinking on this subject has benefited from writing a joint paper with Bob Jessop on 'Social order, reform, and revolution' (University of Cambridge). For a recent, interesting article, see Lawrence (A1972).
56 See Mannheim (1936, pp. 116–17), who argues that such 'theoretical practice' is only necessary in non-traditional societies.
57 It should be noted that no use is made of the concept of charisma; that is because 'the preconception that every form of successful ostensibly personal leadership imparts a religious inspiration' (Marcuse, 1965, p. 13) is precisely the obverse of the claim being made here. Rather, what is necessary is both 'an analysis of the historical conditions and social processes that give rise to charismatic eruptions in the social structure' (Blau, 1963, p. 309), and a specification of whether the societal values are congruent with charismatic dissensual leadership.
58 Arendt (1963, p. 112); see also, Chorley (1943). On the possibility of the 'failure of social control' being tautological, see Dunn (1972, p. 239f).
59 This is less than Smelser (1962) requires from his notion of the 'precipitating factors' of a value-orientated movement.
60 There are interesting similarities between my argument here and David Aberle's fascinating account of the cult of Peyote among the Navaho Indians (A1966). I would not like any of my criticisms of the social comparisons literature in chapter 4 to be taken to be referring to this book.

Part three, chapter 6

1 I will use the term Indonesia to refer to the archipelago irrespective of the particular period under discussion.
2 See Wertheim (B1964, p. 111) and Schrieke (B1955, p. 184f; B1957, p. 217f) on the Dutch East India Company; and Wertheim (B1964, p. 115) on the Dutch.
3 See Weber (1925, p. 711). The evidence presented by Schrieke (B1955, p. 184; B1957, p. 217) bears out Wertheim's claim (B1964, pp. 108–9) that these Asian empires were not strongly centralized units over which the prince exercised 'total power'; on the contrary,

there was a highly significant localization of power (see Benda, B1962a, p. 113).

4 Benda (B1962a, p. 133); see also Benda (B1958a, p. 18); Wertheim (B1956, esp. pp. 62–8) and 'The Bantam Report', in Benda and McVey (B1960, Appendix 1, p. 67).

5 See among others: van Leur (B1955, p. 104f); Benda (B1962a, p. 113); Weber (1964, p. 346f).

6 For a contrary view, see Krom (B1931).

7 See van Leur (B1955, pp. 145–56); the argument here is to raise serious dispute with van Leur's description of Islam as 'a thin and easily disappearing varnish'.

8 See van der Kroef (B1958a, pp. 356–7), especially his comments upon the treaties ratified between the Dutch and Sunan Amangkurat, the ruler of Mataram, 1746–77; see also Glamann (B1958, *passim*).

9 The main thrust of the reforms of the former was the transformation of the Regents from protected rulers into government officials (see Day, B1966, pp. 156–63); the main focus of the latter was the replacement of the compulsory deliveries system by a land-tax (see ibid., pp. 164–202).

10 See ibid., pp. 244–5; by 1830 the government debt was 30 million guilders.

11 See Geertz (B1963a, p. 67) for details of the 'take-off' of sugar and coffee production over this period.

12 See also Lasker (B1950, p. 79).

13 See Vlekke (B1959, pp. 309–10); it is noteworthy that Dutch apologists tend to remove this change of policy out of the general imperialist context and attribute it to specific events such as the publication of *Max Havelaar* by Multatuli (namely, E. Douwes Dekker).

14 See the Table in Callis (B1942, p. 36) and Thompson and Adloff (B1950, p. 164).

15 See also his comments on pre-revolutionary Russia.

16 Day (B1966, p. 426), writing in 1903, commented on how: 'One party to the work is as weak as are necessarily the natives.'

17 This is well illustrated in Kartodirdjo (B1966).

18 See Kartini (B1921, pp. 38–9); and Day (B1966, p. 425) who said: 'At best the faults of native character would disappear but slowly, as new intellectual and moral standards grew up in native society.'

19 For details both of the change and of the regressive system of taxation, see Vlekke (B1959, p. 313).

20 It appears as part of the explanation of various dissensual movements: see for example, Kahin (B1952, p. 44) on the Saminists; van der Kroef (B1965a, p. 113) and Kartodirdjo (B1962, p. 73) on the dissent of the 1920s.

21 In the latter, the Dutch feared that a failure to keep order might bring about takeover by another colonial power.

22 See Worsley (1968) and Hobsbawm (1959) in general; and Kartodirdjo (B1966) in particular.

23 See Reid (B1967, *passim*) as well as Harris to Glanville, 22 July 1873, Foreign Office, 37/534.

24 See Benda (B1958a, pp. 21–2) for discussion of all these points.
25 See van der Kolff (B1929, pp. 123–4) on the sugar industry.
26 Thus the numbers in western primary education rose from 3,000 Indonesians at the turn of the century to 88,000 by 1940; similarly, the numbers in western secondary education rose from 25,000 to 100,000 (see Kahin, B1952, p. 31). It should also be noted: primary education was normally only for three years; most Indonesians receiving secondary education did not receive it to the high school level; there was a predominance of the *prijaji* since tuition was never free for the Indonesians although it customarily was for the Dutch; most of the expansion occurred before 1930; even by 1940, only 10 per cent of Indonesians were literate in any language. For those who did receive it though, the consequences are summarized by Kartini (B1921).
27 See Sitorus (B1951, p. 10); Kerstiens (B1966, p. 93) and Singh (B1961) for an exposition of its history.
28 See Barber (1955, p. 62) who points out that the same was true of the eighteenth-century French bourgeoisie.
29 For details, see Palmier (B1962, p. 28); *Hollandsch-Inlandsch Onderwijs Commissie*, 6a, pp. 73–8; van Niel (B1960, p. 219); Furnivall (B1943, pp. 77–8).
30 See Mansvelt (B1928); van Niel (B1960, pp. 70 and 235). It should be noted that unemployment was a previously almost unheard of phenomenon in the archipelago.
31 See on some or all of these points: van der Kroef (B1951b); van Niel (B1960, p. 202); Schrieke (B1955, p. 132).
32 See Geertz (B1963a, p. 115), see chapter 2 for an account of the *sawah–swidden* distinction. The latter is a diverse, shifting, uncertain, multicrop, ecosystem; the former, a specialized, stable, monocrop, ecosystem with man-made irrigation.
33 There were municipal, provincial and regency councils.
34 See *Verslag van den Economischen Toestand der Inlandsche Bevolking 1924*, 1926, vol. 1, pp. 106–9.
35 See van der Kroef (B1954a, p. 102); note how the colonial representative in Rider Haggard becomes king – the alternative is sacrifice to the gods.
36 See van der Kroef (B1954a, p. 44); Mannoni's analysis of Madagascar is congruent with the situation in Indonesia (1964, p. 114):

> Mixed unions . . . are becoming more and more rare . . . partly because Europeans have learnt from experience to mistrust those they consider to be 'degraded', but more particularly because there now exists in Madagascar a European female population whose presence has completely altered the basis of the problem.

37 As Kartini (B1921, pp. 43–4) asks: 'Why do Hollanders find it unpleasant to converse with us in their own language? Oh yes, now I understand; Dutch is too beautiful to be spoken by a brown mouth.'
38 See Vandenbosch (B1952, p. 182) on its potential for universalization; on the *santri–abangan* split, see Geertz (B1960a).

39 See van der Kroef (B1965a, p. 6; B1963a, pp. 31–2), especially the latter for details of the background of the PKI leadership.
40 Thompson (B1947, p. 158) attributes this to: 'the predominance of peasant agriculture; the prevalence of part-time employment; the very recent development of industrialisation; the government's policy; the inclusion among unions of such strictly non-labour elements as civil servants and government employees generally.'
41 Note how the PKI successfully capitalized upon this form until its shift of policy away from the peasantry in 1924; this is well-discussed in McVey (B1965, pp. 275–89); it is criticized in Dingley (B1926, p. 43).
42 See also Kahin (B1952, p. 90).
43 Just before the outbreak of the Second World War it supplied about one-third of the world's output of copra, rubber and palm oil, about one-fifth of its tin and sisal, as well as practically all of its pepper and quinine, and significant proportions of its tea, cane, sugar and coffee (see Toynbee and Ashton-Gwatkin, B1939, p. 94).
44 Quoted in Elsbree (B1953, p. 76).
45 On the last point, see Thompson (B1946, p. 203).
46 See Elsbree (B1953, p. 53 and 119) and Anderson (B1961, pp. 2–8) for a general statement on Army–Navy conflict.
47 Tojo, *Japanese Year Book*, 1943–4, p. 202.
48 See Aziz (B1955, p. 206); see also pp. 177–81 on the various educational changes.
49 See Kahin (B1952, p. 35); Brugmans and Soenario (B1941, p. 65) suggest that there were 1,961 of these schools in 1938.
50 See Anderson (B1961, pp. 48–50) for details of the different underground movements.
51 See *ibid.*, p. 38, on the conflict between the young and the old. See Smail (B1964, p. 18) on the formation of *Angkatan Muda* (Younger Generation) at the Villa Isola (north of Bandung) in May 1945.
52 See Aziz (B1955, p. 251); and Elsbree (B1953, pp. 53–4). The two main champions of independence were the Tokyo Ministry of Foreign Affairs and the military authorities in Java.
53 See Anderson (B1961, p. 113); see also Soemardi (B1956, p. 339, Table 1) which shows the predominance of older generation nationalists in both the government and the executive up to 1955.
54 See Geertz (B1968) for a discussion of Sunan Kalidjaga and of how Sukarno was part of the same tradition.
55 See Burger (B1956, pp. 26–8) for further details.
56 In west Java, *desa* organization was only established in 1845; as a consequence, the obligatory services were not so well integrated with local customs (see Kartodirdjo, B1966, p. 49).
57 See Benda and McVey (B1960); 'The Bantam Report', in Benda and McVey (B1960, Appendix 1, p. 26); Benda (B1955a); van der Kroef (B1963a; B1965a) for greater elucidation of these points.
58 Similarly, the mobilizing belief of the 1888 revolt was for a return to the sultanate (see Kartodirdjo, B1966, p. 107).

59 For example, Salim, Sjahrir, Hatta, Tan Malaka and Effendi all moved to Java around this period.
60 'The Bantam Report', in Benda and McVey (B1960, Appendix 1, p. 26).
61 Kartodirdjo's judgment on the Bantam rebellion of 1888 (B1966, p. 321) does not seem inappropriate to 1926; it 'was doomed to failure because it relied wholly on supernatural forces and operated along mystico-magical lines which were completely inadequate in facing colonial forces with modern techniques and organization.'

Conclusion

1 See Althusser (1969), as well as his various other works.

Bibliography

Abbreviations

AA	*American Anthropologist*	*HR*	*Human Relations*
AHR	*American Historical Review*	*JAS*	*Journal of Asian*
AJS	*American Journal of Sociology*		*Studies*
APSR	*American Political Science*	*JSEAH*	*Journal of Southeast*
	Review		*Asian History*
ASR	*American Sociological Review*	*JSP*	*Journal of Social*
ASQ	*Administrative Science*		*Psychology*
	Quarterly	*NLR*	*New Left Review*
BJS	*British Journal of Sociology*	*PA*	*Pacific Affairs*
CSSH	*Comparative Studies in*	*POQ*	*Public Opinion Quarterly*
	Society and History	*SF*	*Social Forces*
EJS	*European Journal of Sociology*	*SR*	*Sociological Review*
FEQ	*Far Eastern Quarterly*	*WP*	*World Politics*

(A) Reference groups

NB: There are a number of articles which refer to the reference group literature written within the marketing and advertising field. The most interesting contributions seem to be in the *Journal of Marketing*.

ABERLE, D. F. (A1962), 'A note on relative deprivation as applied to millenarian and other cult movements', in THRUPP, SYLVIA L., *Millennial Dreams in Action; Essays in Comparative Study, CSSH*, Supplement 2, 209–14.

ABERLE, D. F. (A1966), *The Peyote Religion Among the Navaho*, Chicago.

ADAMS, J. B. (A1960), 'Effects of reference groups and status on opinion change', *Journalism Quarterly*, 37, 408–12.

ADAMS STACY, J. (A1965), 'Inequity in social exchange', in Berkowitz, L. (ed.), *Advances in Experimental Social Psychology*, vol. 2, New York, pp. 267–99.

ANDERSON, B. and ZELDITCH, M., Jr (A1964), 'Rank equilibrium and political behaviour', *EJS*, 5, 112–25.

BIBLIOGRAPHY

ANDERSON, B., BERGER, J., ZELDITCH, M., Jr and COHEN, B. P. (A1969), 'Reactions to inequity', *Acta Sociologica*, 12, 1–12.

BAGLEY, C. (A1968), 'Relative deprivation and the working-class racialist', Institute of Race Relations *Newsletter*, June.

BAGLEY, C. (A1970a), 'Race relations and theories of status consistency', *Race*, 11, 267–88.

BAGLEY, C. (A1970b), 'Social structure and prejudice in five English boroughs'; report prepared for the Survey of Race Relations in Britain, to be published by Institute of Race Relations.

BANTON, M. (A1965), *Roles: An Introduction to the Study of Social Relations*, London.

BARBOSA DASILVA, J. F. (A1966), 'Orientacoes de referencia em um grupo etnico de uma comunidade fronteirica' ('Reference orientations in an ethnic group of a frontier community'), *Sociologia*, 27, 193–208.

BARNES, L. B. (A1960), *Organizational Systems and Engineering Groups*, Boston, Mass.

BARRY, B. (A1965), *Political Argument*, London.

BARRY, B. (A1966), 'The roots of social injustice', *Oxford Review*, 3, 33–46.

BARRY, B. (A1967), 'On social justice', *Oxford Review*, 5, 29–53.

BASEHART, H. W. (undated), 'Reference group theory and the analysis of segmentary systems', *55th Annual Meeting of American Anthropological Association*, Santa Monica, California.

BAUER, P. A. (A1968), 'The communicator and the audience', in HYMAN and SINGER (A1968, pp. 430–42).

BEN-DAVID, J. (A1958), 'The professional role of the physician in bureaucratized medicine: a study in role conflict', *HR*, 11, 255–74.

BENNIS, W. G., BERKOWITZ, W., AFFINITO, M. and MALONE, M. (A1958), 'Reference groups and loyalties in the outpatient department', *ASQ*, 2, 481–500.

BERGER, P. (A1966), *Invitation to Sociology*, London.

BERGER, P. and LUCKMANN, T. (A1967), *The Social Construction of Reality*, London.

BERREMAN, G. D. (A1964), 'Aleut reference group alienation, mobility, and acculturation', *AA*, 66, 231–50.

BERTRAND, A. L., JENKINS, Q. L. and WALKER, MARCIA A. (A1967), 'Anomie and fatalism: the backlash of rising expectations', *Proceedings of the Southwestern Sociological Association*, 18, 109–14.

BLAU, P. (A1960), 'Patterns of deviation in work groups', *Sociometry*, 23, 245–61.

BLAU, P. (A1964), *Exchange and Power in Social Life*, New York.

BOTT, ELIZABETH (A1954), 'The concept of class as a reference group', *HR*, 7, 259–85.

BOTT, ELIZABETH (A1956), 'Urban families: the norms of conjugal roles', *HR*, 9, 325–42.

BOTT, ELIZABETH (A1957), *Family and Social Network: Roles, Norms, and External Relationships in Ordinary Urban Families*, London.

BRIM, O. G., Jr (A1966), 'Socialization through the life-cycle', in BRIM,

204

O. G., Jr and WHEELER, S., *Socialization after Childhood: Two Essays*, New York, pp. 1–49.

BROOKS, R. S. (A1967), 'Reference group influence on political party preference', in MANIS, J. G. and MELTZER, B. N. (eds) *Symbolic Interaction* (1967, pp. 472–80). BURNS, T. (A1955), 'The reference of conduct in small groups', *HR*, 8, 467–86.

BURNS, T. (A1958), 'The idea of structure in sociology', *HR*, 11, 217–28.

BURNS, T. (A1966a), 'Review of Runciman, W. G.: *Relative Deprivation and Social Justice*', *BJS*, 17, 430–4.

BURNS, T. (A1966b), 'The study of consumer behaviour', *EJS*, 7, 313–29.

CAIN, MAUREEN (A1968), 'Suggested developments for role and reference group analysis', *BJS*, 19, 191–205.

CAIN, MAUREEN (A1969), 'Conflict and its solution', Ph.D. thesis, University of London.

CAMPBELL, A., CONVERSE, P. E., MILLER, W. E. and STOKES, D. E. (A1960), *The American Voter*, New York.

CAMPBELL, E. Q. (A1958), 'Some social psychological correlates of direction in attitude change', *SF*, 36, 335–40.

CANTRIL, H. (A1965), *The Pattern of Human Concerns*, New Brunswick.

CAPLAN, N. (A1970), 'The new ghetto man: a review of recent empirical findings', *Journal of Social Issues*, 26, 59–73.

CARLSON, R. O. (A1952), 'The influence of the community and the primary group on the reactions of southern negroes to syphilis', Ph.D. thesis, University of Columbia.

CHAPMAN, D. W. and VOLKMANN, J. A. (A1939), 'A social determinant of the level of aspiration', *Journal of Abnormal and Social Psychology*, 34, 225–38.

CHARTERS, W. W., Jr and NEWCOMB, T. M. (A1968), 'Some attitudinal effects of experimentally increased salience of a membership group', in HYMAN and SINGER (A1968, pp. 95–102).

CLOWARD, R. A. and OHLIN, L. E. (A1960), *Delinquency and Opportunity: A Theory of Delinquent Gangs*, New York.

COATES, K. and SILBURN, R. (A1967), *St. Ann's: Poverty, Deprivation and Morale in a Nottingham Community*, Nottingham.

COHEN, A. K. (A1956), *Delinquent Boys: The Cult of the Gang*, London.

COHEN, B. P. (A1962), 'The process of choosing a reference group', in CRISWELL, J. H. *et al.* (eds), *Mathematical Methods in Small Group Processes*, Stanford, pp. 101–18.

COSER, ROSE LAUB (A1966a), 'An encounter between Goffman's role distance and Merton's reference group theory', working paper available from the University of Wisconsin, Milwaukee.

COSER, ROSE LAUB (A1966b), 'Role distance, sociological ambivalence, and transitional status systems', *AJS*, 72, 173–87.

DAHRENDORF, R. (A1968), 'Homo sociologicus', in DAHRENDORF, R., *Essays in the Theory of Society*, London, pp. 19–87.

DAMLE, Y. B. (A1963), 'Reference group theory with regard to mobility in castes', *Social Action* (Poona), 13, 190–9.

205

DAVIS, J. A. (A1959), 'A formal interpretation of the theory of relative deprivation', *Sociometry*, 22, 280–96.

DE SOLA POOL, I. and SHULMAN, I. (A1959), 'Newsman's fantasies, audiences, and newswritings', *POQ*, 23, 145–58.

DEUTSCH, M. and KRAUSS, R. M. (A1965), *Theories in Social Psychology*, New York.

DIAB, L. N. (A1962), 'National stereotypes and the "Reference Group" concept', *JSP*, 57, 339–52.

DIRENZO, G. J. (ed.) (A1966), *Concepts, Theory, and Explanation in the Behavioral Sciences*, New York.

EDELMAN, M. (A1967), *The Symbolic Uses of Politics*, Chicago.

EHRLICH, H. J. (A1966), 'Review of "Reference Groups"' (see Sherif and Sherif, A1964), *Sociological Quarterly*, 7, 92–3.

EHRLICH, H. J., RINEHART, J. W. and HOWELL, J. C. (A1962), 'The study of role conflict – explorations in methodology', *Sociometry*, 25, 85–98.

EISENSTADT, S. N. (A1954a), 'Reference group behavior and social integration: an explorative study', *ASR*, 19, 175–85.

EISENSTADT, S. N. (A1954b), 'The research project on leadership, mobility and communication', *Transactions of the Second World Congress of Sociology*, International Sociological Association, vol. 1, 106–19.

EISENSTADT, S. N. (A1954c), 'Studies in reference group behaviour: 1. Reference norms and the social structure', *HR*, 7, 191–216.

ELLEMERS, J. E. (A1961), 'Sociologie em de studie van acculturatiever – schijnselen: convergentie van disciplines' ('Sociology and the study of acculturation: convergence of disciplines'), *Mens Maat*, 36, 344–66.

ELLIS, R. A. and LANE, W. CLAYTON (A1966), 'Social mobility and career orientation', *Sociology and Social Research*, 50, 280–96.

EMERY, F. E. and KATZ, F. M. (A1951), 'Social theory and minority group behaviour', *Australian Journal of Psychology*, 3, 22–35.

EMERY, F. E. and KATZ, F. M. (A1952), 'Dr. Taft's criticism – a rejoinder', *Australian Journal of Psychology*, 4, 24–7.

EMGE, M. (A1967), 'Fremde gruppen als Bezugagruppen' ('Foreign groups as reference groups'), in *Kolner Zeitschrift fur Soziologie and Sozial-Psychologie*, 19, 246–62.

ENGEL, J. F., KOLLAT, D. T. and BLACKWELL, R. D. (A1968), *Consumer Behavior*, New York.

ENGLAND, G. W. and STEIN, C. I. (A1961), 'The occupational reference group. A neglected concept', *Personnel Psychology*, 14, 299–304.

ETZKORN, P. (A1966), 'On esthetic standards and reference groups of popular songwriters', *Sociological Inquiry*, 36, 39–47.

EULAU, H. (A1968), 'Identification with class and political role behaviour', in HYMAN and SINGER (A1968, pp. 490–503).

FABRIS, G. (A1965), 'Gruppi di riferimento e consumi' ('Reference groups and consumption'), *Studi di Sociologia*, 3, 141–60.

FELLIN, P. (A1961), 'A study of the effects of reference group orientations and bureaucratic careers on neighborhood cohesion', Ph.D. thesis, University of Michigan.

FELLIN, P. and LITWAK, E. (A1963), 'Neighborhood cohesion under conditions of mobility', *ASR*, 28, 364–76.

FENDRICH, J. M. (A1967), 'Perceived reference group support: racial attitudes and overt behavior', *ASR*, 32, 960–9.

FESTINGER, L. (A1968), 'A theory of social comparison processes', in HYMAN and SINGER (A1968, pp. 123–46).

FISHBEIN, M. (A1963), 'The perception of non-members: a test of Merton's reference group theory', *Sociometry*, 26, 271–86.

FLOYD, H. H. and SOUTH, D. R. (A1969), 'Varied reference group orientations and some meaningful correlates', paper submitted to *32nd Annual Meeting of the Southern Sociological Society*.

FOLKMAN, W. S. (A1958), 'Board members as decision makers in farmers' cooperatives', *Rural Sociology*, 23, 239–52.

FORM, W. H. and GESCHWENDER, J. A. (A1968), 'Social reference basis of job satisfaction: the case of manual workers', in HYMAN and SINGER (A1968, pp. 185–98).

FRENCH, J. R. P. Jr and RAVEN, B. (A1959), 'The basis of social power', in CARTWRIGHT, D. (ed.), *Studies in Social Power*, Ann Arbor, Michigan, pp. 150–67.

GALTUNG, J. (A1964), 'A structural theory of aggression', *Journal of Peace Research*, 1, 95–119.

GANS, H. J. (A1957), 'The creator-audience relationship in the mass media: an analysis of movie-making', in ROSENBERG, B. and WHITE, D. M. (eds), *Mass Culture*, Illinois, pp. 315–24.

GERMANI, G. (A1966), 'Social and political consequences of mobility', in SMELSER, N. J. and LIPSET, S. M. (eds), *Social Structure and Mobility in Economic Development*, London, pp. 364–94.

GESCHWENDER, J. A. (A1964), 'Social structure and the negro revolt: an examination of some hypotheses', *SF*, 43, 248–56.

GESCHWENDER, J. A. (A1968), 'Explorations in the theory of social movements and revolutions', *SF*, 47, 127–35.

GLAZER, N. (A1949), '"The American Soldier" as science. Can sociology fulfil its ambitions?', *Commentary*, 5, 487–96.

GOLDTHORPE, J. H. (A1969a), *The Affluent Worker in the Class Structure*, Cambridge.

GOLDTHORPE, J. H. (A1969b), 'Social inequality and social integration in modern Britain', *Advancement of Science*, 26, 190–202.

GOLDTHORPE, J. H. and LOCKWOOD, D. (A1963), 'Affluence and the British class structure', *SR*, 11, 133–63.

GOLDTHORPE, J. H., LOCKWOOD, D., BECHHOFER, F. and PLATT, JENNIFER (A1968), *The Affluent Worker: Industrial Attitudes and Behaviour*, Cambridge.

GOULDNER, A. W. (A1956), 'Some observations on systemic theory, 1945–55', in ZETTERBERG, H. L. (ed.), *Sociology in the USA*, Paris.

GROSS, L. (A1967), 'Note on selected problems in theory construction', in GROSS, L. (ed.), *Sociological Theory: Inquiries and Paradigms*, New York, pp. 254–64.

GURR, T., with RUTTENBERG, C. (A1967), *The Conditions of Civil Violence*, Center of International Studies, Princeton.

HALLORAN, J. D. (A1967), *Attitude Formation and Change*, Leicester.

HAMILTON, R. F. (A1964), 'Income, class, and reference groups', *ASR*, 29, 576–9.

HARGROVE, BARBARA W. (A1966), 'An interdisciplinary approach to role theory', *Rocky Mountain Social Science Journal*, 3, 149–63.

HARTLEY, E. (A1951), 'Psychological problems of multiple group membership', in ROHRER, J. H. and SHERIF, M. (eds), *Social Psychology at the Crossroads*, New York, pp. 371–87.

HARTLEY, E. and HARTLEY, RUTH E. (A1952), *Fundamentals of Social Psychology*, New York.

HARTLEY, RUTH E. (A1956), 'The acceptance of new reference groups', Technical Report (Final Report, 1958), Office of Naval Research, New York.

HARTLEY, RUTH E. (A1960a), 'Personal needs and the acceptance of a new group as a reference group', *JSP*, 52, 349–58.

HARTLEY, RUTH E. (A1960b), 'Relationships between perceived values and acceptance of a new reference group', *JSP*, 51, 181–90.

HARTLEY, RUTH E. (A1968a), 'Norm compatibility, norm preference and the acceptance of new reference groups', in HYMAN and SINGER (A1968, pp. 238–46).

HARTLEY, RUTH E. (A1968b), 'Personal characteristics and acceptance of secondary groups as reference groups', in HYMAN and SINGER (A1968, pp. 247–56).

HARVEY, O. J. (A1953), 'An experimental approach to the study of status relations in informal groups', *ASR*, 18, 357–67.

HASKELL, M. R. (A1960–1), 'Towards a reference group theory of juvenile delinquency', *Social Problems*, 8, 220–30.

HICKMAN, C. A. and KUHN, M. H. (A1956), *Individuals, Groups and Economic Behavior*, New York.

HOLDEN, D. E. W. (A1965), 'Associations as reference groups: an approach to the problem', *Rural Sociology*, 30, 63–74.

HOLLANDER, E. P. (A1967), *Principles and Methods of Social Psychology*, New York.

HOMANS, G. C. (A1961), *Social Behaviour: Its Elementary Forms*, London.

HUGHES, C. C. (A1957), 'Reference group concepts in the study of a changing Eskimo culture', in RAY, V. F. (ed.), *Proceedings of the 1957 Annual Spring Meeting of the American Ethnological Society: Cultural Stability and Cultural Change,* Seattle.

HYMAN, H. H. (A1942), 'The psychology of status', *Archives of Psychology*, 38 (269).

HYMAN, H. H. (A1960), 'Reflections on reference groups', *POQ*, 24, 383–96.

HYMAN, H. H. (A1968), 'Reference groups', in SILLS, D. (ed.), *International Encyclopaedia of the Social Sciences*, New York, 3, 353–61.

HYMAN, H. H. and SINGER, ELEANOR (A1968), *Readings in Reference Group Theory and Research*, New York, Introduction, pp. 3–21.

HYMAN, H. H., WRIGHT, C. R. and HOPKINS, T. K. (A1968), 'Reference groups and the maintenance of changes in attitudes and behaviour', in HYMAN and SINGER (A1968, pp. 387–93).

HYMAN, M. D. (A1967), 'The unpleasant consequences of rank inconsistency: suggestions for a reorientation of theory and research', *Sociological Quarterly*, 8, 383–96.

JACKSON, J. M. (A1959a), 'Reference group processes in a formal organization', *Sociometry*, 22, 307–27.

JACKSON, J. M. (A1959b), 'A space for conceptualizing person-group relationships', *HR*, 12, 3–15.

JACKSON, J. M. and SALZSTEIN, H. D. (A1956), *Group Membership and Conformity Processes*, Ann Arbor, Michigan.

JACKSON, J. M. and SALZSTEIN, H. D. (A1958), 'The effect of person-group relationships on conformity processes', *Journal of Abnormal and Social Psychology*, 57, 17–24.

JACOBSON, E., KUMATA, H. and GULLAHORN, J. E. (A1960), 'Cross-cultural contributions to attitude research', *POQ*, 24, 205–23.

JAHODA, G. (A1953), 'Social class attitudes and levels of occupational aspiration in secondary modern school leavers', *British Journal of Psychology*, 44, 95–107.

KANIN, E. J. (A1967), 'Reference groups and sex conduct norm violations', *Sociological Quarterly*, 8, 495–504.

KAPLAN, N. (A1955), 'Reference group theory and voting behavior', Ph.D. thesis, University of Columbia.

KAPLAN, N. (A1965), 'The role of the research administrator', in KAPLAN, N. (ed.), *Science and Society*, Chicago, pp. 211–28.

KATONA, G. (A1951), *Psychological Analysis of Economic Behavior*, New York.

KATZ, E. (A1957), 'The two-step flow of communication: an up-to-date report on an hypothesis', *POQ*, 21, 61–78.

KELLER, SUZANNE and ZAVALLONI, MARISA (A1964), 'Ambition and social class: a respecification', *SF*, 43, 58–70.

KELLY, H. H. (A1955), 'Salience of membership and resistance to change of group-anchored attitudes', *HR*, 8, 275–89.

KELLY, H. H. (A1968), 'Two functions of reference groups', in HYMAN and SINGER (A1968, pp. 77–83).

KELLY, H. H. and VOLKART, E. H. (A1952), 'The resistance to change of group-anchored attitudes', *ASR*, 17, 455–65.

KEMPER, T. D. (A1966), 'Self-conceptions and the expectations of significant others', *Sociological Quarterly*, 7, 323–43.

KEMPER, T. D. (A1968), 'Reference groups, socialization and achievement', *ASR*, 33, 31–45.

KERCKHOFF, A. C. and MCCORMICK, T. C. (A1955), 'Marginal status and marginal personality', *SF*, 34, 48–55.

KORPI, W. (A1964), 'Social pressures and attitudes in military training', *Stockholm Studies in Sociology*, 2.

KRECH, D., CRUTCHFIELD, R. S. and BALLACHEY, E. L. (A1962), *Individual in Society: A Textbook of Social Psychology*, New York.

KUHN, M. H. (A1954), 'Kinsey's view of human behavior', *Social Problems*, 1, 119–25.

KUHN, M. H. (A1964a), 'Major trends in symbolic interaction theory in the past twenty-five years', *Sociological Quarterly*, 5, 61–84.

KUHN, M. H. (A1964b), 'The reference group reconsidered', *Sociological Quarterly*, 5, 5–21.

KUHN, M. H. and MCPARLTAND, T. S. (A1954), 'An empirical investigation of self-attitudes', *ASR*, 19, 68–76.

LATANE, B. (A1966), 'Studies in social comparison – introduction and overview', *Journal of Experimental Social Psychology*, Supplement 1, 1–5.

LAWRENCE, P. A. (A1972), 'Problems in the theory of revolution', *Sociological Analysis*, 2, 31–7.

LAZARSFELD, P. (A1949), '*The American Soldier* – an expository review', *POQ*, 13, 377–404.

LEACH, E. (A1966), 'Liberty, equality, fraternity', *New Statesman*, 8 July.

LEFCOURT, H. M. and LADWIG, G. W. (A1965), 'The effect of reference groups upon negroes' task persistence in a biracial competitive game', *Journal of Personality and Social Psychology*, 1, 668–71.

LEHMAN, E. C., Jr (A1966), 'Social participation and the community as a reference group', working paper available from the University of Wisconsin, Milwaukee.

LEHMANN, I. J. (A1963), 'Autobiography of a freshman class', in *Measurement in Education* (Yearbook of the National Council on Measurement in Education), New York, pp. 115–23.

LINDESMITH, A. R. and STRAUSS, A. L. (A1968), *Social Psychology*, New York.

LINN, E. L. (A1966), 'Reference groups: a case study in conceptual diffusion', *Sociological Quarterly*, 7, 489–99.

LIPSET, S. M. (A1954), 'The political process in trade unions', in BERGER, M., ABEL, T. and PAGE, C. H. (eds), *Freedom and Control in Modern Society*, New York, pp. 82–124.

LIPSET, S. M. (A1968), 'Social Class', in SILLS, D. (ed.), *International Encyclopaedia of the Social Sciences*, New York, 15, 296–316.

LIPSET, S. M., COLEMAN, J. and TROW, M. (A1956), *Union Democracy: The Internal Politics of the International Typographical Union*, Chicago.

LIPSET, S. M. and TROW, M. (A1957), 'Reference group theory and trade union wage policy', in KOMAROVSKY, MIRRA (ed.): *Common Frontiers of the Social Sciences*, Chicago, pp. 391–411.

LITWAK, E. (A1960), 'Reference group theory, bureaucratic career and neighbourhood primary group cohesion', *Sociometry*, 23, 72–84.

MCCALL, G. J. and SIMMONS, J. L. (A1966), *Identities and Interactions*, New York.

MCINTOSH, A. (A1942), 'Differential effect of the status of the competing group on levels of aspiration', *American Journal of Psychology*, 55, 546–54.

MACK, R. W. (A1969), 'Riot, revolt, or responsible revolution: of reference groups and racism', *Sociological Quarterly*, 10, 147–56.

MANNHEIM, BILHA F. (A1966), 'Reference groups, membership groups and the self-image', *Sociometry*, 29, 265–79.

MARSH, C. P. and COLEMAN, A. L. (A1954), 'Farmers' practice adoption rates in relation to adoption rates of "Leaders"', *Rural Sociology*, 19, 180–3.

MARSH, C. P. and COLEMAN, A. L. (A1956), 'Group influences and agricultural innovations: some tentative findings and hypotheses', *AJS*, 61, 588–94.

MERTON, R. K. (A1957), 'Continuities in the theory of reference groups and social structure', in MERTON, R. K. (1957, pp. 281–386).

MERTON, R. K. and BARBER, ELINOR (A1963), 'Sociological ambivalence', in TIRYAKIN, A. (ed.), *Sociological Theory, Values and Sociocultural Change*, New York, pp. 91–120.

MERTON, R. K. and ROSSI, ALICE S. (A1957), 'Contributions to the theory of reference group behavior', in MERTON, R. K. (1957, pp. 225–80).

MILLER, D. R. (A1963), 'The study of social relationships: situation, identity, and social interaction', in KOCH, S., *Psychology V*, New York, pp. 639–737.

MITCHELL, J. CLYDE (A1955), 'The African middle classes in British Central Africa', working paper, *29th Study Session of the International Institute of Differing Civilizations*, London, pp. 13–16.

NASH, D. J. and WOLFE, A. W. (A1957), 'The stranger in laboratory culture', *ASR*, 22, 400–5.

NELSON, H. A. (A1961), 'A tentative foundation for reference group theory', *Sociology and Social Research*, 45, 274–80.

NETTL, J. P. and ROBERTSON, R. (A1968), *International Systems and the Modernization of Societies*, London.

NEWCOMB, T. M. (A1943), *Personality and Social Change*, New York.

NEWCOMB, T. M. (A1946), 'The influence of attitude climate upon some determinants of information', *Journal of Abnormal and Social Psychology*, 89, 291–302.

NEWCOMB, T. M. (A1951a), 'Review of *Continuities in Social Research: Studies in the Scope and Method of "The American Soldier"*', *AJS*, 57, 90–2.

NEWCOMB, T. M. (A1951b), 'Social psychological theory: integrating individual and social approaches', in ROHRER, J. H. and SHERIF, M. (eds), *Social Psychology at the Crossroads*, New York, pp. 31–49.

NEWCOMB, T. M. (A1952), *Social Psychology*, London.

NEWCOMB, T. M. (A1957), *Personality and Social Change: Attitude Formation in a Student Community*, New York.

NEWCOMB, T. M. (A1968a), 'Attitude development as a function of reference groups; the Bennington study', in HYMAN and SINGER (A1968, pp. 374–86).

NEWCOMB, T. M. (A1968b), 'Persistence and regression of changed attitudes: long-range studies', in HYMAN and SINGER (A1968, pp. 257–67).

NEWCOMB, T. M., KOENIG, KATHRYNE, FLACKS, R. and WARWICK, D. P. (1967), *Persistence and Change: A College and its Students after 25 Years*, New York.

PARKER, S. and KLEINER, R. J. (A1966), *Mental Illness in the Urban Negro Community*, New York.

PARKER, S. and KLEINER, R. J. (A1968), 'Reference group behaviour and mental disorder', in HYMAN and SINGER (A1968, pp. 350–73).

PARSONS, T. (A1964), 'Recent trends in structural-functional theory', in

211

COUNT, G. W. and BOWLES, G. T. (eds), *Fact and Theory in Social Science*, Syracuse, pp. 140–58.

PATCHEN, M. (A1961), *The Choice of Wage Comparisons*, New Jersey.

PATCHEN, M. (A1968a), 'A conceptual framework and some empirical data regarding comparisons of social rewards', in HYMAN and SINGER (A1968, pp. 166–84).

PATCHEN, M. (A1968b), 'The effect of reference group standards on job satisfactions', in HYMAN and SINGER (A1968, pp. 325–38).

PAYNTON, C. T. (A1966), 'A suggestion for reference group theory: ideational referents and group referents', *Canadian Review of Sociology and Anthropology*, 3, 214–223.

PETRIE, J. (A1956) (translator), *The Worker-Priests: A Collective Documentation*, London.

PETTIGREW, T. (A1964), *A Profile of the Negro American*, New York.

PETTIGREW, T. (A1967), 'Social evaluation theory: convergences and applications', Nebraska Symposium on Motivation, 272–300.

PETTIGREW, T. (A1968), 'Actual gains and psychological losses', in HYMAN and SINGER (A1968, pp. 339–49).

PINARD, M. (A1969), 'Mass society and political movements: a new formulation', in DREITZEL, H. P. (ed.), *Recent Sociology, no. 1*, New York, pp. 99–114.

POLLIS, N. P. (A1968), 'Reference group re-examined', *BJS*, 19, 300–7.

RAVEN, B. H. and FISHBEIN, M. (A1965), 'Social referents and self-evaluation in examinations', *JSP*, 65, 89–99.

RAVEN, B. H. and GALLO, P. S. (A1965), 'The effects of nominating conventions, elections, and reference group identification upon the perception of political figures', *HR*, 18, 217–30.

REEDER, L. G., DONOGHUE, G. A. and BIBLARZ, A. (A1960), 'Conceptions of self and others', *AJS*, 66, 153–9.

REISS, A. J. and RHODES, A. L. (A1962), 'Status deprivation and delinquent behaviour', *Sociological Quarterly*, 4, 135–49.

REISSMAN, L. (A1953), 'Levels of aspiration and social class', *ASR*, 18, 233–42.

RILEY, J. W., Jr and RILEY, MATILDA WHITE (A1968), 'Mass communication and the social system', in HYMAN and SINGER (A1968, pp. 443–51).

ROETHLISBERGER, F. J. and DICKSON, W. J. (A1964), *Management and the Worker*, New York.

ROGERS, E. M. (A1958), 'Reference group influences on student drinking behaviour', *Quarterly Journal of Studies on Alcohol*, 19, 244–54.

ROGERS, E. M. (A1960), *Social Change in Rural Society: A Textbook in Rural Sociology*, New York.

ROGERS, E. M. (A1962), *Diffusion of Innovations*, New York.

ROGERS, E. M. and BEAL, G. M. (A1958), 'Reference group influence in the adoption of agricultural technology', *Iowa Agricultural and Home Economics Experiment Station Project*, no. 1236.

ROKEACH, M. (A1964), *The Three Christ's of Ypsilanti*, New York.

ROSE, A. M. (A1962), 'A systematic summary of symbolic interaction theory', in ROSE, A. M. (ed.) (1962, pp. 3–19).

ROSE, E. J. B. (A1969), *Colour and Citizenship*, London.

ROSEN, B. C. (A1955), 'Reference group approach to the parental factor in attitude and behaviour formation', *SF*, 34, 137–44.

ROSEN, B. C. (A1968), 'Conflicting group membership: a study of parent-peer group cross-pressures', in HYMAN and SINGER (A1968, pp. 402–12).

ROSOW, I. (A1970), 'Old people: their friends and neighbors', *American Behavioral Scientist*, 14, 59–70.

ROSSI, P. H. and ALICE S. (A1961), 'Some effects of parochial-school education in America', *Daedalus*, 90, 300–28.

RUNCIMAN, W. G. (A1961), 'Problems of research on relative deprivation', *EJS*, 2, 315–23.

RUNCIMAN, W. G. (A1966), *Relative Deprivation and Social Justice*, London (see also Postscript to 1972 edition).

RUNCIMAN, W. G. (A1967), 'Justice, congruence and Prof. Homans', *EJS*, 8, 115–28.

RUNCIMAN, W. G. and BAGLEY, C. R. (A1969), 'Status consistency, relative deprivation, and attitudes to immigrants', *Sociology*, 3, 359–75.

RUSHING, W. A. (A1964), *The Psychiatric Professions*, Chapel Hill.

RUSHING, W. A. (A1969), 'Two patterns in the relationship between social class and mental hospitalization', *ASR*, 34, 533 41.

SALAMAN, G. S. (A1969), 'Some sociological determinants of occupational communities', Ph.D. thesis, University of Cambridge.

SCHOECK, H. (A1969), *Envy: A Theory of Social Behaviour*, London.

SCHOPLER, J. (A1965), 'Social power', in BERKOWITZ, L. (ed.), *Advances in Experimental Social Psychology*, vol. 2, New York, 177–218.

SCOTT, W. H., BANKS, J., HALSEY, A. H. and LUPTON, T. (A1956), *Technical Change and Industrial Relations*, Liverpool.

SHERIF, M. (A1948), *An Outline of Social Psychology*, New York.

SHERIF, M. (A1953), 'The concept of reference groups in human relations', in SHERIF, M. and WILSON, M. O. (eds), *Group Relations at the Crossroads*, New York, pp. 203–31.

SHERIF, M. (A1962), 'The self and reference groups: meeting ground of individual and group approaches', *Annals of the New York Academy of Sciences*, 96, pp. 797–813.

SHERIF, M. (A1968a), 'Self concept', in SILLS, D. (ed.), *International Encyclopaedia of the Social Sciences*, New York, 14, pp. 150–9.

SHERIF, M. (A1968b), *Social Interaction: Processes and Products*, Chicago.

SHERIF, M. and CANTRIL, H. (A1947), *The Psychology of Ego-Involvements*, New York.

SHERIF, M. and SHERIF, CAROLYN (A1953), *Groups in Harmony and Tension*, New York.

SHERIF, M. and SHERIF, CAROLYN (A1964), *Reference Groups: Exploration into Conformity and Deviation of Adolescents*, New York.

SHERIF, M. and SHERIF, CAROLYN (A1967), 'The adolescent in his group in its setting', in SHERIF, M. (A1968b, pp. 247–309).

SHERIF, M., SHERIF, CAROLYN and NEBERGALL, R. E. (A1965), *Attitude and Attitude Change: The Social Judgment-Involvement Approach*, Philadelphia.

SHERWOOD, J. (A1965), 'Self identity and referent others', *Sociometry*, 28, 66–81.

SHIBUTANI, T. (A1955), 'Reference groups as perspectives', *AJS*, 60, 562–9.

SHIBUTANI, T. (A1962), 'Reference groups and social control', in ROSE, A. M. (ed.) (1962, pp. 128–47).

SHIBUTANI, T. (A1964), *Society and Personality: an Interactionist Approach to Social Psychology*, Englewood Cliffs, New Jersey.

SHIPTON, L. (A1955), 'Reference groups in the formation of public opinion', Ph.D. thesis, University of Harvard.

SIEGEL, ALBERTA E. and SIEGEL, S. (A1968), 'Reference groups, membership groups, and attitude change', in HYMAN and SINGER (A1968, pp. 394–401).

SIMMONS, ROBERTA G. (A1969), 'The experimentally-increased salience of extreme comparative reference groups', *Sociology and Social Research*, 53, 409–19.

SIMPSON, R. (A1962), 'Parental influence, anticipatory socialisation and social mobility', *ASR*, 27, 517–22.

SMITH, M. A. (A1968), 'Process technology and powerlessness', *BJS*, 19, 76–88.

SMITH, M. B., BRUNER, J. S. and WHITE, R. W. (A1956), *Opinions and Personality*, New York.

SOWA, JULIA (A1962), 'Teoria Grup Odniesienia' ('Theory of reference groups'), *Studia Socjologniczne*, 7, 41–70.

SPECTOR, A. J. (A1956), 'Expectations, fulfillment and morale', *Journal of Abnormal and Social Psychology*, 52, 51–6.

STERN, E. and KELLER, SUZANNE (A1968), 'Spontaneous group references in France', in HYMAN and SINGER (A1968, pp. 199–206).

STONE, G. (A1958), 'Review of R. K. Merton: *Social Theory and Social Structure*', *ASQ*, 2, 556–62.

STONE, L. (A1966), 'Theories of revolution', *WP*, 18, 159–76.

STOUFFER, S. A. (A1962), *Social Research to Test Ideas*, New York, 1962.

STOUFFER, S. A. *et al.* (A1965), *The American Soldier: Adjustment During Army Life*, vol. 1, New York.

STRAUSS, A. (A1959), *Mirrors and Masks: The Search for Identity*, Illinois.

STRAUSS, A. (A1964), Introduction to *George Herbert Mead on Social Psychology*, Chicago.

STRAUSS, HELEN (A1968), 'Reference group and social comparison processes among the totally blind', in HYMAN and SINGER (A1968, pp. 222–37).

TAFT, R. (A1952), 'Minority group behaviour and reference group theory – a reply to Emery and Katz', *Australian Journal of Psychology*, 4, 10–23.

TAFT, R. (A1953), 'The shared frame of reference concept applied to the assimilation of immigrants', *HR*, 6, 45–55.

TURNER, R. H. (A1955), 'Reference groups of future-oriented men', *SF*, 34, 130–6.

TURNER, R. H. (A1966), 'Role-taking, role standpoint, and reference-group behavior', in BIDDLE, B. J. and THOMAS, E. J. (eds), *Role Theory: Concepts and Research*, New York, pp. 151–9.

URRY, J. R. (A1971), 'Some notes on the study of the promotion finding in "The American Soldier"', *EJS*, 12, 133–40.

URRY, J. R. (A1972), 'Role-performances and social comparison processes', in JACKSON, J. A. (ed.), *Role, Cambridge Studies in Sociology*, Cambridge; see also, 'Reply to Mr. Urry', by W. G. Runciman in the same book.

VALENTINE, C. A. (A1968), *Culture and Poverty*, Chicago.

VARMA, BAIDYA NATH (A1965), 'Community studies and the concept of caste', *Indian Journal of Social Research*, 6, 251–62.

WAISENEN, F. (A1952), 'Television ownership in a Iowa city: a study in some determinants of social innovation', M.A. thesis, University of Iowa.

WAKEFORD, J. (A1969), *The Cloistered Elite: A Sociological Analysis of the English Public Boarding School*, London.

WALLACE, S. F. (A1966), 'Reference group behaviour in occupational role socialization', *Sociological Quarterly*, 7, 366–72.

WALUM, L. R. (A1968), 'Group perception of threat to non-members', *Sociometry*, 31, 278–84.

WESTERGAARD, J. H. (A1970), 'The rediscovery of the cash nexus', *Socialist Register*, 111–38.

WHYTE, D. H. (A1965), 'Sociological aspects of poverty. A conceptual analysis', *Canadian Review of Sociology and Anthropology*, 2, 175–89.

WILENSKY, H. L. (A1956), *Intellectuals in Labor Unions: Organizational Pressures on Professional Roles*, Chicago.

WILENSKY, H. L. (A1963), 'The moonlighter: a product of relative deprivation', *Industrial Relations*, 3, 105–24.

WILLIAMS, MARGARET A. (A1970), 'Reference groups: a review and commentary', *Sociological Quarterly*, 11, 545–54.

WILSON, R. N. (A1952), 'The American poet: a role investigation', Ph.D. thesis, University of Harvard.

WILSON, W. R. (A1963), 'The incentive value of a promised social standard of comparison', *JSP*, 59, 169–74.

WINTER, E. H. (A1955), *Bwamba Economy*, Kampala, Uganda.

ZALEZNIK, A., CHRISTENSEN, C. R. and ROESTLISBERGER, F. J. (A1959), *The Motivation, Productivity and Satisfaction of Workers: A Prediction Study*, Boston, Mass.

ZEITLIN, M. (A1967), *Revolutionary Politics and the Cuban Working Class*, Princeton.

(B) Indonesia

AIDIT, D. N. (B1955), *A Short History of the Communist Party of Indonesia*, New Delhi.

ALATAS, SYED HUSSEIN (B1963), 'On the need for an historical study of Malaysian Islamisation', *JSEAH*, 4, 62–74.

ALERS, H. J. H. (B1956), *Towards a Red or a Green Merdeka: Ten Years of Internal Politics in Indonesia*, Eindhoven.

ALISJAHBANA, S. TAKDIR (B1949), 'The Indonesian language – by-product of nationalism', *PA*, 23, 388–92.

ALISJAHBANA, S. TAKDIR (B1966), *Indonesia: Social and Cultural Revolution*, London.

ALLEN, G. C. and DONNITHORPE, AUDREY G. (B1957), *Western Enterprise in Indonesia and Malaya*, New York.

ANDERSON, B. R. O'G. (B1961), *Some Aspects of Indonesian Politics Under the Japanese Occupation: 1944–5*, Ithaca, New York.

ANDERSON, B. R. O'G. (B1967), 'The Pemuda revolution, Indonesian politics *1945–6*', Ph.D. thesis, University of Cornell.

ARASARATNAM, S. (B1962), 'The use of Dutch material for southeast Asian historical writing', *JSEAH*, 3, 95–105.

AZIZ, M. A. (B1955), *Japan's Colonialism and Indonesia*, The Hague.

BASTIN, J. (B1957), *The Native Policies of Sir Stamford Raffles in Java and Sumatra*, Oxford.

BAUER, P. T. (B1948), *The Rubber Industry*, Cambridge, Mass.

BECKER, C. (B1951), 'Historical patterns of cultural contact in southern Asia', *FEQ*, 11, 3–15.

BENDA, H. J. (B1955a), 'The communist rebellions of 1926–7 in Indonesia', *Pacific Historical Review*, 24, 139–52.

BENDA, H. J. (B1955b), 'Indonesian Islam under the Japanese occupation, 1942–5', *PA*, 28, 350–62.

BENDA, H. J. (B1956), 'The beginnings of the Japanese occupation of Java', *FEQ*, 15, 541–60.

BENDA, H. J. (B1958a), *The Crescent and the Rising Sun*, The Hague.

BENDA, H. J. (B1958b), 'Christiaan Snouck Hurgronje and the foundations of Dutch Islamic policy in Indonesia', *Journal of Modern History*, 34, 338–47.

BENDA, H. J. (B1962a), 'The structure of southeast Asian history: some preliminary observations', *JSEAH*, 3, 106–38.

BENDA, H. J. (B1962b), 'Non-western intelligentsias as political elites', in KAUTSKY, J. H. (ed.), *Political Change in Underdeveloped Countries: Nationalism and Communism*, New York.

BENDA, H. J. (B1965), 'Decolonialization in India: the problem of continuity and change', *AHR*, 70, 1058–73.

BENDA, H. J. (B1966), 'The pattern of administrative reforms in the closing years of Dutch rule in Indonesia', *JAS*, 25, 589–605.

BENDA, H. J. and MCVEY, R. T. (eds) (B1960), *The Communist Uprisings of 1926–7 in Indonesia: Key Documents*, Ithaca, New York; see 'The governor general's report' (pp. 1–18); 'The Bantam report' (pp. 19–96); 'Political section of the west coast of Sumatra report' (pp. 97–177).

BENDA, H. J. et al. (eds) (B1965), *Japanese Military Administration in Indonesia, Selected Documents*, New Haven.

BERG, C. C. (B1961), 'Javanese histiography, a synopsis of its evolution', in HALL, D. E. G. (ed.), *Historians of Southeast Asia*, London, pp. 164–71.

BOEKE, J. H. (B1942), *The Structure of the Netherlands Indian Economy*, New York.

BOEKE, J. H. (B1946), *The Evolution of the Netherlands Indies Economy*, New York.

216

BOEKE, J. H. (B1953), *Economics and Economic Policy of Dual Societies as Exemplified by Indonesia*, Haarlem.
BOUSQUET, G. H. (B1940), *A French View of the Netherlands Indies*, London.
BOUSQUET, G. H. and SCHACHT, J. (eds) (B1957), *Selected Works of C. Snouck Hurgronje*, Leiden.
BOXER, C. R. (B1959), 'Oost-Indie', *Past and Present*, 15, 82–6.
BRACKMAN, A. C. (B1963), *Indonesian Communism: A History*, New York.
BROEK, JAN O. M. (B1951), 'On the use of Netherlands Indies' statistics', *FEQ*, 10, 277–81.
BRUGMANS, I. J. and SOENARIO (B1941), *Visman Report*, Batavia.
BRUNER, E. M. (B1961), 'Urban and ethnic identity in north Sumatra', *AA*, 63, 508–21.
BURGER, D. H. (B1956), *Structural Changes in Javanese Society: The Supra-village Sphere*, Ithaca, New York.
BURGER, D. H. (B1957), *Structural Changes in Javanese Society: The Village Sphere*, Ithaca, New York.
BURGER, D. H. (B1961), 'The Government's Native Economic Policy', in *Selected Studies on Indonesia, vol. 6: Indonesian Economics*, The Hague, pp. 318–29.
CABATON, A. (B1911), *Java, Sumatra, and the Other Islands of the Dutch East Indies*, London.
CALDWELL, J. A. M. (B1964), 'Indonesian exports and production from the decline of the Culture System to the First World War', in COWAN, C. D. (ed.), *The Economic Development of Southeast Asia: Studies in Economic History and Political Economy*, New York and London, pp. 72–101.
CALDWELL, M. (B1968), *Indonesia*, London.
CALLIS, H. G. (B1942), *Foreign Capital in Southeast Asia*, New York.
CASKEL, W. (B1955), 'Western impact and Islamic civilization', in VON GRUNEBAUM, G. E. (ed.), *Unity and Diversity in Muslim Civilization*, Chicago, pp. 335–361.
Census of 1930 in Netherlands Indies, Batavia (B1933–6).
COOLHAAS, W. PH. (B1960), *A Critical Survey of Studies on Dutch Colonial History*, The Hague.
COOLIE BUDGET COMMISSION (Final Report) (B1956), *Living Conditions of Plantation Workers and Peasants on Java in 1939–40*, Ithaca, New York.
DAHM, B. (B1971), *History of Indonesia in the Twentieth Century*, London.
DAY, C. (B1966), *The Policy and the Administration of the Dutch in Java*, Oxford.
DE DAT ANGELINO, A. D. A. (B1931), *Colonial Policy*, The Hague, 2 vols.
D'ENCAUSSE, HELENE CARRERE and SCHRAM, S. R. (eds) (B1969), *Marxism and Asia*, London.
DE KLERCK, E. S. (B1938), *History of the Netherlands East Indies*, 2 vols.
DE MEEL, H. (B1951), 'Impediments to economic progress in Indonesia', *PA*, 24, 39–51.

217

DE VRIES, E. (B1949), 'Problems of agriculture in Indonesia', *PA*, 22, 130–43.

DE WEERD, K. A. (B1946), *The Japanese Occupation of the Netherlands Indies*, prepared statement, International Prosecution Section, Netherlands Division at the International Military Tribunal, Far East, Process Document 2750.

DINGLEY, S. (B1926), *The Peasants' Movement in Indonesia*, Berlin.

DJAJADININGRAT, IDRUS (B1958), *The Beginnings of the Indonesian-Dutch Negotiations and the Hoge Veluwe Talks*, Ithaca, New York.

DREWES, G. W. J. (B1955), 'Indonesia: mysticism and activism', in VON GRUNEBAUM, G. E. (ed.), *Unity and Diversity in Muslim Civilization*, Chicago, pp. 284–310.

DU BOIS, C. (B1947), *Social Forces in Southeast Asia*, Minnesota and London.

ELSBREE, W. H. (B1953), *Japan's Role in Southeast Asian Movements 1940–5*, Cambridge.

EMERSON, R. (B1942), *The Netherlands Indies and the US*, Boston.

EMERSON, R. (B1946), 'An analysis of nationalism in southeast Asia', *FEQ*, 5, 208–15.

EMERSON, R., MILLS, L. A. and THOMPSON, VIRGINIA (B1942), *Government and Nationalism in Southeast Asia*, New York.

EUDIN, XENIA J. and NORTH, R. C. (B1957), *Soviet Russia and the East, 1920–7: A Documentary Survey*, Stanford.

FEITH, H. (B1962), *The Decline of Constitutional Democracy in Indonesia*, New York.

FRIEDRICH, R. (B1959), *The Civilization and Culture of Bali*, Calcutta.

FURNIVALL, J. S. (B1935), *Studies in the Economic and Social Development of the Netherlands East Indies, III(a) Political Institutions in Netherlands Indies*, Rangoon.

FURNIVALL, J. S. (B1939), *Netherlands Indies*, Cambridge.

FURNIVALL, J. S. (B1941), *Progress and Welfare in Southeast Asia: A Comparison of Colonial Policy and Practice*, New York.

FURNIVALL, J. S. (B1942), *Problems of Education in Southeast Asia*, New York.

FURNIVALL, J. S. (B1943), *Educational Progress in Southeast Asia*, New York.

FURNIVALL, J. S. (B1948), *Colonial Theory and Practice*, Cambridge.

GEERTZ, C. (B1955–6), 'Religious belief and economic behaviour in central Javanese town', *Economic Development and Cultural Change*, 4, 134–58.

GEERTZ, C. (B1957), 'Ritual and social change: a Javanese example', *AA*, 59, 32–54.

GEERTZ, C. (B1959), 'The Javanese village', in SKINNER, G. W. (ed.) (B1959, pp. 34–41).

GEERTZ, C. (B1960a), *The Religion of Java*, New York.

GEERTZ, C. (B1960b), 'The Javanese Kiaji: the changing role of a cultural broker', *CSSH*, 2, 228–49.

GEERTZ, C. (B1963a), *Agricultural Involution: the Process of Ecological Change in Indonesia*, California.

GEERTZ, C. (B1963b), *Peddlars and Princes: Social Change and Economic Modernization in Two Indonesian Towns*, Chicago.

GEERTZ, C. (B1964), '"Internal Conversion" in Contemporary Bali', in BASTIN, J. and ROOLVINK, R. (eds), *Malayan and Indonesian Studies: Essays presented to Sir Richard Winstedt*, Oxford, pp. 208–302.

GEERTZ, C. (B1965), *The Social History of an Indonesian Town*, Cambridge, Mass.

GEERTZ, C. (B1966a), 'Modernization in a Muslim society: the Indonesian case', in BELLAH, R. N. (ed.), *Religion and Progress in Modern Asia*, New York, pp. 93–108.

GEERTZ, C. (B1966b), *Person, Time, and Conduct in Bali: an Essay in Cultural Analysis*, New Haven.

GEERTZ, C. (B1967), 'Politics past, politics present', *EJS*, 8, 1–14.

GEERTZ, C. (B1968), *Islam Observed*, Chicago.

GEERTZ, MILDRED (B1959a), 'The vocabulary of emotion', *Psychiatry*, 22, 225–37.

GEERTZ, MILDRED (B1959b), 'The Balinese village', in SKINNER, G. W. (ed.) (B1959, pp. 24–33).

GEERTZ, MILDRED (B1961), *The Javanese Family: a Study of Kinship and Socialisation*, New York.

GIBB, H. A. R. (ed.) (B1932), *Whither Islam? A Survey of Modern Moslem Movements in the Moslem World*, London.

GILLIN, J. (B1952), 'Ethos and cultural aspects of personality', in TAX, S. (ed.), *Heritage of Conquest*, New York, pp. 193–212.

GLAMANN, K. (B1958), *Dutch-Asiatic Trade, 1620–1740*, Copenhagen and The Hague.

GONGGRIJP, G. (B1949), *Schets Ener Economische Geschiedenis van Nederlands-Indie*, Haarlem.

HAGEN, E. E. (B1964), *On the Theory of Social Change*, London.

HARRISON, B. (B1963), *Southeast Asia: A Short History*, London.

HEINE-GELDERN, R. (B1942), 'Conceptions of state and kingship in southeast Asia', *FEQ*, 2, 15–30.

HERMANS, ELIZABETH and HERMANS, P. W. (B1967), 'Indonesian terms of address in a situation of rapid social change', *SF*, 46, 48–51.

HILL, A. H. (B1963), 'The coming of Islam to north Sumatra', *JSEAH*, 4, 6–21.

HIGGINS, B. (B1958), 'Western enterprise and the economic development of southeast Asia: review article', *PA*, 31, 74–87.

HOLLAND, W. L. (ed.) (B1953), *Asian Nationalism and the West*, New York.

HURGRONJE, C. SNOUCK (B1924), *Collected Writings, Part 2*, Bonn and Leipzig.

INDONESIAN DEPARTMENT OF INFORMATION (B1961), *The Indonesian Revolution, Basic Documents and the Era of Guided Democracy*, Djakarta.

JACOBY, E. H. (B1948), *Agrarian Unrest in South East Asia*, New York.

JASPAN, M. A. (B1961), *Social Stratification and Social Mobility in Indonesia: a Trend Report and Annotated Bibliography*, Djakarta.

JASPAN, M. A. (B1969), 'Leadership and elite groups in Indonesia: a

219

study of unstable symbiosis', *South-East Asian Journal of Sociology*, 2, 27–43.

JOHNS, A. H. (B1961), 'Sufism as a category in Indonesian literature and history', *JSEAH*, 2, 10–23.

JONES, F. C. (B1954), *Japan's New Order in East Asia; Its Rise and Fall, 1937–45*, Oxford.

KAHIN, G. MCT. (B1952), *Nationalism and Revolution in Indonesia*, New York.

KARTINI, R. A. (B1921), *Letters of a Javanese Princess*, London.

KARTODIRDJO, S. (B1962), 'Some problems on the genesis of nationalism in Indonesia', *JSEAH*, 3, 67–94.

KARTODIRDJO, S. (B1966), *The Peasants' Revolt of Banten in* 1888, s'Gravenhage.

KATTENBURG, P. M. (B1951), *A Central Javanese Village in 1950*, Ithaca, New York.

KENNEDY, R. (B1942), *The Ageless Indies*, New York.

KENNEDY, R. (B1943), 'Acculturation and administration in Indonesia', *AA*, 45, 185–92.

KENNEDY, R. (B1945), 'The colonial crisis and the future', in LINTON, R. (ed.), *The Science of Man in the World Crisis*, New York, pp. 306f.

KERSTIENS, T. (B1966), *The New Elite in Asia and Africa*, New York.

KOENTJARANINGRAT (ed.) (B1967), *Villages in Indonesia*, New York.

KROM, M. J. (B1931), *Hindoe-Javaansche Geschiedenis*.

LANDON, K. (B1949), *Southeast Asia: Crossroads of Religion*, Chicago.

LANTERNARI, V. (B1963), *The Religions of the Oppressed*, London.

LASKER, B. (B1950), *Human Bondage in Southeast Asia*, Chapel Hill.

LEGGE, J. D. (B1964), *Indonesia*, New Jersey.

LEVY, R. (B1957), *The Social Structure of Islam*, Cambridge.

LOGEMANN, J. H. A. (B1947), 'The Indonesian problem', *PA*, 20, 30–41.

MCVEY, RUTH T. (B1965), *The Rise of Indonesian Communism*, New York.

MANSVELT, W. W. F. (B1928), 'Onderwijs en communisme', *Koloniale Studien*, 203–25.

MINTZ, J. S. (B1965), *Mohammed, Marx and Marhaen, The Roots of Indonesian Socialism*, London.

NASUTION, ABDUL H. (B1965), *Fundamentals of Guerrilla Warfare*, London.

NEYTELL DE WILDE, A. and MOLL, J. TH. (B1936), *The Netherlands Indies During the Depression*, Amsterdam.

NISHIJIMA, S. and KISHI, K. (B1963), *Japanese Military Administration in Indonesia*, translation prepared by US Department of Commerce, Joint Publications Research Service.

PALMER, ANDREA W. (B1959), 'The Sundanese village', in SKINNER, G. W. (ed.) (B1959, pp. 42–51).

PALMIER, L. H. (B1955), 'Aspects of Indonesia's social structure', *PA*, 28, 117–31.

PALMIER, L. H. (B1957), 'Sukarno, the nationalist', *PA*, 30, 101–19.

PALMIER, L. H. (B1960a), *Social Status and Power in Java*, London.

PALMIER, L. H. (B1960b), 'The Javanese nobility under the Dutch', *CSSH*, 2, 197–227.

PALMIER, L. H. (B1962), *Indonesia and the Dutch*, London.

PALMIER, L. H. (B1965), *Indonesia*, London.

PAUKER, G. J. (B1958), *Indonesian Images of their National Self*, California.

PAUKER, G. J. (B1962), 'The military in Indonesia', in JOHNSON, J. J. (ed.), *The Role of the Military in Under-developed Countries*, Princeton, pp. 185–230.

PELZER, K. J. (B1951), 'Western impact on East Sumatra and North Tapahuli: the roles of the planter and the missionary', *JSEAH*, 2, 66–71.

PIGEAUD, TH. (B1960–3), *Java in the Fourteenth Century: A Study in Cultural History*, The Hague, 5 vols.

PLUVIER, J. (B1965), 'Dutch-Indonesian relations, 1940–1', *JSEAH*, 6, 33–47.

PLUVIER, J. (B1968), 'The Indonesian revolution of 1945', paper presented to a conference on twentieth-century political revolutions at King's College, Cambridge, June 1968.

PRINGGODIGDO, A. K. (B1950), *Sedjarah Pergerakan Rakjat Indonesia*, Djakarta.

PURCELL, V. (B1951), *The Chinese in Southeast Asia*, London.

RAY, J. K. (B1967), *Transfer of Power in Indonesia, 1942–9*, Bombay.

REID, A. (B1967), 'Nineteenth-century Pan-Islam in Indonesia and Malaysia', *JAS*, 26, 267–83.

REINSMA, R. (B1955), *Het Verval van het Cultuurstelsel*, s'Gravenhage.

ROMEIN, J. (B1962), *The Asian Century: A History of Modern Asian Nationalism*, London.

SARDESI, D. R. and SARDESI, B. D. (B1970), *Theses and Dissertations on Southeast Asia*, Switzerland.

SCHRIEKE, B. (B1929), 'Native society in the transformation period', in SCHRIEKE, B. (ed.), *The Effect of Western Influence on Native Civilizations in the Malay Archipelago*, Batavia, pp. 236–47.

SCHRIEKE, B. (B1955; B1957), *Indonesian Sociological Studies*, parts 1 and 2, The Hague and Bandung.

SELOSOEMARDJAN (B1962), *Social Changes in Jogjakarta*, Ithaca, New York.

SINGH, V. (B1961), 'The Rise of Indonesian political parties', *JSEAH*, 2, 43–65.

SITORUS, I. M. (B1951), *Sedjatah Pergerakan Kebangsaan Indonesia*, Djakarta.

SITSEN, P. H. W. (B1942), *Industrial Development of the Netherlands Indies*, New York.

SJAHRIR, S. (B1946), *Our Struggle*, Amsterdam.

SJAHRIR, S. (B1949), *Out of Exile*, New York.

SJAHRIR, S. (B1956), *Indonesian Socialism*, Rangoon.

SKINNER, G. W. (ed.) (B1959), *Local, Ethnic and National Loyalties in Village Indonesia*, Yale University, South-East Asian Studies, Cultural Report Series, no. 8.

SMAIL, J. R. W. (B1961), 'On the possibility of an autonomous history of modern southeast Asia', *JSEAH*, 2, 72–102.

SMAIL, J. R. W. (B1964), *Bandung in the Early Revolution, 1945–6; A Study of the Social History of the Indonesian Revolution*, Ithaca, New York.

SMITH, W. C. (B1957), *Islam in the Modern World*, Princeton.

SOEDJATMOKO, *et al*. (B1965), *An Introduction to Indonesian Historiography*, Ithaca, New York.

SOEMARDI, S. (B1956), 'Some aspects of the social origins of Indonesian political decision-makers', *Transactions of the Third World Congress of Sociology*, vol. 3, London, pp. 338–48.

TEDJASUKMANA, I. (B1959), *The Political Character of the Indonesian Trade Union Movement*, Ithaca, New York.

THOMPSON, VIRGINIA (B1946), 'Japan's blueprint for Indonesia', *FEQ*, 5, 200–7.

THOMPSON, VIRGINIA (B1947), *Labor Problems in Southeast Asia*, New York.

THOMPSON, VIRGINIA and ADLOFF, R. (B1950), *The Left Wing in Southeast Asia*, New York.

TIE, KHOUW BIAN (B1955), 'The development of a middle class in Indonesia', in *Development of a Middle Class in Tropical and Sub-Tropical Countries*, Record of the XXIVth Session of the International Institute of Differing Civilizations, pp. 303–13.

TOYNBEE, A. J. and ASHTON-GWATKIN, F. T. (B1939), *The World in March, 1939*, Survey of International Affairs.

UBANI, B. A., DURRANI, O. K. and MOEIN, M. (B1946), *The Indonesian Struggle for Independence*, Bombay.

VANDENBOSCH, A. (B1942), *The Dutch East Indies: Its Government, Problems and Politics*, Berkeley.

VANDENBOSCH, A. (B1952), 'Nationalism and religion in Indonesia', *Far Eastern Survey*, 21, 181–5.

VANDENBOSCH, A. (B1960), 'Review of H. J. Benda and C. A. O. van Nieuwenhuize', *CSSH*, 2, 257–61.

VAN DER KOLFF, G. H. (B1929), 'European influence on native agriculture', in SCHRIEKE, B. (ed.), *The Effect of Western Influence on Native Civilizations in the Malay Archipelago*, Batavia, pp. 103–25.

VAN DER KOLFF, G. H. (B1936), *The Historical Development of the Labour Relationships in a Remote Corner of Java as they apply to the Cultivation of Rice*, Batavia.

VAN DER KROEF, J. M. (B1949), 'Prince Diponegoro: progenitor of Indonesian Nationalism', *FEQ*, 8, 424–50.

VAN DER KROEF, J. M. (B1950), 'Economic origins of Indonesian nationalism', in TALBOT, P. (ed.), *South Asia in the World Today*, Chicago, pp. 174–201.

VAN DER KROEF, J. M. (B1951a), 'The Hinduization of Indonesia reconsidered', *FEQ*, 11, 17–30.

VAN DER KROEF, J. M. (B1951b), 'The Indonesian revolution in retrospect', *WP*, 3, 369–98.

VAN DER KROEF, J. M. (B1951c), 'Indonesia and the origins of Dutch colonial sovereignty', *FEQ*, 10, 151–69.

VAN DER KROEF, J. M. (B1951d), 'Reply to Mr. Broek', *FEQ*, 10, 281–4.

VAN DER KROEF, J. M. (B1952a), 'The Messiah in Indonesia and Malaysia', *Scientific Monthly*, 75, 161–5.

VAN DER KROEF, J. M. (B1952b), 'Society and culture in Indonesian nationalism', *AJS*, 58, 11–24.

VAN DER KROEF, J. M. (B1954a), *Indonesia in the Modern World*, 2 vols, Bandung.

VAN DER KROEF, J. M. (B1954b), 'Communism and Islam in Indonesia', *India Quarterly*, 314–52.

VAN DER KROEF, J. M. (B1956a), 'The colonial deviation in Indonesian history', *East and West*, pp. 251–61.

VAN DER KROEF, J. M. (B1956b), 'The changing class structure of Indonesia', *ASR*, 21, 138–48.

VAN DER KROEF, J. M. (B1958a), 'On the writing of Indonesian history', *PA*, 31, 352–71.

VAN DER KROEF, J. M. (B1958b), 'Indonesia's military and the state', *Far Eastern Economic Review*, 24, 683–7.

VAN DER KROEF, J. M. (B1958c), 'The role of Islam in Indonesian nationalism and politics', *Western Political Quarterly*, 11, 33–54.

VAN DER KROEF, J. M. (B1960), 'Indonesian Communist Party and the Sixth Party Congress', *PA*, 33, 227–49.

VAN DER KROEF, J. M. (B1962), 'An Indonesian ideological lexicon', *Asian Survey*, 2, 24–30.

VAN DER KROEF, J. M. (B1963a), 'Peasant and land reform in Indonesian communism', *JSEAH*, 4, 30–61.

VAN DER KROEF, J. M. (B1963b), 'Indonesia and the Dutch', *PA*, 36, 290–3.

VAN DER KROEF, J. M. (B1963c), *The Dialectic of Colonial Indonesian History*, Amsterdam.

VAN DER KROEF, J. M. (B1965a), *The Communist Party of Indonesia*, Vancouver.

VAN DER KROEF, J. M. (B1965b), 'National and international dimensions of Indonesian history', *JSEAH*, 6, 17–32.

VAN DER KROEF, J. M. (B1968), 'Sukarno, the ideologue', *PA*, 41, 245–61.

VAN DER WAL, S. L. (ed.) (B1963), *Het onderwijsbeleid in Nederlandsch Indie 1900–40: Een bronnenpublikatie* (*Education Policy in the Netherlands Indies 1900–40*), Groningen.

VAN KLAVEREN, J. J. (B1953), *The Dutch Colonial System in the East Indies*, The Hague.

VAN LEUR, J. C. (B1955), *Indonesian Trade and Society*, The Hague and Bandung.

VAN MOOK, H. J. (B1958), 'Kuta Gede', in WERTHEIM, W. F. *et al.* (B1958, pp. 277–331).

VAN NIEL, R. (B1960), *The Emergence of the Modern Indonesian Elite*, Bandung.

VAN NIEUWENHUIJZE, C. A. O. (B1968), *Aspects of Islam in Post-Colonial Indonesia*, The Hague and Bandung.

VAN WOUDEN, P. A. E. (B1968), *Types of Social Structure in Eastern Indonesia*, The Hague.

VAN WULLFLEN-PATHE, P. M. (B1949), *Psychological Aspects of the Indonesian Problem*, Leiden.

VAN ZYLL DE JONG, ELLEN (B1942), *The Netherlands East Indies and Japan*, Netherlands Information Bureau.

VERDOORN, J. A. (B1946), 'Indonesia at the crossroads', *PA*, 19, 339–50.

VLEKKE, B. H. M. (B1949a), 'Communism and nationalism in south east Asia', *International Affairs*, 25, 149–56.

VLEKKE, B. H. M. (B1949b), 'Indonesia in retrospect', *PA*, 22, 290–5.

VLEKKE, B. H. M. (B1957), *Indonesia in 1956, Political and Economic Aspects*, The Hague.

VLEKKE, B. H. M. (B1959), *Nusantara: A History of the East Indian Archipelago*, Cambridge, Mass.

WEATHERBEE, D. E. (B1966), *Ideology in Indonesia: Sukarno's Indonesian Revolution*, New Haven.

WEHL, D. (1948), *The Birth of Indonesia*, London.

WERTHEIM, W. F. (B1953a), 'The Coolie Budget Report', *PA*, 26, 158–64.

WERTHEIM, W. F. (B1953b), 'The changing structure of eastern society', *Eastern and Western World*, The Hague and Bandung, pp. 39–53.

WERTHEIM, W. F. (B1955), 'Changes in Indonesia's social stratification', *PA*, 28, 41–52.

WERTHEIM, W. F. (B1956), *Indonesian Society in Transition*, The Hague.

WERTHEIM, W. F. (B1964), *East-West Parallels*, The Hague.

WERTHEIM, W. F. *et al.* (eds) (B1958), *The Indonesian Town: Studies in Urban Sociology*, The Hague and Bandung.

WILLIAMS, L. E. (B1961), 'The ethical programme and the Chinese of Indonesia', *JSEAH*, 2, 35–42.

WOLF, C., Jr (B1948), *The Indonesian Story; The Birth, Growth and Structure of the Indonesian Republic*, New York.

WOLF, E. C. (B1957), 'Closed corporate peasant communities in Meso-America and central Java', *Southwestern Journal of Anthropology*, 13, 1–18.

WOODMAN, DOROTHY (B1955), *The Republic of Indonesia*, New York.

ZINKIN, M. (B1953), *Asia and the West*, London.

(C) Other works

ABRAMS, P. (1968), 'The revolutionary as a social type', paper prepared for seminar on twentieth-century political revolution held at King's College, Cambridge.

ABRAMS, P. (1970), 'Rites de Passage. The conflict of generations in industrial society', *Journal of Contemporary History*, 5, 175–90.

ADLER, A. (1938), *Social Interest: A Challenge to Mankind*, London.

ADLER, A. (1965), *Superiority and Social Interest: A Collection of Later Writings*, ed. by H. L. ANSBACHER and ROWENA R. ANSBACHER, London.

ALAVI, H. (1965), 'Peasants and revolution', *Socialist Register*, 241–77.

ALBERONI, F. (1946), *Consumi e Societá*, Bologna.

224

BIBLIOGRAPHY

ALLEN, S. (1968), 'Some theoretical problems in the study of youth', SR, 16, 319–31.
ALLPORT, G. (1955), Becoming: Basic Considerations for a Psychology of Personality, New Haven.
ALTHUSSER, L. (1967), 'Contradiction and overdetermination', NLR, 41, 15–35.
ALTHUSSER, L. (1969), For Marx, London.
ARENDT, HANNAH (1963), On Revolution, London.
ARISTOTLE (1942), Rhetorica, in The Works of Aristotle, Oxford.
ARISTOTLE (1962), Politics, London.
ARISTOTLE (1963), Ethics, London.
ARISTOTLE (1968), Poetics, Englewood Cliffs, New Jersey.
AVINERI, S. (1968), The Social and Political Thought of Karl Marx, Cambridge.
BACON, FRANCIS (1911), The Essays, or Counsels Civil and Moral of Francis Bacon, Oxford.
BACHRACH, P. and BARATZ, M. S. (1962), 'Two faces of power', APSR, 56, 947–52.
BAGEHOT, W. (1963), The English Constitution, London.
BALDWIN, A. L. (1963), 'The Parsonian theory of personality', in BLACK, M. (ed.), The Social Theories of Talcott Parsons, Englewood Cliffs, New Jersey, pp. 153–90.
BALDWIN, J. M. (1911), The Individual and Society, or Psychology and Sociology, London.
BARBER, ELINOR (1955), The Bourgeoisie in Eighteenth-Century France, Princeton.
BARNES, J. A. (1969), 'Graph theory and social networks: a technical comment on connectedness and connectivity', Sociology, 3, 215–32.
BARRY, B. (1970), Sociologists, Economists and Democracy, London.
BATESON, G., JACKSON, D. D., HALEY, J., WEAKLAND, J. and WEAKLAND, J. (1956), 'Towards a theory of schizophrenia', Behavioural Science, 1, 251–64.
BECKER, H. (1963), Outsiders: Studies in the Sociology of Deviance, New York.
BECKER, H. (1964), 'Personal change in adult life', Sociometry, 27, 40–53.
BECKER, H. and CARPER, J. W. (1956), 'The development of identification with an occupation', AJS, 61, 289–98.
BECKER, H. and STRAUSS, A. (1956), 'Careers, personality and adult socialization', AJS, 62, 253–63.
BENDIX, R. (1966), Max Weber: An Intellectual Portrait, London.
BENDIX, R. and LIPSET, S. M. (1963), Social Mobility in Industrial Society, Berkeley, California.
BENDIX, R. and LIPSET, S. M. (eds) (1966), Class, Status and Power, London.
BERGER, J., ANDERSON, B. and ZELDITCH, M., Jr (eds) (1966), Sociological Theories in Progress, Boston.
BERGER, P. (1965), 'Towards a sociological understanding of psychoanalysis', Social Research, 32, 26–41.

225

BIBLIOGRAPHY

BERGER, P. (1966), 'Identity as a problem in the sociology of knowledge', EJS, 7, 105–15.

BERGER, P. and PULLBERG, P. (1966), 'Reification and the sociological critique of consciousness', NLR, 35, 56–71.

BERGSON, H. (1913), Time and Free Will, New York.

BERKE, J. (ed.) (1969), Counter Culture, London.

BETTLEHEIM, B. (1958), 'Individual and mass behavior in extreme situations', in MACCOBY, ELEANOR (ed.), Readings in Social Psychology, New York, pp. 300–10.

BIENEN, H. (1968), Violence and Social Change, Chicago.

BLACKBURN, R. (1969), 'A brief guide to bourgeois ideology', in COCKBURN, A. and BLACKBURN, R. (eds), Student Power, Problems, Diagnosis, Action, London, pp. 163–213.

BLALOCK, H. (1966), 'The identification problem and theory building', ASR, 31, 52–61.

BLAU, P. (1963), 'Critical remarks on Weber's theory of authority', APSR, 57, 305–16.

BLUM, A. F. (1966), 'Social structure, social class and participation in primary relationships', in GOODE, W. J. (ed.), Dynamics of Modern Society, New York, pp. 77–86.

BLUMER, H. (1966), 'Sociological implications of the thought of George Herbert Mead', AJS, 71, 534–44.

BOBER, M. M. (1948), Karl Marx's Interpretation of History, Cambridge, Mass.

BOTTOMORE, T. B. and RUBEL, M. (eds) (1963), Karl Marx: Selected Writings in Sociology and Social Philosophy, London.

BOX, S. and FORD, JULIENNE (1969), 'Some questionable assumptions in the theory of status inconsistency', SR, 17, 187–201.

BRIM, O. G. (1960), 'Personality development as role learning', in ISCOE, I., and STEVENSON, H. (eds) Personality Development in Children, Austin, Texas, pp. 127–59.

BRINTON, C. (1953), The Anatomy of Revolution, London.

BRONFENBRENNER, U. (1963), 'Parsons' theory of identification', in BLACK, M. (ed.), The Social Theories of Talcott Parsons, Englewood Cliffs, New Jersey, pp. 191–213.

BROUWER, M. (1962), 'Mass communication and the social sciences: some neglected areas', International Social Science Journal, 14, 303–19.

BROWN, JULIA S. and GILMARTIN, B. G. (1969), 'Sociology today: lacunae, emphases, and surfeits', The American Sociologist, 4, 283–91.

BROWN, N. O. (1968), Life against Death, London.

BRUYN, S. T. (1966), The Human Perspective in Sociology: The Methodology of Participant Observation, Englewood Cliffs, New Jersey.

BUCKLEY, W. (1967), Sociology and Modern Systems Theory, Englewood Cliffs, New Jersey.

CAIN, L. D. Jr (1964), 'Life course and social structure', in FARIS, R. E. L. (ed.), Handbook of Modern Sociology, Chicago, pp. 272–309.

CAMPBELL, E. Q. (1964), 'The internalization of moral norms', Sociometry, 27, pp. 391–412.

CARMICHAEL, S. and HAMILTON, C. V. (1969), Black Power, London.

226

CASSIRER, E. (1944), *An Essay on Man: An Introduction to a Philosophy of Human Culture*, New Haven.
CHASIN, G. (1964), 'George Herbert Mead. Social Psychologist of the moral society', *Berkeley Journal of Sociology*, 9, 95–117.
CHILD, A. (1941), 'The theoretical possibilities of the sociology of knowledge', *Ethics*, 51, 392–418.
CHINOY, E. (1955), *Automobile Workers and the American Dream*, New York.
CHORLEY, KATHARINE C. (1943), *Armies and the Art of Revolution*, London.
CICOUREL, A. V. (1964), *Method and Measurement in Sociology*, New York.
CLEAVER, ELDRIDGE (1968), *Soul on Ice*, New York.
COHN, N. (1957), *The Pursuit of the Millennium*, London.
COLE, R. (1966), 'Structural-functional theory, the dialectic and social change', *Sociological Quarterly*, 7, 39–58.
CONVERSE, P. E. (1964), 'The nature of belief systems in mass publics', in APTER, D. E. (ed.), *Ideology and Discontent*, New York, pp. 206–61.
COOLEY, C. H. (1956a), *Human Nature and the Social Order*, Chicago.
COOLEY, C. H. (1956b), *Social Organization: A Study of the Larger Mind*, Chicago.
COOLEY, C. H. (1966), *Social Process*, Southern Illinois.
COSER, L. (1955), 'The functions of small group research', *Social Problems*, 3, 1–6.
COSER, ROSE LAUB (1966), 'Role distance, sociological ambivalence, and transitional status systems', *AJS*, 72, 173–87.
CROMBIE, A. C. (1962), *An Examination of Plato's Doctrines*, London.
DAHRENDORF, R. (1959), *Class and Class Conflict in Industrial Society*, London.
DAHRENDORF, R. (1961), 'Über einige Probleme der soziologischen Theorie der Revolution', *EJS*, 2, 153–62.
DAHRENDORF, R. (1967), *Conflict After Class: New Perspectives on the Theory of Social and Political Conflict*, the Noel Buxton Lecture at the University of Essex, London.
DAI, B. (1969), 'A socio-psychiatric approach to personality organization', in SPITZER, S. P. (ed.), *The Sociology of Personality*, New York, pp. 72–82.
DAVIES, A. F. (1967), *Images of Class: An Australian Study*, Sydney.
DAVIES, J. C. (1962), 'The theory of revolution', *ASR*, 27, 5–19.
DE KADT, I. (1965), 'Conflict and power in society', *International Journal of the Social Science*, 17, 454–71.
DEMERATH, N. J. (1967), 'Synecdoche and structural-functionalism', in DEMERATH, N. J. and PETERSON, R. A. (eds), *System, Change, and Conflict*, New York.
DENNIS, N., HENRIQUES, F. and SLAUGHTER, C. (1956), *Coal is Our Life*, London.
DE TOCQUEVILLE, A. (1933), *The Ancien Régime and the French Revolution*, Oxford.
DE TOCQUEVILLE, A. (1966), *Democracy in America*, 2, New York.

BIBLIOGRAPHY

DEWEY, J. (1925), *Experience and Nature*, Chicago.

DEWEY, J. (1927), *The Public and Its Problems*, New York.

DIGGORY, J. (1966), *Self-evaluation: Concepts and Studies*, New York.

DOREIAN, P. and STOCKMAN, N. (1969), 'A critique of the multi-dimensional approach to stratification', *SR*, 17, 47–65.

DUESENBERRY, J. S. (1967), *Income, Saving and the Theory of Consumer Behavior*, New York.

DUNN, J. (1972), *Modern Revolutions: An Introduction to the Analysis of a Political Phenomenon*, Cambridge.

DURKHEIM, E. (1952), *Suicide*, London.

ECKSTEIN, H. (1964) (ed.), *Internal War*, New York.

ECKSTEIN, H. (1965), 'On the etiology of internal wars', *History and Theory*, 4, 133–63.

EDWARDS, L. P. (1927), *The Natural History of Revolution*, Chicago.

EISENSTADT, S. N. (1956), *From Generation to Generation*, Chicago.

EISENSTADT, S. N. (1962), 'Religious organizations and political processes in centralized empires', *JAS*, 21, 271–94.

ENGELS, F. (1889), 'Letter to F. A. Sorge, December 7', in Marx and Engels, *On Britain* (1962), Moscow.

ENGELS, F. (1962), 'Letter to Joseph Bloch, 21st September, 1890', *Marx and Engels Selected Works*, 2, Moscow.

ERIKSON, E. H. (1968a), 'Identity, psychosocial', in SILLS, D. (ed.), *International Encyclopaedia of the Social Sciences*, 7, New York, pp. 61–5.

ERIKSON, E. H. (1968b), *Identity: Youth and Crisis*, London.

ERIKSON, E. H. (1969), *Childhood and Society*, Harmondsworth.

ETZIONI, A. (1965), *A Comparative Analysis of Complex Organisations*, New York.

FALLDING, H. (1968), *The Sociological Task*, Englewood Cliffs, New Jersey.

FANON, F. (1967), *The Wretched of the Earth*, London.

FATHI, A. (1965), 'Effect of latent positions on interaction', *Sociology and Social Research*, 49, 190–200.

FESTINGER, L. (1953), 'An analysis of compliant behavior', in SHERIF, M. and WILSON, M. O. (eds), *Group Relations at the Crossroads*, New York, pp. 232–56.

FIRTH, R. (1964), *Essays on Social Organization and Values*, London.

FLETCHER, C. (1970), 'On replication: notes on the notions of a replicability quotient and a generalizability quotient', *Sociology*, 4, 51–69.

FOOTE, N. (1951), 'Identification as the basis for a theory of motivation', *ASR*, 16, 14–21.

FOSTER, J. O. (1967), 'Capitalism and class consciousness in earlier nineteenth-century Oldham', Ph.D. thesis, University of Cambridge.

FREUD, S. (1960), *Group Psychology and the Analysis of the Ego*, New York.

FRIEDMAN, N. (1967), *The Social Nature of Psychological Research: The Psychological Experiment as a Social Interaction*, New York.

GARFINKEL, H. (1960), 'The rational properties of scientific and common-sense activities', *Behavioural Science*, 5, 72–83.

GARFINKEL, H. (1967), *Studies in Ethnomethodology*, Englewood Cliffs, New Jersey.

GEARY, R. (1969), 'Karl Kautsky and the development of Marxism', Ph.D. thesis, University of Cambridge.

GERGEN, K. J. (1968), 'Personal consistency and the presentation of self', in GORDON, C. and GERGEN, K. J. (eds), *The Self in Social Interaction*, 1, pp. 299–308.

GERTH, H. H. and MILLS, C. WRIGHT (1954), *Character and Social Structure*, London.

GIDDENS, A. (1968), '"Power" in the recent writings of Talcott Parsons', *Sociology*, 2, 257–72.

GLASER, B. G. and STRAUSS, A. L. (1968), *The Discovery of Grounded Theory*, London.

GLOCK, C. Y. (1964), 'The role of deprivation in the origin and evolution of religious groups', in LEE, R. and MARTY, M. E. (eds), *Religion and Social Conflict*, New York, pp. 24–36.

GLUCKSMAN, M. (1962), 'Les rites de passage', in GLUCKSMAN, M. (ed.), *Essays on the Ritual of Social Relations*, Manchester, pp. 1–52.

GODELIER, M. (1967), 'System, structure and contradiction in "Capital"', *Socialist Register*, 91–119.

GOFFMAN, E. (1961), *Encounters*, New York.

GOFFMAN, E. (1962), 'On cooling the mark out: some aspects of adaptation to failure', in ROSE, A. M. (ed.) (1962, pp. 482–505).

GOFFMAN, E. (1963), *Stigma*, London.

GOFFMAN, E. (1968), *Asylums*, London.

GOLDBERG, M. M. (1941), 'A qualification of the marginal man theory', *ASR*, 6, 52–8.

GOLDMANN, L. (1964), *The Hidden God*, London.

GOLDMANN, L. (1969), *The Human Sciences and Philosophy*, London.

GOODE, W. J. (1960), 'A theory of role strain', *ASR*, 25, 483–96.

GORDON, C. and GERGEN, K. J. (eds) (1968), *The Self in Social Interaction*, New York.

GORZ, A. (1965), 'Work and consumption', in ANDERSON, P. and BLACKBURN, R. (eds), *Towards Socialism*, London, pp. 317–53.

GORZ, A. (1967), *Strategy for Labor*, Boston.

GOTTSCHALK, L. (1944), 'Causes of revolution', *AJS*, 50, 1–8.

GOULDNER, A. W. (1955), *Wildcat Strike; a Study of an Unofficial Strike*, London.

GOULDNER, A. W. (1960), 'The norm of reciprocity', *ASR*, 25, pp. 161–78.

GOULDNER, A. W. (1967), 'Reciprocity and autonomy in functional theory', in DEMERATH, N. J. and PETERSON, R. A. (eds), *System, Change, and Conflict*, New York, pp. 141–69.

GRAMSCI, A. (1957), *The Modern Prince and Other Writings*, translated by L. MARKS, New York.

GUEVARA, CHE (1969), *Guerrilla Warfare*, London.

HALL, O. (1948), 'The stages of a medical career', *AJS*, 53, 327–36.

HAMILTON, R. F. (1967), *Affluence and the French Worker in the Fourth Republic*, Princeton.

HARRELL, B. (1967), 'Symbols, perception, and meaning', in GROSS, L.

(ed.), *Sociological Theory: Inquiries and Paradigms*, New York, pp. 104–27.

HEIDER, F. (1967), *The Psychology of Interpersonal Relations*, New York.

HERZBERG, F. (1968), *Work and the Nature of Man*, London.

HINKLE, R. C. (1967), 'Charles Horton Cooley's general sociological orientation', *Sociological Quarterly*, 8, 5–20.

HOBSBAWM, E. (1959), *Primitive Rebels*, Manchester.

HOFFER, E. (1964), *The Ordeal of Change*, New York.

HOGGART, R. (1957), *The Uses of Literacy*, London.

HOLMES, R. (1965), 'Freud and social class', *BJS*, 16, 48–67.

HOPPER, R. D. (1950), 'The revolutionary process: a frame of reference for the study of revolutionary movements', *SF*, 28, 270–9.

HUGHES, E. C. (1937), 'Institutional office and the person', *AJS*, 43, 404–13.

HUGHES, E. C. (1945), 'Dilemmas and contradictions of status', *AJS*, 50, 353–9.

HUGHES, E. C. (1949), 'Social change and status protest: an essay on the marginal man', *Phylon*, 10, 58–65.

HUGHES, E. C. (1958), *Men and Their Work*, Chicago.

HUGHES, E. C. (1962), 'What other?' in ROSE, A. M. (ed.) (1962, pp. 119–28).

HUME, D. (1962), *A Treatise of Human Nature*, vol. 1, London.

HYMAN, H. H. (1966), 'The value systems of different classes', in BENDIX, R. and LIPSET, S. M. (eds) (1966, pp. 488–99).

HYPPOLITE, J. (1969), *Studies on Marx and Hegel*, London.

INGHAM, G. K. (1969), 'Plant size: political attitudes and behaviour', *SR*, 17, 235–49.

ISAJIW, W. W. (1968), *Causation and Functionalism in Sociology*, London.

JAMES, W. (1890), *Principles of Psychology*, vol. 1, London.

JAMES, W. (1892), *Psychology: Briefer Course*, New York.

KALDOR, N. (1964), *Essays on Economic Policy*, vol. 1, London.

KANT, L. (1922), *The Metaphysics of Morals*, in *Samtliche Werke*, vol. 3, Leipzig.

KATZ, E. and LAZARSFELD, P. (1960), *Personal Influence: the part played by people in the flow of mass communications*, Chicago.

KAUTSKY, K. J. (1909), *The Social Revolution and on the Morrow of the Social Revolution*, London.

KELLY, G. A. (1963), *A Theory of Personality; The Psychology of Personal Constructs*, New York.

KERR, C. and SIEGEL, A. (1954), 'The inter-industry propensity to strike – an international comparison', in KORNHAUSER, A. *et al.* (eds), *Industrial Conflict*, New York, pp. 189–212.

KEY, V. O. (1956), *Politics, Parties, and Pressure Groups*, New York.

KEYNES, J. M. (1961), *The General Theory of Employment, Interest and Money*, London.

KOLB, W. L. (1967), 'A critical evaluation of Mead's "I" and "Me" concepts', in MANIS, J. G. and MELTZER, B. N. (1967, pp. 241–50).

KRIESBERG, M. (1949), 'Cross pressures and attitudes: a study of conflicting propaganda on opinions regarding American-Soviet relations', *POQ*, 13, 5–16.

KUMAR, K. (ed.) (1971), *Revolution*, London.

LAING, R. D. (1967), *The Politics of Experience*, London.

LANE, R. (1959), 'The fear of equality', *APSR*, 53, 35–51.

LAPIERE, R. T. (1934), 'Attitudes versus actions', *SF*, 13, 230–7.

LASKY, M. J. (1970a), 'The birth of a metaphor: on the origins of utopia and revolution (1)', *Encounter*, 34, 35–45.

LASKY, M. J. (1970b), 'The birth of a metaphor: on the origins of utopia and revolution (2)', *Encounter*, 34, 30–42.

LEACH, E. (1954), *The Political Systems of Highland Burma: A Study in Kachin Social Structure*, London.

LECKY, P. (1951), *Self-Consistency: A Theory of Personality*, New York.

LECKY, P. (1968), 'The theory of self-consistency', in GORDON, C. and GERGEN, K. J. (eds), *The Self in Social Interaction*, New York, pp. 297–8.

LEFEBVRE, H. (1968), *The Sociology of Marx*, London.

LEGGETT, J. C. (1968), *Class, Race and Labor*, New York.

LENSKI, G. (1954), 'Status crystallization: a non-vertical dimension of social status', *ASR*, 19, 405–13.

LENSKI, G. (1966), *Power and Privilege*, New York.

LEWIS, L. S. (1965), 'Class consciousness and the salience of class', *Sociology and Social Research*, 49, 173–82.

LIGHT, I. V. (1969), 'The social construction of uncertainty', *Berkeley Journal of Sociology*, 14, 189–99.

LOCKWOOD, D. (1958), *The Blackcoated Worker*, London.

LOCKWOOD, D. (1964), 'Social integration and system integration', in ZOLLSCHAN, G. K. and HIRSCH, W. (eds), *Explorations in Social Change*, London, pp. 244–57.

LOCKWOOD, D. (1966), 'Sources of variation in working-class images of society', *SR*, 14, 249–67.

LOPREATO, J. (1968), 'Authority relations and class conflict', *SF*, 47, 70–9.

LUKACS, G. (1923), *Geschichte und Klassenbewusstein*, Berlin.

LYND, HELEN (1958), *On Shame and the Search for Identity*, London.

MACINTYRE, A. (1967), *A Short History of Ethics*, London.

MACINTYRE, A. (1969), 'The self as work of art', *New Statesman*, 28 March.

MCLELLAN, D. (1971), *Marx's Grundrisse*, London.

MALLET, S. (1963), *La Nouvelle Classe Ouvriere*, Paris.

MANDEL, E. (1962), *Marxist Economic Theory*, vol. 1, London.

MANDEVILLE, B. (1970), *The Fable of the Bees*, London.

MANIS, J. G. and MELTZER, B. N. (1963), 'Some correlates of class consciousness among textile workers', *AJS*, 69, 77–84.

MANIS, J. G. and MELTZER, B. N. (1967), *Symbolic Interaction: A Reader in Social Psychology*, Boston.

MANN, M. (1970), 'The social cohesion of liberal democracy', *ASR*, 30, 423–39.

MANNHEIM, K. (1936), *Ideology and Utopia*, London.

MANNHEIM, K. (1952), *Essays on the Sociology of Knowledge*, London.

MANNONI, O. (1964), *Prospero and Caliban. The Psychology of Colonialization*, New York.

MAO-TSE-TUNG (1966), *Four Essays on Philosophy*, Peking.

MAREK, F. (1969), *Philosophy of World Revolution*, London.

MARCUSE, H. (1965), 'Industrialization and capitalism', *NLR*, 30, 3–17.

MARCUSE, H. (1969a), *Eros and Civilisation*, London.

MARCUSE, H. (1969b), 'Re-examination of the concept of revolution', *NLR*, 56, 27–34.

MARCUSE, H. (1969c), 'Repressive tolerance', in WOLFF, R. P., MOORE, BARRINGTON Jr and MARCUSE, H., *A Critique of Pure Tolerance*, London, pp. 95–137.

MARSH, R. M. (1967), *Comparative Sociology*, New York.

MARX, K. (1909), *Capital*, vol. 1, Chicago.

MARX, K. (1919), *Theorien Uber den Mehrwert*, vol. 2, Stuttgart.

MARX, K. (1922), *Die Inauguraladresse der internationalen Arbeiter-Association*, ed. by K. KAUTSKY, Berlin.

MARX, K. (1926), *The Eighteenth Brumaire of Louis Bonaparte*, London.

MARX, K. (1933), *Wage-Labour and Capital*, London.

MARX, K. (1954), *Capital*, vol. 1, Moscow.

MARX, K. (1956), *Capital*, vol. 2, Moscow.

MARX, K. (1959), *Economic and Philosophic Manuscripts of 1844*, Moscow.

MARX, K. and ENGELS, F. (1888), *Manifesto of the Communist Party*, Moscow.

MARX, K. and ENGELS, F. (1956), *The Holy Family, or Critique of Critical Critique*, Moscow.

MARX, K. and ENGELS, F. (1965), *The German Ideology*, Moscow.

MAY, R. (1958), Introduction to MAY, R., ANGEL, E., ELLENBERGER, H. F. (eds), *Existence: A New Dimension in Psychiatry and Psychology*, New York, pp. 1–36.

MEAD, G. H. (1912), 'The mechanism of social consciousness', *Journal of Philosophy, Psychology and Scientific Methods*, 9, 401–6.

MEAD, G. H. (1930), 'Cooley's contribution to American social thought', *AJS*, 35, 693–706.

MEAD, G. H. (1932), *The Philosophy of the Present*, Chicago.

MEAD, G. H. (1934), *Mind, Self, and Society*, Chicago.

MEAD, G. H. (1936), *Movements of Thought in the Nineteenth Century*, Chicago.

MEAD, G. H. (1938), *The Philosophy of the Act*, Chicago.

MERLEAU-PONTY, M. (1962), *Phenomenology of Perception*, London.

MERTON, R. K. (1957), *Social Theory and Social Structure*, Chicago.

MILLS, C. WRIGHT (1963), *Power, Politics and People*, New York.

MILLS, C. WRIGHT (1967), *The Sociological Imagination*, New York.

MISHAN, E. (1969), *The Costs of Economic Growth*, London.

MITCHELL, R. E. (1964), 'Methodological notes on a theory of status crystallization', *POQ*, 28, 315–25.

MIZRUCHI, E. H. (1963), *Success and Opportunity: a Study of Anomie*, New York.

MIZRUCHI, E. II. (1967), 'Aspiration and poverty: a neglected aspect of Merton's anomie', *Sociological Quarterly*, 8, 439–46.

MOORE, BARRINGTON Jr (1958), *Political Power and Social Theory*, Cambridge, Mass.

MOORE, BARRINGTON Jr (1967), *Social Origins of Dictatorship and Democracy*, London.

MOORE, BARRINGTON Jr (1969), 'Revolution in America', *New York Review of Books*, 30 January, 6–12.

MOORE, W. (1960), 'Reconsideration of theories of social change', *ASR*, 25, 810–18.

MORRIS, C. (1934), Introduction to MEAD, G. H. (1934).

MORRIS, R. T. and MURPHY, R. J. (1966), 'A paradigm for the study of class consciousness', *Sociology and Social Research*, 50, 297–313.

MOUSTAKAS, C. E. (ed.) (1956), *The Self*, New York.

NADEL, G. (1960), 'The logic of "The anatomy of revolution", with reference to the Netherlands revolt', *Comparative Studies in Society and History*, 2, 473–84.

NATANSON, M. (1956), *The Social Dynamics of George H. Mead*, Washington.

NEWTON, K. (1965), 'British Communism: The Sociology of a Radical Political Party', Ph.D. thesis, Cambridge,

NIETZSCHE, F. (1909), *Thus Spake Zarathrusta*, 2, Edinburgh.

NIETZSCHE, F. (1910), *The Will to Power*, 2, Edinburgh.

NIETZSCHE, F. (1911a), *The Dawn of Day*, Edinburgh.

NIETZSCHE, F. (1911b), *Human, All-too-Human*, 2, Edinburgh.

NIETZSCHE, F. (1956), *The Genealogy of Morals*, New York.

NURKSE, R. (1953), *Problems of Capital Formation in Underdeveloped Countries*, Oxford.

OESER, O. A. and HAMMOND, S. B. (1954), *Social Structure and Personality in a City*, London.

OSSOWSKI, S. (1963), *Class Structure in the Social Consciousness*, London.

PARK, R. E. (1928), 'Human migration and the marginal man', *AJS*, 33, 881–93.

PARSONS, H. L. (1965), 'Existentialism and Marxism in dialogue (a review of Sartre's *Problem of Method*)', in APTHEKER, H. (ed.), *Marxism and Alienation*, New York, pp. 89–124.

PARSONS, T. (1954), 'Psychology and sociology', in GILLIN, J. (ed.), *For a Science of Social Man*, New York, pp. 67–101.

PARSONS, T. (1955), 'The mechanisms of personality functioning with special reference to socialization', in PARSONS, T. *et al.*, *Family, Socialization and Interaction Process*, Chicago, pp. 187–257.

PARSONS, T. (1957), 'Power in American society', *WP*, 10, 123–43.

PARSONS, T. (1960), *Structure and Process in Modern Society*, New York.

PARSONS, T. and OLDS, J. (1964), *Social Structure and Personality*, London.

PARSONS, T. and SHILS, E. (eds) (1951), *Towards a General Theory of Action*, Cambridge, Mass.

PARSONS, T. and SMELSER, N. J. (1956), *Economy and Society*, London.

PFUETZE, P. E. (1954), *The Social Self*, New York.

233

PLATO (1955), *Republic*, London.

PLOWMAN, D. E. G., MINCHINGTON, W. E. and STACEY, MARGARET (1962), 'Local social status in England and Wales', *SR*, 10, 161–202.

POPITZ, H., BAHRDT, H. P., JUERES, E. A. and KESTING, H. (1957), *Das Gesellschaftsbild des Arbeiters*, Tubingen.

POTTER, D. M. (1954), *People of Plenty: Economic Abundance and the American Character*, Chicago.

PRESSEY, S. L. and KUHLEN, R. G. (1957), *Psychological Development Through the Life-Span*, New York.

PUGH, D. (1966), 'Role activation conflict: a study of industrial inspection', *ASR*, 31, 835–42.

RANULF, S. (1938), *Moral Indignation and Middle Class Psychology: a Sociological Study*, Copenhagen.

REX, J. (1961), *Key Problems in Sociological Theory*, London.

RIESMAN, D. (1951), 'Some observations concerning marginality', *Phylon*, 113–27.

RILEY, MATILDA W. and FLOWERMAN, S. H. (1951), 'Group relations as a variable in communications research', *ASR*, 16, 174–80.

ROBBINS, M. (1965), *The Railway Age*, London.

RODMAN, H. (1963), 'The lower-class value stretch', *SF*, 42, 205–15.

RODNER, K. (1967), 'Logical foundations of social change theory', *Sociology and Social Research*, 51, 287–301.

ROGIN, M. P. (1967), *The Intellectuals and McCarthy: The Radical Specter*, Cambridge, Mass.

ROSE, A. M. (ed.) (1962), *Human Behaviour and Social Processes*, London.

ROSENBERG, M. (1953), 'Perceptual obstacles to class consciousness', *SF*, 32, 22–7.

ROSENBERG, M. (1967), 'Psychological selectivity in self-esteem formation', in SHERIF, CAROLYN and SHERIF, M. (eds), *Attitude, Ego-involvement, and Change*, New York, pp. 26–50.

ROSZAK, T. (1969), *The Making of a Counter Culture*, New York.

RUDE, G. (1959), *The Crowd in the French Revolution*, London.

RUDNER, R. S. (1966), *Philosophy of Social Science*, Englewood Cliffs, New Jersey.

RUNCIMAN, W. G. (1965), *Social Science and Political Theory*, Cambridge.

RUNCIMAN, W. G. (1967), 'Social Equality', *Philosophical Quarterly*, 17, 221–30.

RUNCIMAN, W. G. (1968), 'Class, status and power?' in JACKSON, J. A. (ed), *Social Stratification*, Cambridge, pp. 25–61.

RUNCIMAN, W. G. (1970), 'Social stratification: a rejoinder to Mr. Ingham', *Sociology*, 4, 246–8.

RUSTIN, J. (1967), 'A way out of the exploding ghetto', *New York Magazine*, 13 August.

SAMPSON, E. E. (1966), 'Status congruency and cognitive consistency', in BACKMAN, C. and SECORD, P. F. (eds), *Readings in Social Psychology*, New York, pp. 218–26.

SARBIN, T. (1954), 'Role theory', in LINDZEY, G. (ed.), *Handbook of Social Psychology*, vol. 1, Reading, Mass., pp. 223–58.

SCHATZ, O. and WINTER, E. F. (1967), 'Alienation, Marxism and humanism (a Christian viewpoint)', in FROMM, E. (ed), *Socialist Humanism*, London, pp. 291–308.

SCHATZMAN, L. and STRAUSS, A. (1955), 'Social class and modes of communication', *AJS*, 60, 329–38.

SCHELER, M. (1961), *Ressentiment*, New York.

SCHUTZ, A. (1944), 'The stranger: an essay in social psychology', *AJS*, 49, 499–507.

SCHUTZ, A. (1962), *Collected Papers*, 1, The Hague.

SCHUTZ, A. (1964), *Collected Papers*, 2, The Hague.

SCHUTZ, A. (1966), *Collected Papers*, 3, The Hague.

SCHUTZ, A. (1967), *The Phenomenology of the Social World*, Pittsburgh.

SCOTT, J. F. (1963), 'The changing foundations of the Parsonian action scheme', *ASR*, 28, 716–735.

SCOTT, J. P. (1958), *Animal Behavior*, Chicago.

SEGAL, D. R. (1969), 'Status consistency, cross pressures, and American political behavior', *ASR*, 34, 352–9.

SHILS, E. (1968), 'Deference', in JACKSON, J. A. (ed.), *Social Stratification*, Cambridge, pp. 104–32.

SIMMEL, G. (1955), *Conflict and the Web of Group-Affiliations*, New York.

SMELSER, N. J. (1962), *The Theory of Collective Behaviour*, London.

SMELSER, N. J. and SMELSER, W. T. (1963), *Personality and Social Systems*, New York.

SMITH, D. H. (1967), 'A parsimonious definition of "Group": toward conceptual clarity and scientific utility', *Sociological Inquiry*, 37, 141–67.

SNOW, V. F. (1962), 'The concept of revolution in seventeenth-century England', *Historical Journal*, 5, 167–74.

SOREL, G. (1950), *Reflections on Violence*, New York.

SOROKIN, P. (1925), *The Sociology of Revolution*, Philadelphia.

SOROKIN, P. (1964), *Social and Cultural Mobility*, New York.

SPEIER, M. (1967), 'Phenomenology and social theory: discovering actors and social acts', *Berkeley Journal of Sociology*, 12, 193–211.

SPROTT, W. (1958), *Human Groups*, London.

STONE, G. P. and FARBERMAN, H. A. (1967), 'On the edge of rapprochement: was Durkheim moving toward the perspective of symbolic interaction?' *Sociological Quarterly*, 8, 149–64.

STONE, G. P. and FARBERMAN, H. A. (1970), *Social Psychology Through Symbolic Interaction*, Waltham, Mass.

STONEQUIST, E. V. (1937), *The Marginal Man*, New York.

STRAUSS, A. (1962), 'Transformations of Identity', in ROSE, A. M. (ed.) (1962, pp. 63–85).

STRAUSS, A. (1964), Introduction to *George Herbert Mead on Social Psychology*, Chicago.

STRAUSS, A. (1968), 'Some neglected properties of status passage', in BECKER, H. S. *et al.* (eds), *Institutions and the Person: Papers Presented to E. C. Hughes*, Chicago, pp. 265–71.

SULLIVAN, H. S. (1955a), *Conceptions of Modern Psychiatry*, London.

SULLIVAN, H. S. (1955b), in PERRY, HELEN S. and GARVEL, MARY L. (eds), *The Interpersonal Theory of Psychiatry*, London.

SUPEK, R. (1967), 'Freedom and polydeterminism in cultural criticism', in FROMM, E. (ed.), *Socialist Humanism*, London, pp. 257–74.

THOMAS, W. I. (1966), *On Social Organization and Social Personality*, Chicago.

THOMPSON, E. P. (1968), *The Making of the English Working Class*, London.

TOURAINE, A. and RAGAZZI, O. (1961), *Ouvriers d'origine agricole*, Paris.

TROTSKY, L. (1965), *History of the Russian Revolution*, London.

TURNER, R. H. (1962), 'Role-taking: process versus conformity', in ROSE, A. M. (ed.) (1962, pp. 20–40).

TURNER, R. H. (1968), 'The self-conception in social interaction', in GORDON, C. and GERGEN, K. J. (eds) (1968, pp. 93–106).

ULAM, A. (1960), *The Unfinished Revolution*, Cambridge, Mass.

URRY, J. R. (1970), 'Role analysis and the sociological enterprise', *SR*, 18, 351–63.

URRY, J. R. (1973), Introduction to URRY, J. R. and WAKEFORD, J. (eds), *Power in Britain*, London, p. 1f.

VAN DEN BERGHE, P. L. (1967), 'Dialectic and functionalism: towards a synthesis', in DEMERATH, N. J. and PETERSON, R. A. (eds), *System, Change, and Conflict*, New York, pp. 293–306.

VEBLEN, T. (1899), *The Theory of the Leisure Class*, New York.

WARRINER, C. K. (1962), 'Groups are real: a reaffirmation', in STOODLEY, B. H. (ed.), *Society and Self*, New York, pp. 29–38.

WEBER, M. (1925), *Wirtschaft und Gesellschaft*, Tübingen.

WEBER, M. (1930), *The Protestant Ethic and the Spirit of Capitalism*, London.

WEBER, M. (1948), *From Max Weber; Essays in Sociology*, translated and ed. by H. H. GERTH and C. WRIGHT MILLS, London.

WEBER, M. (1964), *The Theory of Social and Economic Organization*, ed. by T. PARSONS, New York.

WEBER, M. (1965), *The Sociology of Religion*, London.

WEDDERBURN, DOROTHY (1970), 'Workplace inequality', *New Society*, 9 April, 593–5.

WILENSKY, H. L. (1969), 'Work, careers and social integration', in BURNS, T. (ed.), *Industrial Man*, London, pp. 110–39.

WILLENER, A. (1957), *Images de la société et classes sociales*, Bern.

WILLER, D. (1967), *Scientific Sociology*, Englewood Cliffs, New Jersey.

WILLER, D. and ZOLLSCHAN, G. K. (1964), 'Prolegomenon to a theory of revolutions', in ZOLLSCHAN, G. K. and HIRSCH, W. (eds), *Explorations in Social Change*, London, pp. 125–51.

WILLIAMS, R. M. (1963), *American Society: A Sociological Interpretation*, New York.

WILLIAMS, R. M. (1968), 'The concept of norms', in SILLS, D. (ed.), *International Encyclopaedia of the Social Sciences*, New York, 11, pp. 204–8.

WINNICOTT, D. W. (1965), *The Family and Individual Development*, London.

WOLFF, R. P. (1969), 'Beyond Tolerance', in WOLFF, R. P., MOORE,

BARRINGTON, Jr and MARCUSE, H., *A Critique of Pure Tolerance*, London, pp. 9–61

WOLPE, H. (1970), 'Some problems concerning revolutionary consciousness', *Socialist Register*, 251–80.

WORSLEY, P. (1968), *The Trumpet Shall Sound*, London.

WRONG, D. (1966), 'The oversocialized conception of man in modern sociology', in COSER, L. A. and ROSENBERG, B. (eds), *Sociological Theory*, second ed., New York, pp. 112–22.

WYLIE, RUTH (1961), *The Self Concept*, Lincoln.

YINGER, M. (1960), 'Contraculture and subculture', *ASR*, 25, 625–35.

YOUNG, M. and WILLMOTT, P. (1962), *Family and Kinship in East London*, London.

ZETTERBURG, H. (1962), *Social Thought and Social Practice*, New Jersey.

ZNANIECKI, F. (1967), *Social Actions*, New York.

237

Index

International Library of
Sociology

Edited by

John Rex
University of Warwick

Founded by

Karl Mannheim
as The International Library of Sociology
and Social Reconstruction

*This Catalogue also contains other Social Science
series published by Routledge*

Routledge & Kegan Paul   London and Boston

68-74 Carter Lane London EC4V 5EL
9 Park Street Boston Mass 02108

Contents

● *Books so marked are available in paperback*
All books are in Metric Demy 8vo format (216 × 138mm approx.)

GENERAL SOCIOLOGY

Belshaw, Cyril. The Conditions of Social Performance. *An Exploratory Theory. 144 pp.*

Brown, Robert. Explanation in Social Science. *208 pp.*

● Rules and Laws in Sociology.

Cain, Maureen E. Society and the Policeman's Role. *About 300 pp.*

Gibson, Quentin. The Logic of Social Enquiry. *240 pp.*

Gurvitch, Georges. Sociology of Law. *Preface by Roscoe Pound. 264 pp.*

Homans, George C. Sentiments and Activities: *Essays in Social Science. 336 pp.*

Johnson, Harry M. Sociology: *a Systematic Introduction. Foreword by Robert K. Merton. 710 pp.*

Mannheim, Karl. Essays on Sociology and Social Psychology. *Edited by Paul Keckskemeti. With Editorial Note by Adolph Lowe. 344 pp.*
Systematic Sociology: *An Introduction to the Study of Society. Edited by J. S. Erös and Professor W. A. C. Stewart. 220 pp.*

Martindale, Don. The Nature and Types of Sociological Theory. *292 pp.*

● **Maus, Heinz.** A Short History of Sociology. *234 pp.*

Mey, Harald. Field-Theory. *A Study of its Application in the Social Sciences. 352 pp.*

Myrdal, Gunnar. Value in Social Theory: *A Collection of Essays on Methodology. Edited by Paul Streeten. 332 pp.*

Ogburn, William F., and **Nimkoff, Meyer F.** A Handbook of Sociology. *Preface by Karl Mannheim. 656 pp. 46 figures. 35 tables.*

Parsons, Talcott, and **Smelser, Neil J.** Economy and Society: *A Study in the Integration of Economic and Social Theory. 362 pp.*

● **Rex, John.** Key Problems of Sociological Theory. *220 pp.*

Urry, John. Reference Groups and the Theory of Revolution.

FOREIGN CLASSICS OF SOCIOLOGY

● **Durkheim, Emile.** Suicide. *A Study in Sociology. Edited and with an Introduction by George Simpson. 404 pp.*
Professional Ethics and Civic Morals. *Translated by Cornelia Brookfield. 288 pp.*

● **Gerth, H. H.,** and **Mills, C. Wright.** From Max Weber: *Essays in Sociology. 502 pp.*

Tönnies, Ferdinand. Community and Association. *(Gemeinschaft und Gesellschaft.) Translated and Supplemented by Charles P. Loomis. Foreword by Pitirim A. Sorokin. 334 pp.*

SOCIAL STRUCTURE

Andreski, Stanislav. Military Organization and Society. *Foreword by Professor A. R. Radcliffe-Brown. 226 pp. 1 folder.*

3

Coontz, Sydney H. Population Theories and the Economic Interpretation. *202 pp.*

Coser, Lewis. The Functions of Social Conflict. *204 pp.*

Dickie-Clark, H. F. Marginal Situation: *A Sociological Study of a Coloured Group. 240 pp. 11 tables.*

Glass, D. V. (Ed.). Social Mobility in Britain. *Contributions by J. Berent, T. Bottomore, R. C. Chambers, J. Floud, D. V. Glass, J. R. Hall, H. T. Himmelweit, R. K. Kelsall, F. M. Martin, C. A. Moser, R. Mukherjee, and W. Ziegel. 420 pp.*

Glaser, Barney, and **Strauss, Anselm L.** Status Passage. *A Formal Theory. 208 pp.*

Jones, Garth N. Planned Organizational Change: *An Exploratory Study Using an Empirical Approach. 268 pp.*

Kelsall, R. K. Higher Civil Servants in Britain: *From 1870 to the Present Day. 268 pp. 31 tables.*

König, René. The Community. *232 pp. Illustrated.*

● **Lawton, Denis.** Social Class, Language and Education. *192 pp.*

McLeish, John. The Theory of Social Change: *Four Views Considered. 128 pp.*

Marsh, David C. The Changing Social Structure of England and Wales, 1871-1961. *288 pp.*

Mouzelis, Nicos. Organization and Bureaucracy. *An Analysis of Modern Theories. 240 pp.*

Mulkay, M. J. Functionalism, Exchange and Theoretical Strategy. *272 pp.*

Ossowski, Stanislaw. Class Structure in the Social Consciousness. *210 pp.*

SOCIOLOGY AND POLITICS

Hertz, Frederick. Nationality in History and Politics: *A Psychology and Sociology of National Sentiment and Nationalism. 432 pp.*

Kornhauser, William. The Politics of Mass Society. *272 pp. 20 tables.*

Laidler, Harry W. History of Socialism. *Social-Economic Movements: An Historical and Comparative Survey of Socialism, Communism, Co-operation, Utopianism; and other Systems of Reform and Reconstruction. 992 pp.*

Mannheim, Karl. Freedom, Power and Democratic Planning. *Edited by Hans Gerth and Ernest K. Bramstedt. 424 pp.*

Mansur, Fatma. Process of Independence. *Foreword by A. H. Hanson. 208 pp.*

Martin, David A. Pacificism: *an Historical and Sociological Study. 262 pp.*

Myrdal, Gunnar. The Political Element in the Development of Economic Theory. *Translated from the German by Paul Streeten. 282 pp.*

Wootton, Graham. Workers, Unions and the State. *188 pp.*

FOREIGN AFFAIRS: THEIR SOCIAL, POLITICAL AND ECONOMIC FOUNDATIONS

Mayer, J. P. Political Thought in France from the Revolution to the Fifth Republic. *164 pp.*

4

CRIMINOLOGY

Ancel, Marc. Social Defence: *A Modern Approach to Criminal Problems. Foreword by Leon Radzinowicz. 240 pp.*

Cloward, Richard A., and **Ohlin, Lloyd E.** Delinquency and Opportunity: *A Theory of Delinquent Gangs. 248 pp.*

Downes, David M. The Delinquent Solution. *A Study in Subcultural Theory. 296 pp.*

Dunlop, A. B., and **McCabe, S.** Young Men in Detention Centres. *192 pp.*

Friedlander, Kate. The Psycho-Analytical Approach to Juvenile Delinquency: *Theory, Case Studies, Treatment. 320 pp.*

Glueck, Sheldon, and **Eleanor.** Family Environment and Delinquency. *With the statistical assistance of Rose W. Kneznek. 340 pp.*

Lopez-Rey, Manuel. Crime. *An Analytical Appraisal. 288 pp.*

Mannheim, Hermann. Comparative Criminology: *a Text Book. Two volumes. 442 pp. and 380 pp.*

Morris, Terence. The Criminal Area: *A Study in Social Ecology. Foreword by Hermann Mannheim. 232 pp. 25 tables. 4 maps.*

● **Taylor, Ian, Walton, Paul,** and **Young, Jock.** The New Criminology. *For a Social Theory of Deviance.*

SOCIAL PSYCHOLOGY

Bagley, Christopher. The Social Psychology of the Epileptic Child. *320 pp.*

Barbu, Zevedei. Problems of Historical Psychology. *248 pp.*

Blackburn, Julian. Psychology and the Social Pattern. *184 pp.*

● **Brittan, Arthur.** Meanings and Situations. *224 pp.*

● **Fleming, C. M.** Adolescence: Its Social Psychology. *With an Introduction to recent findings from the fields of Anthropology, Physiology, Medicine, Psychometrics and Sociometry. 288 pp.*

● The Social Psychology of Education: *An Introduction and Guide to Its Study. 136 pp.*

Homans, George C. The Human Group. *Foreword by Bernard DeVoto. Introduction by Robert K. Merton. 526 pp.*

Social Behaviour: *its Elementary Forms. 416 pp.*

Klein, Josephine. The Study of Groups. *226 pp. 31 figures. 5 tables.*

Linton, Ralph. The Cultural Background of Personality. *132 pp.*

Mayo, Elton. The Social Problems of an Industrial Civilization. *With an appendix on the Political Problem. 180 pp.*

Ottaway, A. K. C. Learning Through Group Experience. *176 pp.*

Ridder, J. C. de. The Personality of the Urban African in South Africa. *A Thematic Apperception Test Study. 196 pp. 12 plates.*

● **Rose, Arnold M.** (Ed.). Human Behaviour and Social Processes: *an Interactionist Approach. Contributions by Arnold M. Rose, Ralph H. Turner, Anselm Strauss, Everett C. Hughes, E. Franklin Frazier, Howard S. Becker, et al. 696 pp.*

Smelser, Neil J. Theory of Collective Behaviour. *448 pp.*
Stephenson, Geoffrey M. The Development of Conscience. *128 pp.*
Young, Kimball. Handbook of Social Psychology. *658 pp. 16 figures. 10 tables.*

SOCIOLOGY OF THE FAMILY

Banks, J. A. Prosperity and Parenthood: *A Study of Family Planning among The Victorian Middle Classes. 262 pp.*
Bell, Colin R. Middle Class Families: *Social and Geographical Mobility. 224 pp.*
Burton, Lindy. Vulnerable Children. *272 pp.*
Gavron, Hannah. The Captive Wife: *Conflicts of Household Mothers. 190 pp.*
George, Victor, and **Wilding, Paul.** Motherless Families. *220 pp.*
Klein, Josephine. Samples from English Cultures.
  1. Three Preliminary Studies and Aspects of Adult Life in England. *447 pp.*
  2. Child-Rearing Practices and Index. *247 pp.*
Klein, Viola. Britain's Married Women Workers. *180 pp.*
  The Feminine Character. *History of an Ideology. 244 pp.*
McWhinnie, Alexina M. Adopted Children. *How They Grow Up. 304 pp.*
Myrdal, Alva, and **Klein, Viola.** Women's Two Roles: *Home and Work. 238 pp. 27 tables.*
Parsons, Talcott, and **Bales, Robert F.** Family: Socialization and Interaction Process. *In collaboration with James Olds, Morris Zelditch and Philip E. Slater. 456 pp. 50 figures and tables.*

SOCIAL SERVICES

Bastide, Roger. The Sociology of Mental Disorder. *Translated from the French by Jean McNeil. 260 pp.*
Carlebach, Julius. Caring For Children in Trouble. *266 pp.*
Forder, R. A. (Ed.). Penelope Hall's Social Services of England and Wales. *352 pp.*
George, Victor. Foster Care. *Theory and Practice. 234 pp.*
  Social Security: *Beveridge and After. 258 pp.*
● **Goetschius, George W.** Working with Community Groups. *256 pp.*
Goetschius, George W., and **Tash, Joan.** Working with Unattached Youth. *416 pp.*
Hall, M. P., and **Howes, I. V.** The Church in Social Work. *A Study of Moral Welfare Work undertaken by the Church of England. 320 pp.*
Heywood, Jean S. Children in Care: *the Development of the Service for the Deprived Child. 264 pp.*
Hoenig, J., and **Hamilton, Marian W.** The De-Segration of the Mentally Ill. *284 pp.*
Jones, Kathleen. Mental Health and Social Policy, 1845-1959. *264 pp.*

King, Roy D., Raynes, Norma V., and **Tizard, Jack.** Patterns of Residential Care. *356 pp.*
Leigh, John. Young People and Leisure. *256 pp.*
Morris, Mary. Voluntary Work and the Welfare State. *300 pp.*
Morris, Pauline. Put Away: *A Sociological Study of Institutions for the Mentally Retarded. 364 pp.*
Nokes, P. L. The Professional Task in Welfare Practice. *152 pp.*
Timms, Noel. Psychiatric Social Work in Great Britain (1939-1962). *280 pp.*
● Social Casework: *Principles and Practice. 256 pp.*
Young, A. F., and **Ashton, E. T.** British Social Work in the Nineteenth Century. *288 pp.*
Young, A. F. Social Services in British Industry. *272 pp.*

SOCIOLOGY OF EDUCATION

Banks, Olive. Parity and Prestige in English Secondary Education: a Study in Educational Sociology. *272 pp.*
Bentwich, Joseph. Education in Israel. *224 pp. 8 pp. plates.*
● **Blyth, W. A. L.** English Primary Education. *A Sociological Description.*
  1. Schools. *232 pp.*
  2. Background. *168 pp.*
Collier, K. G. The Social Purposes of Education: *Personal and Social Values in Education. 268 pp.*
Dale, R. R., and **Griffith, S.** Down Stream: *Failure in the Grammar School. 108 pp.*
Dore, R. P. Education in Tokugawa Japan. *356 pp. 9 pp. plates*
Evans, K. M. Sociometry and Education. *158 pp.*
Foster, P. J. Education and Social Change in Ghana. *336 pp. 3 maps.*
Fraser, W. R. Education and Society in Modern France. *150 pp.*
Grace, Gerald R. Role Conflict and the Teacher. *About 200 pp.*
Hans, Nicholas. New Trends in Education in the Eighteenth Century. *278 pp. 19 tables.*
● Comparative Education: *A Study of Educational Factors and Traditions. 360 pp.*
Hargreaves, David. Interpersonal Relations and Education. *432 pp.*
● Social Relations in a Secondary School. *240 pp.*
Holmes, Brian. Problems in Education. *A Comparative Approach. 336 pp.*
King, Ronald. Values and Involvement in a Grammar School. *164 pp.*
  School Organization and Pupil Involvement. *A Study of Secondary Schools.*
● **Mannheim, Karl,** and **Stewart, W. A. C.** An Introduction to the Sociology of Education. *206 pp.*
Morris, Raymond N. The Sixth Form and College Entrance. *231 pp.*
● **Musgrove, F.** Youth and the Social Order. *176 pp.*
● **Ottaway, A. K. C.** Education and Society: An Introduction to the Sociology of Education. *With an Introduction by W. O. Lester Smith. 212 pp.*
Peers, Robert. Adult Education: *A Comparative Study. 398 pp.*

Pritchard, D. G. Education and the Handicapped: *1760 to 1960. 258 pp.*
Richardson, Helen. Adolescent Girls in Approved Schools. *308 pp.*
Stratta, Erica. The Education of Borstal Boys. *A Study of their Educational Experiences prior to, and during Borstal Training. 256 pp.*

SOCIOLOGY OF CULTURE

Eppel, E. M., and **M.** Adolescents and Morality: *A Study of some Moral Values and Dilemmas of Working Adolescents in the Context of a changing Climate of Opinion. Foreword by W. J. H. Sprott. 268 pp. 39 tables.*
● **Fromm, Erich.** The Fear of Freedom. *286 pp.*
   The Sane Society. *400 pp.*
Mannheim, Karl. Essays on the Sociology of Culture. *Edited by Ernst Mannheim in co-operation with Paul Kecskemeti. Editorial Note by Adolph Lowe. 280 pp.*
Weber, Alfred. Farewell to European History: *or The Conquest of Nihilism Translated from the German by R. F. C. Hull. 224 pp.*

SOCIOLOGY OF RELIGION

Argyle, Michael. Religious Behaviour. *224 pp. 8 figures. 41 tables.*
Nelson, G. K. Spiritualism and Society. *313 pp.*
Stark, Werner. The Sociology of Religion. *A Study of Christendom.*
   Volume I. *Established Religion. 248 pp.*
   Volume II. *Sectarian Religion. 368 pp.*
   Volume III. *The Universal Church. 464 pp.*
   Volume IV. *Types of Religious Man. 352 pp.*
   Volume V. *Types of Religious Culture. 464 pp.*
Watt, W. Montgomery. Islam and the Integration of Society. *320 pp.*

SOCIOLOGY OF ART AND LITERATURE

Jarvie, Ian C. Towards a Sociology of the Cinema. *A Comparative Essay on the Structure and Functioning of a Major Entertainment Industry. 405 pp.*
Rust, Frances S. Dance in Society. *An Analysis of the Relationships between the Social Dance and Society in England from the Middle Ages to the Present Day. 256 pp. 8 pp. of plates.*
Schücking, L. L. The Sociology of Literary Taste. *112 pp.*

SOCIOLOGY OF KNOWLEDGE

Mannheim, Karl. Essays on the Sociology of Knowledge. *Edited by Paul Kecskemeti. Editorial Note by Adolph Lowe. 353 pp.*
Remmling, Gunter W. (Ed.). Towards the Sociology of Knowledge. *Origins and Development of a Sociological Thought Style.*
Stark, Werner. The Sociology of Knowledge: *An Essay in Aid of a Deeper Understanding of the History of Ideas. 384 pp.*

URBAN SOCIOLOGY

Ashworth, William. The Genesis of Modern British Town Planning: *A Study in Economic and Social History of the Nineteenth and Twentieth Centuries. 288 pp.*
Cullingworth, J. B. Housing Needs and Planning Policy: *A Restatement of the Problems of Housing Need and 'Overspill' in England and Wales. 232 pp. 44 tables. 8 maps.*
Dickinson, Robert E. City and Region: *A Geographical Interpretation. 608 pp. 125 figures.*
The West European City: *A Geographical Interpretation. 600 pp. 129 maps. 29 plates.*
● The City Region in Western Europe. *320 pp. Maps.*
Humphreys, Alexander J. New Dubliners: *Urbanization and the Irish Family. Foreword by George C. Homans. 304 pp.*
Jackson, Brian. Working Class Community: *Some General Notions raised by a Series of Studies in Northern England. 192 pp.*
Jennings, Hilda. Societies in the Making: *a Study of Development and Re-development within a County Borough. Foreword by D. A. Clark. 286 pp.*
● **Mann, P. H.** An Approach to Urban Sociology. *240 pp.*
Morris, R. N., and **Mogey, J.** The Sociology of Housing. *Studies at Berinsfield. 232 pp. 4 pp. plates.*
Rosser, C., and **Harris, C.** The Family and Social Change. *A Study of Family and Kinship in a South Wales Town. 352 pp. 8 maps.*

RURAL SOCIOLOGY

Chambers, R. J. H. Settlement Schemes in Tropical Africa: *A Selective Study. 268 pp.*
Haswell, M. R. The Economics of Development in Village India. *120 pp.*
Littlejohn, James. Westrigg: *the Sociology of a Cheviot Parish. 172 pp. 5 figures.*
Mayer, Adrian C. Peasants in the Pacific. *A Study of Fiji Indian Rural Society. 248 pp. 20 plates.*
Williams, W. M. The Sociology of an English Village: *Gosforth. 272 pp. 12 figures. 13 tables.*

SOCIOLOGY OF INDUSTRY AND DISTRIBUTION

Anderson, Nels. Work and Leisure. *280 pp.*
● **Blau, Peter M.,** and **Scott, W. Richard.** Formal Organizations: *a Comparative approach. Introduction and Additional Bibliography by J. H. Smith. 326 pp.*
Eldridge, J. E. T. Industrial Disputes. *Essays in the Sociology of Industrial Relations. 288 pp.*
Hetzler, Stanley. Applied Measures for Promoting Technological Growth. *352 pp.*
Technological Growth and Social Change. *Achieving Modernization. 269 pp.*
Hollowell, Peter G. The Lorry Driver. *272 pp.*
Jefferys, Margot, *with the assistance of Winifred Moss.* Mobility in the Labour Market: *Employment Changes in Battersea and Dagenham. Preface by Barbara Wootton. 186 pp. 51 tables.*
Millerson, Geoffrey. The Qualifying Associations: *a Study in Professionalization. 320 pp.*
Smelser, Neil J. Social Change in the Industrial Revolution: *An Application of Theory to the Lancashire Cotton Industry, 1770-1840. 468 pp. 12 figures. 14 tables.*
Williams, Gertrude. Recruitment to Skilled Trades. *240 pp.*
Young, A. F. Industrial Injuries Insurance: *an Examination of British Policy. 192 pp.*

DOCUMENTARY

Schlesinger, Rudolf (Ed.). Changing Attitudes in Soviet Russia.
2. The Nationalities Problem and Soviet Administration. *Selected Readings on the Development of Soviet Nationalities Policies. Introduced by the editor. Translated by W. W. Gottlieb. 324 pp.*

ANTHROPOLOGY

Ammar, Hamed. Growing up in an Egyptian Village: *Silwa, Province of Aswan. 336 pp.*
Brandel-Syrier, Mia. Reeftown Elite. *A Study of Social Mobility in a Modern African Community on the Reef. 376 pp.*
Crook, David, and **Isabel.** Revolution in a Chinese Village: *Ten Mile Inn. 230 pp. 8 plates. 1 map.*
Dickie-Clark, H. F. The Marginal Situation. *A Sociological Study of a Coloured Group. 236 pp.*
Dube, S. C. Indian Village. *Foreword by Morris Edward Opler. 276 pp. 4 plates.*
India's Changing Villages: *Human Factors in Community Development. 260 pp. 8 plates. 1 map.*

Firth, Raymond. Malay Fishermen. *Their Peasant Economy. 420 pp. 17 pp. plates.*

Gulliver, P. H. Social Control in an African Society: a Study of the Arusha, Agricultural Masai of Northern Tanganyika. *320 pp. 8 plates. 10 figures.*

Ishwaran, K. Shivapur. *A South Indian Village. 216 pp.*
Tradition and Economy in Village India: *An Interactionist Approach. Foreword by Conrad Arensburg. 176 pp.*

Jarvie, Ian C. The Revolution in Anthropology. *268 pp.*

Jarvie, Ian C., and **Agassi, Joseph.** Hong Kong. *A Society in Transition. 396 pp. Illustrated with plates and maps.*

Little, Kenneth L. Mende of Sierra Leone. *308 pp. and folder.*
Negroes in Britain. *With a New Introduction and Contemporary Study by Leonard Bloom. 320 pp.*

Lowie, Robert H. Social Organization. *494 pp.*

Mayer, Adrian C. Caste and Kinship in Central India: *A Village and its Region. 328 pp. 16 plates. 15 figures. 16 tables.*

Smith, Raymond T. The Negro Family in British Guiana: *Family Structure and Social Status in the Villages. With a Foreword by Meyer Fortes. 314 pp. 8 plates. 1 figure. 4 maps.*

SOCIOLOGY AND PHILOSOPHY

Barnsley, John H. The Social Reality of Ethics. *A Comparative Analysis of Moral Codes. 448 pp.*

Diesing, Paul. Patterns of Discovery in the Social Sciences. *362 pp.*

Douglas, Jack D. (Ed.). Understanding Everyday Life. *Toward the Reconstruction of Sociological Knowledge. Contributions by Alan F. Blum. Aaron W. Cicourel, Norman K. Denzin, Jack D. Douglas, John Heeren, Peter McHugh, Peter K. Manning, Melvin Power, Matthew Speier, Roy Turner, D. Lawrence Wieder, Thomas P. Wilson and Don H. Zimmerman. 370 pp.*

Jarvie, Ian C. Concepts and Society. *216 pp.*

Roche, Maurice. Phenomenology, Language and the Social Sciences. *About 400 pp.*

Sahay, Arun. Sociological Analysis.

Sklair, Leslie. The Sociology of Progress. *320 pp.*

International Library of Anthropology
General Editor Adam Kuper

Brown, Paula. The Chimbu. *A Study of Change in the New Guinea Highlands.*

Van Den Berghe, Pierre L. Power and Privilege at an African University.

International Library of Social Policy

General Editor Kathleen Jones

Holman, Robert. Trading in Children. *A Study of Private Fostering.*
Jones, Kathleen. History of the Mental Health Services. *428 pp.*
Thomas, J. E. The English Prison Officer since 1850: *A Study in Conflict. 258 pp.*

Primary Socialization, Language and Education

General Editor Basil Bernstein

Bernstein, Basil. Class, Codes and Control. *2 volumes.*
  1. *Theoretical Studies Towards a Sociology of Language. 254 pp.*
  2. *Applied Studies Towards a Sociology of Language. About 400 pp.*
Brandis, Walter, and **Henderson, Dorothy.** Social Class, Language and Communication. *288 pp.*
Cook-Gumperz, Jenny. Social Control and Socialization. *A Study of Class Differences in the Language of Maternal Control.*
Gahagan, D. M., and **G. A.** Talk Reform. *Exploration in Language for Infant School Children. 160 pp.*
Robinson, W. P., and **Rackstraw, Susan, D. A.** A Question of Answers. *2 volumes. 192 pp. and 180 pp.*
Turner, Geoffrey, J., and **Mohan, Bernard, A.** A Linguistic Description and Computer Programme for Children's Speech. *208 pp.*

Reports of the Institute of Community Studies

Cartwright, Ann. Human Relations and Hospital Care. *272 pp.*
  Parents and Family Planning Services. *306 pp.*
  Patients and their Doctors. *A Study of General Practice. 304 pp.*
● **Jackson, Brian.** Streaming: *an Education System in Miniature. 168 pp.*
Jackson, Brian, and **Marsden, Dennis.** Education and the Working Class: *Some General Themes raised by a Study of 88 Working-class Children in a Northern Industrial City. 268 pp. 2 folders.*
Marris, Peter. The Experience of Higher Education. *232 pp. 27 tables.*
Marris, Peter, and **Rein, Martin.** Dilemmas of Social Reform. *Poverty and Community Action in the United States. 256 pp.*
Marris, Peter, and **Somerset, Anthony.** African Businessmen. *A Study of Entrepreneurship and Development in Kenya. 256 pp.*
Mills, Richard. Young Outsiders: *a Study in Alternative Communities.*

Runciman, W. G. Relative Deprivation and Social Justice. *A Study of Attitudes to Social Inequality in Twentieth Century England. 352 pp.*

Townsend, Peter. The Family Life of Old People: *An Inquiry in East London. Foreword by J. H. Sheldon. 300 pp. 3 figures. 63 tables.*

Willmott, Peter. Adolescent Boys in East London. *230 pp.*

The Evolution of a Community: *a study of Dagenham after forty years. 168 pp. 2 maps.*

Willmott, Peter, and Young, Michael. Family and Class in a London Suburb. *202 pp. 47 tables.*

Young, Michael. Innovation and Research in Education. *192 pp.*

● Young, Michael, and McGeeney, Patrick. Learning Begins at Home. *A Study of a Junior School and its Parents. 128 pp.*

Young, Michael, and Willmott, Peter. Family and Kinship in East London. *Foreword by Richard M. Titmuss. 252 pp. 39 tables.*

The Symmetrical Family.

Reports of the Institute for Social Studies in Medical Care

Cartwright, Ann, Hockey, Lisbeth, and Anderson, John L. Life Before Death.

Dunnell, Karen, and Cartwright, Ann. Medicine Takers, Prescribers and Hoarders. *190 pp.*

Medicine, Illness and Society

General Editor W. M. Williams

Robinson, David. The Process of Becoming Ill.

Stacey, Margaret. *et al.* Hospitals, Children and Their Families. *The Report of a Pilot Study. 202 pp.*

Monographs in Social Theory

General Editor Arthur Brittan

Bauman, Zygmunt. Culture as Praxis.

Dixon, Keith. Sociological Theory. *Pretence and Possibility.*

Smith, Anthony D. The Concept of Social Change. *A Critique of the Functionalist Theory of Social Change.*

13

Routledge Social Science Journals

The British Journal of Sociology. *Edited by Terence P. Morris. Vol. 1, No. 1, March 1950 and Quarterly. Roy. 8vo. Back numbers available. An international journal with articles on all aspects of sociology.*

Economy and Society. *Vol. 1, No. 1. February 1972 and Quarterly. Metric Roy. 8vo. A journal for all social scientists covering sociology, philosophy, anthropology, economics and history. Back numbers available.*

Year Book of Social Policy in Britain, The. *Edited by Kathleen Jones. 1971. Published Annually.*

Printed in Great Britain by Lewis Reprints Limited
Brown Knight & Truscott Group, London and Tonbridge   1373